20th CENT

Duncan Fallowell is the author of two novels, the biography of a transsexual, the highly acclaimed travel book *To Noto* and the libretto of the opera *Gormenghast*. His most recent book, *One Hot Summer In St Petersburg*, is published by Jonathan Cape. He lives in London.

Duncan Fallowell

20th CENTURY
CHARACTERS

VINTAGE

Published by Vintage 1994

2 4 6 8 10 9 7 5 3 1

First published in Great Britain by Vintage 1994

Vintage
Random House, 20 Vauxhall Bridge Road, London SW1V 2SA

Random House Australia (Pty) Limited
20 Alfred Street, Milsons Point, Sydney
New South Wales 2061, Australia

Random House New Zealand Limited
18 Poland Road, Glenfield,
Auckland 10, New Zealand

Random House South Africa (Pty) Limited
PO Box 337, Bergvlei, South Africa

Random House UK Limited Reg. No. 954009

A CIP catalogue record for this book
is available from the British Library

ISBN 009947041 1

Typeset by Deltatype Ltd, Ellesmere Port, Wirral
Printed and bound in Great Britain by
Cox & Wyman, Reading, Berkshire

TO THE INSOMNIACS

CONTENTS

PREFATORY NOTE

LA BRUYÈRE. JOHN Aubrey. Vasari. Plutarch. Theophrastus. The tradition of collecting character studies goes back a long way. Perhaps one may even include Freud and Jung in whose case histories the play of archetypal and individual features helps us to identify not so much the mad as the living. There are no absolute rules governing these forms of interaction. My own approach has been flexible (especially in the degree to which I challenge the views of the other). The intention is to paint a composite portrait of the 20th century through a range of its characteristic personalities.

Even though quite a few of them are dead now, heartfelt thanks are given to all the individuals who agreed to meetings. I consider myself to have been very fortunate in this respect. None subsequently complained – at least, not to my face – and I'd like to think that this is because, believing in original sin, but believing in original virtue also, I managed to render them authentically, albeit in a concentrate. No politician is represented here – they allow themselves too little spontaneity. And no one from the world of classical music – since it plays a very significant role in my life, I'm at a loss to explain why. But this is a book of voices and ideas and places, and so politics and music find their way in quite naturally.

In preparing the contents for book publication, I have made some deletions and alterations where I seemed silly or unjust. But sometimes it is important not to change anything – for example, in those references to Russia made before the collapse of Communism. Many of the pieces are published for the first time at full length, and several have not been published at all. However I should like to acknowledge the editors of *The Times*, the *Independent Magazine*, *Playboy*, *Penthouse*, *Harper's & Queen*, the *Sunday Correspondent*, *Deluxe*, *Time Out*, *Tatler*, *Woman's Journal*, *Marie Claire*, *Modern Painters*, the *American Scholar*, the *Paris Review*, *Vanity Fair*, *European Travel & Life*, the *Irish Times*, *Tip*, *Brigitte*, *Tages Anzeiger*, *Avenue*, *La Repubblica*, the *Sydney Morning Herald*, and *The Age*, in which some of this material has appeared.

CLASSICAL WITH GROTTOES

ANTHONY POWELL AND LADY VIOLET NEAR FROME

JUNE 9TH, 4PM. Deeply sunk in Somerset verdure, Mr Anthony Powell and his wife Lady Violet are at home at the Chantry on a hot afternoon.

'I'd absolutely hate to live abroad,' says Tony (as his friends call him – and he is a friendly man).

'Are you good at foreign languages?'

'Frightfully bad. I'm frightfully good at Broken English.'

'Yes, he's very good at that,' says Lady Violet, swinging in with a loaded tea tray, 'and very good at getting foreigners to speak English – even when they can't.'

He wears a hound's-tooth check jacket, with exceptionally wide lapels like the wings of a manta ray. He holds himself upright but with ease on a high sofa and tends to talk out of the side of his face in a way that is both cheerful and slightly conspiratorial. As man and writer he lives very close to the edge – of a giggle.

Lady Violet, having poured and distributed, decides to lie full length on a lower, more frayed sofa, so low indeed that it appears to be collapsing into the floor. Her feet are up in their running shoes, and so is her hair in an informal bluish bush, and she is needlepointing a cushion cover – another cushion cover, for the house is padded with her industry. Lady Violet is Anglo-Irish, the sister of Lord Longford, but seems very settled here.

'I have the strongest possible dislike for Ireland,' declares Mr Powell. 'I dislike that awful national egotism, always going on about what it means to be Irish. But this is very unEnglish of me, I know. Wyndham Lewis said that the Irish resembled the English in being sentimental about the Irish. You asked me earlier if I had any eccentricities. This is the sort of thing I'm eccentric about. Would you say, Violet, I was eccentric?'

Violet, who has tied up her needle for the moment, waves a bit of Custard Cream biscuit from her collapsing island and mumbles something that is negative but not positively so, then bursts out 'Trelawney, stop it . . . ! You don't mind cats, do you?' Trelawney is their Cornish Rex who periodically destroys pieces of upholstery.

'Do you know *The Education of Henry Adams* by Henry Adams?' asks Anthony. 'It's the best book that any American has ever produced. He was a friend of Henry James. His father was American Minister in London during the Civil War. I have – oh, how very tiresome, I think I threw away only the other day this thing an American sent me about Adams. Americans love sending me photocopies of things. Anyway it's a very enjoyable book – perhaps it tails off a bit at the end but . . .'

'But why do you refer to this book?'

'Oh yes, what I was coming on to was – Adams says that the great point about real eccentrics is that they are trying to be tremendously ordinary. I was always brought up to be tremendously ordinary, which can perhaps lead to sort of – but I don't think I have any peculiar habits.'

'What is this Anthony Powell Society in America?'

'Oh, that is simply, well, there is this society at Kalamazoo in Michigan and they bring out a thing called *AP Communications* once a year with information in it about, er, me. I gather that the membership tends to be growing, rather than the reverse. The very nice lady who runs it, Miss Nancy Cutbirth, which I believe is simply a wonderful form of Cuthbert, she sent a photograph of, er, they have sort of conferences of academics, and she sent me a photograph of all the people who were reading papers on my, um, work and it looked exactly like the–um the–um First Politburo of 1917. The thing is I always rather enjoy myself when I go to America. In my early days in 1937 I tried to get a job in Hollywood as a scriptwriter and failed to do so. The only interesting thing that happened was that I met Scott Fitzgerald. He was drinking milk then and

2

we gave him lunch at MGM and that night was the night he and Sheila Graham became lovers. He was scripting *A Yank at Oxford* which was the film I hoped to get in on and didn't. But he had been totally forgotten. 10 years later every one of his books was in print. By that time of course he'd died.'

'Sheila Graham had some kind of wrestling match with his corpse after he died – she wanted the body and some other people wanted it too and I believe they got it from her in the end.'

'Did she? Yes, she would. He's that very rare thing in my opinion: a bad writer who really did turn himself into a good writer.'

'Are you a traveller by nature?'

'I s'pose I like touring about in sort of civilised places. I like to know where I'm going. India is marvellous over and above the other places one knows, although once or twice we felt—at Amritsar they murdered a whole lot of muslims after we left. I'm always very fascinated by their army because they manage to be more British than it's possible to imagine. They've got this curious business of looking very smart and being very languid at the same time – which is so English.'

Anthony Powell's father was a soldier. Sometimes one has the impression that Powell himself is a man of public affairs – commerce, diplomacy, or the forces – accidentally deflected into books.

'No, I don't think being a man of action was ever quite my thing. To extend it a bit, the writer-cum-man-of-action is rare in England but he's quite a figure abroad, like Malraux or Mailer or Mishima. They all seem to be "M"s.'

'Isn't it extraordinary they're all "M"s,' says Violet, stabbing away with her needle.

'Yes, it *is* extraordinary, isn't it,' echoes Tony, as if they had just unearthed a wondrous fragment of Attic pottery. The atmosphere is very rural, taken to the subtly exotic point where 'Powell' is pronounced 'pole' – and where 'Pole' indeed would be pronounced 'Pool'. And the Chantry is near Frome which is pronounced 'Froom'. Auberon Waugh has called the 'Pole' pronunciation a provincial pretension to gentility.

'Auberon Waugh lives at least 50 miles away,' says Tony

with a bewildered air, 'and should we meet, he always goes out of his way to be rude to me. Perhaps it's because I was a friend of his father's.'

'Trelawney, stop it!' commands Violet, lifting a threatening foot-in-running-shoe with absolutely ineffectual results. The cat continues to tear at a ragged armrest.

'Though never one of his intimate friends,' he adds, 'whom he of course used to behave abominably to, such as Christopher Sykes.'

Cyril Connolly, in his published journal, makes the following, only semi-comprehensible reference to an evening on the eve of the Second World War: *Powells to dinner, very nice. He asked for an opinion on him and Evelyn. I said I thought Tony had more talent and Evelyn more vocation. Tony is likely to dry up and Evelyn to make mistakes, but you can learn from mistakes, you can't learn from drying up.*

'Oh, Cyril . . .' Tony cogitates a little. 'Now that he's dead, I really can't tell even myself quite what his thing was, quite why one wanted to see him, because he could be fearfully sort of tiresome. There was something slightly hypnotic about him. He was of course very intelligent indeed but I think intellectually . . . *corrupt* is perhaps going a bit far, but still . . .'

Both the Powells are fascinated by family names, gossip, social connections. Various worn volumes of Burke's Peerage, Baronetage, Gentry are so placed on the bookshelves as to be grabbable at one lunge from where Lady Violet subsides on the sofa. Powell's social curiosity, emphasised by his being a first generation Etonian, resembles more the lepidopterist's concern for markings than it does the Proustian snobbery of intense values, and therefore the art built upon it is not intense. He thinks that to express feelings too richly or directly is to be rude and he does not want to be rude. Powell wrote a review of Painter's biography of Proust and this is his version of a rave: *Mr Painter has done his work so well that it is hard to speak in moderate terms of his skill and unobtrusive wit.* Hard but not impossible apparently. Powell is civilised without being effete, amusing without excoriation, intelligent without being dangerous: the Englishman's idea of a fine writer.

4

'Your books have a designed, not emotional character. Almost abstract.'

'I would say I was quite keen on form, yes.'

And he has never been a controversial writer. But perhaps he's been sued?

'The only time something I've written has attracted the law was when I reviewed a novel of Sartre's for the *Times Literary Supplement*. Have you ever had the misfortune to read any of his novels? In this book, I can't remember which one it was, he dealt with the Munich Agreement and a lot of it was a blow-by-blow account of the real people written in a so-called modernistic style. Anyway somebody called Ashton-Gwatkin, who was part of Chamberlain's staff, was in it and there was a suggestion of involvement with a Russian girl called Suevitch or something and I quoted – in not total innocence – the sentence in which this suggestion arose as a very outdated example of so-called modernistic writing. This brought the roof down because Ashton-Gwatkin had just retired from the Foreign Office and was alleged to have a very jealous wife and immediately writs flew. *The Times* and Hamish Hamilton were absolutely *craven* about it and agreed to pay any sum, though Sartre wanted to come to London to defend the book.'

'Quite obviously Sartre thought it all ludicrously funny,' says Violet.

'But the curious thing was Ashton-Gwatkin himself. It later transpired that he had written a slightly near-the-knuckle paperback called *Kimono* about brothels in Japan. He was also the only person who'd ever been called Ashton-Gwatkin; he'd taken the name on himself. And by an extraordinary coincidence we'd been in the same house at Eton. And he won the Newdigate Prize at Oxford – for a poem on the subject of Michelangelo.'

Powell's main work, the 12 volume novel *A Dance to the Music of Time*, a contrapuntal picture of the upper(ish) classes from the beginning of the century to the 1970s, took him 25 years to write – and in what way is he unhappy with it?

'Oh, I see, yes, *un*happy, um – I don't think that anything went radically wrong at any stage, er, rightly or wrongly.'

But surely he must have experienced a great sense of comedown after dispatching the final volume.

'No, I didn't, as a matter of fact. I experienced an enormous feeling of relief, that I'd managed to get to the end of the thing without running out of steam.'

What then does he consider his particular virtue as a writer?

'I should have thought I'd got a certain amount of staying-power.'

Dance, as he calls it, has parallels to certain musical structures and suggests that music is important to him.

'I'm totally not musical. Couldn't be less. I can often tell with certain books whether the author's musical or not – there's this curious kind of flow. You get it in Kierkegaard.'

'Garcia Marquez is very musical.'

'Oh, really? I haven't read that book *One Hundred Years of . . .* something. I ought to read it, ought I?'

'If not in Spanish, he has a fabulous translator into English. You didn't dry up.'

'Well, then I wrote 4 volumes of memoirs and after that I really thought I would rather like to get back to novel writing which is a more, you know, honourable profession – also more enjoyable. The problem is – one really *doesn't* know what to do with one's mornings. I was talking about this to our daughter-in-law the other day and she said oh, absolutely, after you've tidied up your room for the 20th time, what do you do? It's true. You can't just keep hanging about down-stairs.'

'Here's what I'd call a French question.'

'Oh, should I leave the room?' flutes Violet, allowing her needle to pause in mid-air.

'No, not that sort of French. The question is: what have you sacrificed for your art?'

'Stop it, Trelawney, no!'

'Um – rather a lot of time actually. I have fairly often *not* gone to parties because I was writing. If I had been up to London one night, I pretty well never went up again for another party immediately the next night, even if it was something rather tempting. We're about 12 miles from Westbury which has a fairly decent line, Paddington in an hour and three-quarters, though there is sometimes a fast train that gets you there in an hour and 10 minutes.'

Born in London in 1905, Powell lived his adult life there until 1952 when they moved to the country.

'I didn't know if I'd be able to stand the country at all because I loved going to nightclubs and so on, but London was frightfully disagreeable after the war with all the bombed bits and coal shortages and then the phone goes morning, noon and night, and you answer it and it turns out to be for your wife but you can't very well hang up and the whole bloody morning's gone. I've always liked to write in the mornings when I feel after-breakfast-like. I've never been able to write after even so much as half a glass of sherry – although I have a glass of Guinness at luncheon usually. Violet always liked the idea of living in the country. Then I was left a small amount of money which made it possible to buy a house. We looked at dozens and dozens and dozens. Really we wanted to live on the Wiltshire/Hampshire border but houses are very expensive there – seemed so then – it's now what you'd expect to pay for dinner for 4 people. This was a bit further out than we wanted to go and in a pretty broken down condition when we moved in and an absolute jungle outside. We have 90 acres here which is more than we need but it's easy to let.'

The Chantry is a Regency house, small, with the occasional pair of pillars, and although the Powells are not rich, it is pending manorial in that it has that all-important lodge at the entrance to the drive. Outside there are a lake and 2 grottoes. Inside it is done up in the English squire style whose integrating idea is that nothing should match anything else and there should be plenty of it to dispel a chilly atmosphere; most but not all of the furniture should be old; here and there notes of appalling taste should be struck. In the Powells' case, a bohemian effect is introduced by lurid black and crimson wallpaper in the hall – bohemian that is, until, going up close, you realise that it is a design of printed soldiers.

'Do you go hunting, shooting? Are you to be found on a riverbank week after week?'

Mirth breaks out between them.

'I sometimes potter about and do a bit of – when I say gardening it's really just hacking things down.'

'Has Eton been an advantage to you?'

'Not in the sense of getting on.'

'I meant personally.'

'I would say yes. There are all sorts of amusing things connected with having been at the school. I don't think any of my contemporaries became what I would call *close* friends but with an awful lot of people of different ages whom one meets – it does give a connection. It's probably more true of Oxford than of Eton but I didn't really in a way enjoy Oxford, you know. I mean, one went to parties. There were several very rich people, none of them Etonians, mostly of rather obscure origins, and you really would be invited to a party for 30 with a bottle of champagne placed in front of each guest. There was a man called Lulu Waters-Welch who entertained in this fashion. And somebody called Romney Somers who actually had been up and couldn't bring himself to go down. But this didn't mean that a lot of the time one didn't feel awfully depressed and lonely because one did.'

'You seem very even-tempered – like your books. I can't imagine you suffering from insomnia, for example.'

'Oh, wrong! At one time almost permanent insomnia! Never slept a wink! I'm better than I used to be – I think it was largely from drinking too much. I've given up spirits because they make one so fat.'

'Yours was the barbiturate era – you never took to sleeping pills?'

'No, never. I'm tremendously anti-medicine. I think taking one aspirin is being hooked on drugs.'

'You don't seem a pessimist. Unusual in your literary generation.'

'Well, I mean, I think I'm *generally*, er fairly, you certainly wouldn't describe, I don't know, that's to say, well, the fact that one can go on existing at all must be pretty optimistic, don't you think? You asked about fear and I would have to say that fear wasn't particularly one of my big things – without setting up in the least as being brave,' and he bites into a brown Bourbon biscuit, sips a little tea.

He is changeless, reassuring. He must always have looked 50, as he looks it still. Even the hair has refused to fall out in the slightest. What living writers does he enjoy?

'Yes, I see, *living* writers. Most of the ones I read are dead. The older one gets – you say I really ought to read Marquez?'

'Well, it's not an order.'

'But let me write it down. Do you know a Peruvian character called Vargas Llosa? Wrote a book about trying to establish a military brothel somewhere up the Amazon. *Quite* funny – rather laboured.'

'Have you ever been involved with the Secret Service?'

'Never. I must be the only man in England, I mean, I hardly know anybody who hasn't been involved in some way.'

Politics?

'Tory. Always. Our local MP is Bob Boscawen, a good back-bencher, Military Cross in the war, Cornish family, you'll find him in the Peerage under *Falmouth*. He stopped the car the other day and got out and said "There's something I've been meaning to tell you for years, I'm a trustee of the Widmerpool Estate in Nottinghamshire" and drove on.'

Margaret Thatcher?

'I love her! I find her quite incredibly attractive. Um, yes, sexually. It's not at all uncommon. I was at a dinner the other day – Al Alvarez was there, Isaiah Berlin, people like that – and *they* found her enormously sexually attractive too.'

Knighthood in the offing? Unless Powell has already refused one, as Evelyn Waugh is reputed to have refused one (because he admired only hereditary titles), but that would seem to be very out of character. What is Powell's character? He appears to be a gentleman who isn't a bore. But this is an illusion. A gentleman has interests not obsessions. Anthony Powell is a writer and a writer is only as good as his obsessions. Hence the element of concealment, not so much of inconvenient truths in the outer world (though there is that) as of self from self.

'I'm not a great examiner of myself,' he says, trying to decide between a Custard Cream and a Bourbon. 'I think people are very much divided into those who are interested in themselves and those who are interested in other people, which has nothing to do with being selfish or virtuous or anything, it's just the way one's mind works.'

The sun, given a wide berth by several plump clouds as they advance across the blue, pulses through the tall bay window, heating the room. The external world cannot always be so threatless, so merely objective, can it? People cannot for long be divided into these simple categories, can they? Powell's wish to believe it so, to make it so, is his great forte as a writer, or to put it another way, his great weakness. Do the more complex dramas of the blood and the psyche and the landscape draw no response?

'Well, do you know Dunne's theory of dreams?' he asks.

'The poet?'

Trelawney scratches on. Lady Violet lifts a threatening foot.

'No. D-u-n-n-e, I think it is. Don't know what his initials are, no. He had this theory that you had prophetic dreams. I did keep my dreams for a while, which is an awful bore because you have to write them down the second you wake up, but I did have a few vaguely prophetic – but I believe Dunne's theory is totally exploded now, *totally* exploded. But of course,' he continues, looking sideways with eyebrows raised, 'there are things that are not understood.'

'Do you believe in life after death?'

'Generally speaking – not. But I s'pose it is not absolutely inconceivable that maybe sort of quite *odd* things might happen . . . later.'

(1983)

10

NATURE STRIP

GERMAINE GREER

GERMAINE GREER IS animated, warm, large, intelligent, and talks in vivid phrases with a slight but definite Australian accent. She has a lot to say on every subject. Much of what she says is unusual and valuable, most of it is deeply felt. She also goes out on limbs – if you question her, she'll qualify what she says – otherwise the generalisation, the speculation, the assertion will sweep ever outwards, a movement of emotion rather than of argument. She often generalises from a particular and like the good Catholic she was brought up to be (but has not become) she seeks to turn personal preferences or wishes into commandments for all. She has a compulsion for issuing diktats: people must do this, must not do that. And in doing so she is frequently more generous than others so compelled. Nonetheless this is at odds with her ostensible avowal of pluralism.

She has her Rabelaisian side – something she encourages – which, paradoxically, draws attention to another characteristic, shyness or delicacy of feeling. There is sweetness and kindness here but she tries to avoid being genteel. To edit the vulgarisms out of her talk would be to misrepresent her grossly. She has the gift of languages and speaks English, Spanish, Italian, French, Portuguese. She is a notable gardener and cook; her hands bear the marks of labour. Loosed from exclusive cultural imprinting herself, she admires most the opposite type, the most specifically imprinted type, that is, peasant women and especially those from the Latin cultures she knows. She is a great romantic. She has a very creative

11

conflict between this and her almost equally great intellectuality. She can illuminate in unexpected ways. Despite her veneration for peasant women, and despite her strong Catholic sense of evil, the interview takes place in the velvety luxury of the Montcalm Hotel in London's West End, and she drinks champagne throughout.

DF: You were born in Australia. What did it give you that was good?

GG: It gave me a hunger, which Australians have in great measure, for beauty. Because we're not surrounded by it. We have the ugliest domestic architecture in the world.

DF: You have landscape.

GG: But we don't live in it. We live in endless suburbs. With *nature strips*. Which is a bit of grass down the middle of the road which you have to mow – it's called mowing the nature strip. The best descriptions of Australia, I think, are D. H. Lawrence's – because he has that strange naked eyeball that sees all these small things which don't seem to mean anything but which add up to the real tedium and emptiness of suburban life in Australia. Which is Mrs Thatcher's blueprint for Great Britain, by the way: an endless suburb.

DF: You went to a convent. What remains in you to-day of your Catholic upbringing?

GG: I am still a nun. I am still made in their likeness, the childishness of nuns, the girlishness of them. They show you there's another way of living. You don't have to be a wife and mother. It was very interesting to be with these crazy women who laughed all the time.

DF: What about the Pope?

GG: The Pope! The Pope is an abominable, publicity-seeking, sanctimonious shit!

DF: You have brothers and sisters?

GG: I'm 6 years older than my little sister and so I was used by my mother as my sister's nanny. So I hated my sister. I began to rediscover and delight in her when I went back to Australia in 1978 and since then I've got closer and

12

closer to her. She's the mother of 2 boys, married into a very rich and well-connected Australian Catholic family and she's thoroughly caught up in that but she's fantastic. We're both foul-mouthed – you should hear her playing tennis with her posh friends! She has a huge passionate heart and is a fitness freak. She is also panicked at growing old, I think.

DF: Are you?

GG: Not really. But I don't want to be incapacitated too soon. My father died of a degenerative disease, his brain just turned to soup, and since I'm very like him, I think it's very likely that will happen to me too.

DF: I know you didn't get on with your mother. Have you repaired that relationship too?

GG: My mother doesn't care whether I repair it or not.

DF: No, but do you?

GG: Not really. I don't like her. I'm sorry. When I talk to my mother, my heart starts to pound because she doesn't obey *any rules* of discourse. She uses language as a goad. And I start to think I'm drowning, that that way lies unreason, immorality.

DF: Obviously there's a deeper feeling at work here than your mother's contempt for the rules of discourse.

GG: You can't laugh at your mother. My mother spent her entire life getting a tan.

DF: Was your father important to you?

GG: . . . I think he must've been. I've written a book about my relationship with him. For all gifted girls, the father is the spur. I partly invented my father. And I need to uninvent him. I'm going to be hypnotised to remember what relationship I had with him before the War. He died in 1983.

DF: So this attempt to recover something can't take place in the flesh.

GG: The greatest grief of my whole life was realising it was too late . . . I'm not mentioned in my father's will, for example. Not at all.

DF: Your parents seem to have been freaked out by you.

GG: No. It's this strange Australian indifference. The families are very nuclear, very fragmented.

DF: I know there's an enormous homosexual displacement in Australian society. I don't know about lesbians.

GG: The cult of masculinity is so *vicious* in Australia, so unrelenting, it insists on this terrible coarseness and gluttony and distortion, that the fall-out is enormous. It's like prison. The number of homosexuals in prison increases because of the way criminal society emphasises power and masculinity.

DF: Oh no, no. With prison, it's more because most men want sex and they'll get it with whatever's around.

GG: That's part of the rapist's mythology, that the erect cock is to be worshipped.

DF: No, no, no, all that sort of stuff is secondary, not primary. A healthy sex life is an unblocking.

GG: The new purity is to discharge your sexual energy regularly – like colonic lavage. A very British approach. The notion of a healthy sex life is completely protean.

DF: Of course. A healthy sex life is a healthy relationship with one's sexuality. Which can be many things.

GG: Well, our society has established that you must have recurrent sexual desire. More people are guilty now about *not* feeling desire than about feeling it.

DF: Guilt mechanisms – that is another question. You live near Cambridge. Do you ever feel deracinated?

GG: . . . I don't know that human beings have roots. Until recently Australians weren't interested in roots. The other day somebody said to me about my father 'He didn't want you to know about him. He wanted a *new life*.' The whole point about going to a new country to start a new life is – that's what you have to do. But now I want to know who he was, because all sorts of things about him are thrilling to me.

DF: What did he do for a living?

GG: Daddy? The worst thing you could imagine . . . . .

DF: What's that? Killing horses?

GG: . . . He sold advertising space. I thought it was the worst thing. It's the quintessence of hucksterism.

DF:	It occurs to me that you live near Cambridge because your old university provides you with a root, a physical anchor on the planet – and an anchor you are prepared to identify with.

By this I mean not any old identity but one which she doesn't find embarrassing, one which doesn't define her as the daughter of a man who sold advertising space in Australia.

GG:	Something like that is going on. There was a great moment for me when I went back to the Cambridge University Library 5 years ago and said 'My name is Germaine Greer, I'm a Cambridge Ph.D, and I'd like to use the library. Is that all right? What do I have to do?' And the man behind the counter said 'Dr Greer, this is *your* library. Please come in.' I burst into tears. It was the nicest thing anybody ever said to me! And recently the Principal of Newnham wrote to me saying I hadn't kept in touch with my old college and would I like to go to dinner? Which I did. But remember the nunnery angle – very important to me. It's very hard to find an analogue to that in the world.
DF:	Newnham is the intelligent sisterhood.
GG:	Oh, I don't give a stuff about the intelligent bit!
DF:	I'm sure you do. I know you've written about how you were drawn to the poor women of Calabria but –
GG:	They weren't stupid.
DF:	No, certainly they weren't stupid. But there is a very strong intellectual, mentally sportive dimension to you – it's one of your most obvious characteristics. These Calabrian women were many things – but they weren't that. They questioned nothing. This oppressed, thick, treacly, *heavy* femaleness of the deep south, it's terribly tethered to the earth – and to death. It's wonderful in many ways – but it's terribly limited, suffocating. Did you not feel that ever?
GG:	I have a little farm in Tuscany – I will retire there – and

my housekeeper, Lisa, can't read or write but she's one of my best friends. She can't even tell the time. But once when I was cursing a basil plant which had died on me, she said 'Basilico e geloso, mori subito'. Basil is jealous, it dies at once. And I thought – aw shit, I can't teach this woman *anything*!

It is interesting that Germaine Greer thought she might be in a position to teach Lisa things. Having been disabused of this by the exchange on basil, Germaine Greer goes to the other extreme and invests Lisa's poetic folk wisdom with unerring mystique. But is it not error to abase oneself before any group or class or idea? Germaine Greer seems to live theoretically; that is, while performing an act she sees it as exemplifying some concept. If you do this without thinking, it is called ritual. But Germaine Greer is thinking most of the time. The terrific charm of Lisa is that she is not thinking. She is living ritualistically. Lisa is raw material – but intelligent raw material. The society which produced Lisa is matriarchal and for Germaine Greer this is sufficient recommendation. But matriarchal societies (which she calls heterosexual), which are all obsessed with death and mortality, are not less stultifying than patriarchal societies (which she calls homosexual), which are obsessed with life and immortality. Perhaps the clue to her romancing of the Calabrian peasant in particular is that it was part of her sexual awakening.

GG: No. I really noticed all that stuff about the women because the man I was having an affair with dumped me. I felt really raw and went off to Calabria . . . and one of the first things that happened was that this boy brought me a selection of men to choose from – at first I didn't realise that was what he was doing. One of them was a fisherman, very smart, sexy, witty – all Italians are intelligent – who was sure he would get it. Then there was this other man who was a bit of a fool, shy, awkward, sensitive, uncertain. I knew I was supposed to go for the fisherman – so I went for the awkward one. And that was that. No one else took any liberties with me. The difficulty was to find a place to fuck. It was impossible – even when we went into the fields, a dog always followed us . . . But maybe I've never been sexually awakened at all . . . The Pope says it's possible to commit adultery with your wife if you treat her in a certain way – in my view that is absolutely right. If my husband said to me 'We're losing interest in each other, I've got a limp dick, we're going to look at this porn book', I would walk straight out the door! The debasement of the sexual currency between us would cut me to the heart.

Oh this high-minded priggishness! She provokes me. She says – Do it *my* way, it is the only *correct* way. Why shouldn't a couple do kooky things if *they* want to? What business is it of ours? Just because Germaine Greer, or the Pope, feels debased, have we *all* got to feel debased? Fantasy is part of love and the essential characteristic of fantasy is that it is not limited. Surely love can flower in many surprising ways?

DF: Have you been married?
GG: Yes, for 3 weeks.
DF: 3 weeks is hardly giving it a fair crack of the whip.
GG: I realised he hated me. One of the strange things about men is that they can fuck the gizzards out of you because they hate you.
DF: Oh yes. It often helps. Love can queer the pitch there.
GG: I love the pitch being queered.
DF: Where did you meet your husband?
GG: On the pavement outside Finch's in the Portobello Road. I married him 3 weeks later – and ran away 3 weeks after that. This was 196 . . . 8, I think.
DF: Do you live alone?
GG: I don't have a partner. But I have a household. I'm so proud of the household at the moment! It really is the Abbaye de Thélèmes. Music, painting, laughter, gardening, extremely sensual, very Mediterranean. There's

Rita. James and Tom – they're graduate students at Cambridge. Christopher and Shanghai Jim – they're 2 cats. Livingstone, the parrot. Cecil, the gardener. Paul, the gardener's boy. There should be Elaine as well. My ambition is to run a secular monastery of refined pleasures. But I am perfectly happy to be by myself. The great luxury is to be utterly alone.

DF: That's because you're successful. If you were ignored, it would be different.

GG: That's not true actually. What people are *not* after me for is dinner parties, dropping in. I have to work quite hard to create a semblance of a social life for myself.

DF: Who is the most remarkable man you've ever met?

GG: Man? . . . Met . . . Fellini. But he's a friend of mine – remarkably stimulating. I disagree with almost everything he says. Funnily enough, he talks rather like you do. But the most impressive man I've ever *seen* – I was in the Press Gallery – is Fidel Castro. I was attending the Conference of the Legion of Cuban Women. So was he. He joined in the discussions with this strange, high-pitched, totally uncharismatic voice – but he brought everything so alive. Sometimes he would deliberately say provocative things if he thought the women were being too submissive. You know, people in Cuba can read and write, do have medical care, glasses, false teeth, clean water supply, all the things nobody in the Third World has. They've *done* it! What with? With cash credits from the Soviet Union – but what else would you use the Soviet Union for? It's realpolitik.

DF: I want to talk to you about men. By nationality.

GG: Why?

DF: Because I'm very interested at the moment in cultural variations, unfair though such generalisations might sometimes be.

GG: You mean sexually?

DF: No, not necessarily. How would you characterise the Australian man?

GG: Australian men have inherited the homosexuality of the Englishmen. They are ill at ease with women, shy with

18

them, and comfortable with each other. Australian women are the most complaisant women in the world, Australian women will do *anything* for a sign of affection. But I like Australian men. I grew up with them, I can deal with them, My brother's one and I love my brother.

DF: How would you characterise the Englishman?

GG: I think English culture is basically homosexual in the sense that the men only really care about other men. They find it very difficult to treat women as people. And they don't have any machinery of gallantry to incorporate women even as tokens. But for the most part, there is no genital element in their homosexuality – because Englishmen are worried by their genitals too. One of the reasons they don't like women is because women are the recipients of their genital attentions. Women are, as it were, ambulant spittoons.

DF: Kathy Acker said that American men treat their women like toilets.

GG: What do American men say? Pussy-whipped. They are frightened of women – but they're terrific lovers because they *try so hard*. But after a while the fact that they're trying so hard becomes really depressing. One thing American men do that I've never experienced anywhere else is that they will lie on their backs with a full erection and roll you backwards and forwards over this erection, without penetration, until you – or they – have a climax. They love to do that. And I've never known anyone other than Americans to do it. It's extremely effective. And bewildering.

DF: Bewilderment is good. It helps to release the inner person. A German friend of mine said that for him 'people' are other men and that a woman is something to seduce, to fuck, or to disregard. He is not in any sense afraid of women.

GG: I'd never fuck a German, are you kidding?

DF: The Frenchman.

GG: The Frenchman is *so vain* that you cannot penetrate his psychic space at all. Even while fucking you, he'll be watching *himself*.

19

DF: The Italian.

GG: I think Italian men are genuinely heterosexual, mainly because their mothers ate them alive when they were babies and convinced them that they were utterly adorable. And they know – which the Englishman doesn't know – that making love is a matter of fantasy and language and not a genital performance.

DF: Well, I think the genitals are probably involved in it somewhere. And it isn't difficult to have very thrilling sexual experiences without love. But with love, if you take care of the love-making, the genital performance takes care of itself.

GG: Exactly. I think the Italians are the best lovers in the world. They are quite likely to be inadequate when it comes to the button-twiddling and so on. But the point is they create the ethos of being in love. They can also turn it off, of course. They are totally hypocritical. But that's all right. The important thing is not to let it be banal when it's happening – and they never do. They are utterly absorbed.

DF: The African.

GG: Ha . . . . . If we're talking about black sex, West Indian men believe that they can tell if they've impregnated you. I did it this time, they'll say, you're fixed! And they're never right. One of the things I like about black men is that they know that they've got this rammist image, so one of the first things they do is say 'OK, let's just cool it right out. Let's just relax. This may take all night. And several joints.'

DF: The Arab.

GG: Arabs are 'no hands'. It's really depressing. Don't touch me there, they say. They don't like *anything* being touched. And they don't touch you. It's all narrowly genital, all the Sword of Islam. They're desolate fucks. *Desolate.*

DF: Orientals?

GG: Don't know.

DF: Do you have any phobias?

GG: Yes, I can't stand spiders. Boy, they're revolting.

DF: What things terrify you deep down?

GG: Nothing.

DF: What makes you feel guilty?

GG: Lying.

DF: What's your big vice?

GG: Impatience.

DF: Did you want to have children?

GG: Yes. But it's the great twentieth century tragedy. By the time I wanted to have them, it was too late.

DF: You could adopt.

GG: I don't believe a child should be separated from its mother.

DF: Aren't there loads of orphans?

GG: Not any more.

DF: But overseas.

GG: You mustn't take a child out of its culture. When I was in Ethiopia I wanted to put them inside my dress, bring them back, hold them against my skin . . . but I would've been put in prison by that monster in Cleveland, wouldn't I. I think that woman who's conducting the crusade against child abuse is so evil. The commonest form of child abuse in England is children who've never been kissed and held and made to feel lovable. And here is this insane creature deciding that because children have battered labia they must've been screwed by their fathers. Most children with battered labia batter them by themselves.

DF: And then this ghastly British prurience comes into it. Sex is wrong – all touching is a form of sexual approach – so touching is wrong – be on the lookout for sinister touching. Soon we'll be frightened to touch anyone for any reason. And now as a result of this hysterical child abuse witch-hunt, the Government has found it necessary to issue a statement to parents saying it's OK to touch your children! The true sickness is the Anglo-Saxon terror of the body.

GG: It is going to get worse. The only emotional relationship people will accept is that between spouses. Do you know what my father did when I approached to kiss him? He

21

screwed up his face as if bracing himself for a slap. But I insisted on kissing him. I have all my Italian genes – and Jewish too, I hope – as well as my father's poor, stitched-up Ulster genes.

DF: What about the menopause? Do you have any observations on that?

GG: I've been into it for 2 years now. One of the things that happens is that you can't get to sleep. I don't mind being awake and dreamy in bed – that's nice. But when you're wide awake and exhausted and not free-associating . . . then you start to think. Should I have done this? I wish I hadn't done that. What am I going to do about the VAT? And suddenly a wild card among all these – *My life is finished*. And I thought – is it? Where did that card come from? I don't really believe that. I didn't ask for that. And I sort of exorcised it. Then it popped up again. *This is it – after this, it's all downhill*. Oh, come on, I'm just beginning to find out what it's all about. Go away . . . It was really strange. And you have to take the decision not to act on any of this stuff, that you won't take yourself seriously. But that also compounds the thing of – you are a middle-aged woman, *nobody* takes you seriously, you're a joke figure. What nobody really tells you is that the menopause is *extremely* stressful. I've ruined all my teeth, clenching my teeth at night-time, grinding them. Because my super-ego is much more powerful than it was when I was younger, I'm not *allowing* myself to act on any of the craziness, I'm trying to push it all away. After 2 years I'm still all over the place, I'm still behaving as if I've only just stopped ovulating. I've finally given in and I'm having hormone therapy. But it's hard. Really hard. The menopause is the hardest thing I've ever done.

(1987)

FAST FRAMES, SLOW DRAWL
WILLIAM BURROUGHS, LAWRENCE, KANSAS

IT'S VERY HOT. Grandparents' Day in the United States.

'Did you read this about a professor at Gainesville, Florida?' asks Mr Burroughs. 'Murdered by 3 gay boys. They had a smother party – *the head of the 41 year old bachelor was wrapped in canvas, with sheets, a pillow and a bag of ice tied over his face so there was no chance he could breathe.* Dumb jerks. I hate criminals. They're stupid! One of the 3, a very good-looking boy, he's going to get his arse fucked off in prison, then beaten up, then fucked, then beaten –'

'Excuse me.' It's Wayne, the plumber, who props himself in the doorway in paint-spattered denim. 'Will that be all, Bill?'

'I guess so, Wayne,' says Mr Burroughs, twitching wildly about the mouth. 'Are you going out to John's? I've got to go out there and fetch my .45 automatic.'

'No, I'm going to take a shower and get back to you guys and talk about getting this place secure with some door and window locks.'

'Yeah. Big ones.'

William Burroughs – ex-drug fiend, cat lover, America's most something writer – has moved house. He's been in the new one 3 days but the hot water doesn't work. The flat in New York (which was the shower-and-locker-room floor of a converted YMCA building, complete with latrines) has been turned over to a friend. Burroughs then moved to a stone farmhouse a few miles outside Lawrence, Kansas – 'Very convenient for shooting. I blasted my sculptures there, shotguns blasting sheets of plywood which produces very innaresting splitting. Then I sign em.'

Now he has moved into this small one-floor weatherboard house on the edge of Lawrence itself. Last night he was woken up – 'I'm a *very* light sleeper' – by a possum eating the cat's food on the back porch. 'I may have to shoot it with my air rifle. Did you know that in the old days, air guns had to be pumped up by an assistant before they could be used? I say, Carruthers, some ruffians are approaching – where is my pump boy?'

'Have you met your neighbours?'

Burroughs convulses violently – is it laughter or a cry for help? 'Not really,' he says, jabbing an electric cattle prod in the air. 'I spoke to the woman next door – over the fence. I asked her if there'd been any burglars round here. And she said no. And I said good, let's keep it that way. I haven't seen her since then. I'm getting some *real* locks put on the doors –anyone could pick these silly little things with a fucking paperclip.'

He speaks in a low drawl which is at first almost incomprehensible but which reveals elegant characteristics when you tune in. It comes out of a long lugubrious mask of a face crisscrossed round the eyes by creases which resemble the markings of a clown. Burroughs' basic facial expression is one of infinite disappointment.

He grew up in St Louis. The countryside in this part of Kansas is geographically similar. It is almost coming home after long absences in Central and South America, North Africa and Europe. 'But I've never been further east than Athens – I was married first time in the American consulate in Athens.'

What about father? 'He was very distant. He knew about my addictions to hard drugs – his brother was a morphine addict. It was just about the only thing which ran in the family. About the homosexual stuff – sex in any shape or form embarrassed him acutely,' and Burroughs begins furiously polishing the table with a dirty rag.

'Contrary to a rumour put out by Jack Kerouac, I was never rich. My parents gave me an allowance of 200 dollars a month. I couldn't have written my books without it. All this about millions from the Burroughs Adding Machine is nonsense. It never came my way. Now half my income is produced by these public readings – and you don't just pick up any old thing and start reading it. I rehearse. Usually I concentrate on the comic stuff – like where the captain of the sinking ship gets up in women's clothes and rushes into the first lifeboat. You mustn't go on too long. At that poetry festival out on the beach near Rome – this 81 year old poet got sand thrown at him by 10,000 people and well, I said that's not going to happen to me and we did 3 minutes. We had some trouble one night and Yevtushenko refused to go on.'

DF: What's Yevtushenko like?
WB: He's charming. He's a great performer and performed in English eventually in front of the Italians and just wowed them. The actual content of the poem didn't sound so great but he put it across. McLuhan's 'the medium is the message'.
DF: I disagree with McLuhan on that. There is something called the core of meaning.
WB: Oh, good heavens, yes. McLuhan also said we're all travelling at the speed of light. What the hell does that mean? I don't know and I don't think he did.
DF: Perhaps he meant that light is travelling at the speed of people.
WB: Well, if we were travelling at the speed of light we wouldn't age.
DF: But we wouldn't have mass either. This is one of the problems of advanced space technology – people disappear.
WB: That's no obstacle.
DF: Well . . . do you speak any foreign languages fluently?
WB: No. I come as close to being at home with Spanish as any other – 3 years in Mexico and about 5 years in Tangier where Spanish is a second language. I'd like to take refuge in Bernard Shaw – he who is at home in his own language will never be at home in any other. But that's not true. Joyce was a brilliant linguist. And some very

25

stupid people too can make good linguists, just sort of smack it out at the airport. English is very useful. You can do more with it than with almost any other language. French is a very poor language for any sort of verbal experimentation. You can hardly cut up French.

Burroughs is happy to be no longer living in New York. 'It isn't true that I spent my time there going to parties with Andy Warhol. I hate parties, I hardly know Mick Jagger, I don't know those pop people – well, I know Chris Stein and Blondie – they visited me out here and we had a very pleasant afternoon shooting guns and fooling around – he's into guns and knives and stuff.'

But why Lawrence of all places?

'My assistant, James Grauerholz, lives here. I have a doctor here, a lawyer, someone to look after the cat when I'm away, very little crime here – although James had some things stolen out of his car the other day, some tear gas cartridges and stuff. And I hear the Indian college down the road can be dangerous. I must look into that. They have a bad reaction to alcohol, Indians do.'

'You've never wanted to live in California?'

'Hell, no.'

'What's wrong with it?'

'Everything's wrong with it! They have the most ridiculous guns and weapons laws in the country.' He is twitching up against one of the walls at the moment, then slowly zig-zags across to an ancient air-conditioning device in the middle of a bare wall. He turns it on and the ensuing racket almost drowns out the conversation. 'On the West Coast it's a misdemeanour to carry a gun but a felony if you carry a knife and you have to go on a course before you can even carry a tear gas gun which is a lot of nonsense.'

In 1951 Burroughs accidentally killed his second wife with a pistol in Mexico City but it didn't put him off. 'It isn't a question of the gun,' he says, piling sugar into a cup of tea, 'it's a question of carelessness.' The couple were looning around, playing William Tell with a glass on her head – he shot at it and

26

missed. 'We were together about 5 years. She was very intuitive, one of the more intelligent people I've known.' But not sufficiently intuitive and intelligent, it seems, to have avoided this death, a curious amalgam of whimsy and tragedy. At the time she was a confirmed alcoholic and amphetamine addict. Burroughs himself was into all sorts of substances, including the exotic *yage* (pronounced 'yah-hay') from Amazonia.

DF: How did marriage square with your homosexuality?

WB: When I was younger I wasn't exclusively homosexual.

DF: So when did you realise you preferred boys to girls?

WB: Oh, when I was 13 or 14.

DF: What is your relationship with your son these days?

WB: He's dead.

DF: Oh . . . how did that happen?

WB: He had cirrhosis of the liver and had a liver transplant and lived about 5 years after the transplant. After a transplant the anti-rejection drugs they give you have very bad side effects. It makes people self-righteous. You are dealing with the whole immunity mechanism – if you reduce the body's ability to reject, you get a paranoid reaction. The person, feeling himself to be vulnerable, will react with self-righteousness and terrible rigidity of character.

DF: His book *Speed* was quite successful.

WB: I hate speed. I hate anything that makes me chew the carpet.

He walks the room in ever-decreasing circles and eventually reaches a point of introspection. Silent thoughts for a while.

'This is an excellent cup of tea – very English.'

'Glad you like it,' he says. 'Well, I lived in London for 10 years, 5 of them behind Fortnum & Mason. But when I left London I was never more glad to get out of a place in my entire life!'

'Did you use the Piccadilly boys?'

27

'Certainly. Who wouldn't? I like boys 18 to 25. I can go as low as 15, perhaps 14 in exceptional circumstances. Wordsworth was mad about little girls. Have you read the Lucy poems? Outrageous!'

Victor Bockris has transcribed an encounter between Burroughs and Andy Warhol.

Bockris: The English are very odd sexually.
Warhol: They're really odd, but they're so sophisticated, that's why . . .
Burroughs: They like to be beaten with rulers and hairbrushes.
Bockris: I think the English . . .
Warhol: . . . are the sexiest people.
Bockris: Did you ever have any really good sex in England?
Warhol: Oh yeah, the best.
Burroughs: Yeeesss . . .

Bill says 'I notice circumcision is on the wane in Europe. Is this wise? Most American boys are still circumcised. Virtually all the uncircumcised boys in my high school were Roman Catholics – this goes back to the old days when they wanted to distinguish themselves from the Arabs in Spain and places. I'm circumcised myself. I like boys who are circumcised. When my son came along the doctor said do you want him circumcised? and I said sure, let's have it off, it's a very sanitary thing. Hum, then everything got so expensive in London and went downhill fast – this was in the 70s. When I got to New York everything was a helluva lot cheaper – it hasn't necessarily stayed that way. And in New York there's this violence problem which I rather like. It kinda tones you up to sort through your weapons before you go out visiting friends. I carry the lot there – except a gun of course.'

'Guns are illegal in New York?'

'Good God, are they ever! And they always were,' he adds, picking a crust of uncertain origin off his dark green nylon trousers. Burroughs' body is painfully thin but very much alive. Indeed he never stops moving about. Even if he's standing still some part of him will be twitching, curling, jerking. 'A mandatory gaol sentence of a year if you're caught with a gun in New York. My dear, incarceration in an overcrowded zoo! In New York they're absolute . . . animals. I don't like prison and always get myself bailed out. But Kansas is very much gun territory.'

Writers are often chameleons. They can partake of their surroundings without surrendering any essential part of the self. Burroughs has this. In London he is the Harvard avant-garde writer, in Tangier a junkie, in Paris a beat, in New York a member of café society, and in Lawrence, Kansas, he becomes coloured by the old-fashioned frontiersman down on the homestead.

As yet there is hardly any furniture in the house. Could this be that impossible thing, an American home without a television? 'Well, there's an old black & white out the back. I occasionally flick it on if I'm passing – it might produce some synchronicity.' A few magazines lie about on the shiny wood floor. *Guns, Guns & Arms, Warriors, Science Digest*. And a few paperbacks – *The Mask of Apollo, The Silva Mind Control Method* . . . 'I read a lot of horror,' he says, opening another packet of Player's Navy Cut. He chain smokes them except when, in the evening, one might be displaced by the occasional joint. 'I especially like medical horror.'

After studying English Literature at Harvard, Burroughs studied medicine briefly in Vienna just before World War II – 'Coz there's no way I could have got into an American medical school. Have you read *Brain*? It's by the guy that wrote *Coma*. And *Fever*. Titles are very important. I like those ones in the *Reader's Digest* – "Thank God for my Heart Attack". And "My Eyes Have a Cold Nose" by some writer who went blind,' and we both collapse into choked laughter like muzzled hyaenas.

'They don't give you nightmares?'

'There's a recurring nightmare where I'm attacked by a giant centipede, sometimes a cross between a centipede and a scorpion. In the typical centipede nightmare it suddenly rushes me and fastens onto my leg. Then I wake up kicking the bedclothes off – ugh, centipedes! I have to kill em.'

'Have you worked out the origin of this phobia?'

'It's not a phobia! I can't think of anybody who would have a good word to say for centipedes. Generally I don't have nightmares but dreams. I keep a notepad handy. Maybe 40% of my material comes from dreams – sets and characters. There's no line between the dream world and the actual world. But of course, if you get to the point where you find it difficult to cross the road then you should see a doctor. Ugh, that's a fly! I can't stand a fly that alights anywhere near me. Wait a minute.' He pushes his chair back with a screech.

'Do you have a spray?'

'Sure I got sprays, but this isn't a spray case.' Burroughs, whose gait is a combination of shuffle and hop, takes himself out to the kitchen, scratching his thin grey arms which look like 2 broken pencils, and returns grinning with a large orange plastic swat.

'Where was I?' he wonders, sitting down again, swat erect. 'Yes, from the evolutionary point of view, dreams are very important. Man is an artifact designed for space conditions – and I don't mean going up in, as it were, an aqualung which is all we've done so far. The evolution from land into space is equivalent to the evolution from water onto land and will involve biologic alterations quite as drastic.' Thwack! Missed it . . .

'From where you are sitting, what do you think it'll be like?'

The gristle green needlepoint eyes scan the environment with a measure of fatigue tinged with disgust. 'I'm sitting in time. The transition to space is the escape from time, it's immortality even – because my definition of time is that which runs out. You got water creatures looking up at the land – can they conceive what it's like to live up there? Hardly. The fear of falling means nothing to a fish.' Thwack . . . 'The key to what space is like is to be found in dreams.'

'Interesting.'

'Ha. Gore Vidal said he never heard me say anything interesting. But I have no interest in being interesting. It's what you say to those writers who send you unreadable stuff – very innaresting.'

'Have you ever heard Gore Vidal say anything interesting?'

'He was once asked if he believed in corporal punishment and he said yes, between consenting adults. Dreams are a biological necessity. If animals are deprived of REM sleep they eventually die. This is the clue. One of the big barriers to getting into space is weight. But we have at hand the model of a much lighter body, the dream or astral body which is almost, probably not completely, weightless. Of course very little research is going on in this direction at the present time. You see, man is designed for a purpose. This is the flaw in all utopias – no purpose. How dull it is to rust unburnished, not to shine in use. You know where that's from? *Ulysses.*'

'I didn't know that Joyce – '

'By Tennyson.' Thwack! Got im.

DF: You're pretty expert at this now.

WB: Oh, my dear, I've been in training ever since I was old enough to pick up a fly swatter. In other words, what we call happiness is a by-product of function. Happiness isn't sitting on your arse some place. Would you care for a drink? I can only drink Coca Cola and vodka. But I always drink them simultaneously.

DF: Are you alone in this dream theory?

WB: Maybe Governor Jerry Brown will be up there. He believes the future of the race is in space. That's the only thing I agree with him on – he's a gun control person.

DF: You're pretty gun crazy.

WB: I don't think crazy is quite the word. I just *like* guns. Some people like butterflies, some people like . . . knife collections are very popular, you know. For me to be justified in shooting someone, he has to be using what is legally known as *deadly force*. The deadly force hasn't come at me yet, and I don't expect it will, but it doesn't do any good to be wise after the event.

DF: What don't you like?

WB: I don't like centipedes and I don't like flies. Flies are dangerous, they can lay eggs in your ear, then the larvae hatch out and eat into the brain and kill people. If you are ever in the South Seas and see a tiny blue octopus on

31

the beach, don't pick it up – they bite and everyone who's been bitten by the blue ring octopus has been dead within the hour. There's no antidote. I'm going to do a book of things you mustn't do. It gets very cold in Kansas in winter. If it's 16 below zero and there's a slight wind, say 30mph, that makes it the equivalent of 60 below. My dear, several people round here in the winter popped out to collect their mail and a little wind came up and poop, they never came back.

But to-day the temperature is in the mid 80s in the heart of America and the crickets whirr like a Lancashire mill. We are in the garden now and Burroughs is dancing slowly along the perimeter of his property, waving the long, pink cattle prod.

WB: It packs 5,000 volts. Enough to make any trespasser apologise. It works best if there's a little water around – perhaps you should spit on em first!

DF: Are you healthy? I mean physically.

WB: Very healthy. I've never had a major illness in my life. I used to do martial arts, judo, but this bit of jumping up 6 feet into the air and kicking your opponent in the back of the head, my arthritis gets in the way. I go walking round Lawrence.

DF: Is there a conflict in you between the writer and the man of action?

WB: This is an artificial dichotomy, although Hemingway's determination to act out the least interesting facets of his own character posed serious limitations on his writing.

DF: This conflict – is this why he committed suicide?

WB: Oh, he was out of his head. I was convinced he suffered organic brain damage when he had that crash and had to butt his way out of the plane. The best thing he ever wrote was *The Snows of Kilimanjaro*, a story about death which he had a particular feeling for. He could smell it on others.

DF: Have you ever wanted to commit suicide?

WB: Never. I can't see that suicide is bettering one's position at all.

DF: Do you believe in an afterlife?

WB: Certainly. I never doubted the possibility of an afterlife, nor the existence of gods –

DF: But an afterlife presupposes –

WB: Hold on – wait a minute – I'm quoting from *The Place of Dead Roads*, a book of mine. *Kim never doubted the possibility of an afterlife or the existence of gods. He thought that immortality was the only goal worth fighting for and he knew it was not something you just automatically get from believing some rubbish or other like Christianity or Islam. It was something you had to work and fight for like everything else in this life or another.* I do feel that Christianity is the most virulent spiritual poison ever administered to a disaster-prone planet. It is parasitic, fastens onto people, and the essence of evil is parasitism.

DF: So what is your function as a writer?

'The function of all art,' he shouts from the other side of the garden as he crawls playfully on all fours round a tree after the cat, 'and by that I include creative scientific thought, is to make people aware of what they know and don't know they know, coz you can't tell anybody anything that they don't know already on some level.'

'Do you cry easily, Bill?'

'Not easily – but I do cry. It's not necessarily a question of getting upset – it's something that hits you, something that moves you. I cried not so long ago.'

'Is loneliness ever a problem?'

'No, it isn't. I gave a course in creative writing at New York City College. I don't believe it can be taught. But I said there are certain prerequisites. One, you have to be able to spend hours at a typewriter in solitude – if you can't, forget about being a writer.'

'What are the other prerequisites?'

'A lot of reading. I think it was T. S. Eliot who said that if

33

someone has a pretentious literary style it's usually because they haven't read enough books.'

Bill talks very well, for hours, then on through the next day. Why is Kansas a dry state? Why is Lawrence called the Paris of the Plains? Where do you get your vice in a place like this? What indeed is the Plains sensibility?

'Good God, these aren't the Plains! The Plains are 300 miles west of here – the most goddam desolate country I've ever seen, not a tree in any direction. The Plains sensibility must be whatever lunacy causes people to carry on living there.'

James Grauerholz, future tender of the shrine, arrives in gold-rimmed spectacles to take us to dinner. Burroughs produces a large shopping bag and starts to fill it with weaponry.

'With these books of yours, the strange worlds and weird sex and so on, you must get a lot of people just turning up on the doorstep making awful suggestions.'

'It's not something I encourage. But I'm prepared,' he says, clanking the shopping bag. 'Some people call it paranoia – but I say a paranoiac is a man in possession of all the facts. Was Pasolini paranoid? That kid murdered Pasolini from behind with a plank with nails sticking out of it. The nails penetrated his skull. I have heard from various people that this kid was hired by a right wing group.'

It's getting dark outside. Magnificent sheets of shocking pink lightning light up patches of the sky and tornadoes are forecast over the next few days.

'Look at this, my favourite, my Charter Arms 2″ Barrel Undercover .38 Special – I'd like to see some dumb fucker with a bag of ice get past that! And look at this,' he says, pulling on a jacket of blue-based tartan in some synthetic material. 'I got it from the Thrift Shop. They're the Salvation Army places. 8 dollars, pretty good, eh? I enjoy a bargain.' And donning very unalluring spectacles, plonking a pork pie hat on his head, he selects a stout walking stick, picks up the clanking shopping bag, and moves keenly into the outside world.

(1982)

WARM PSYCHIATRIST
R. D. LAING IN THE BASEMENT

THIS CONTROVERSIAL PSYCHIATRIST was born in Glasgow in 1927. Now he lives mainly in North London, in a white stucco house which was once a vicarage and has a leafy front garden. A steep flight of steps brings one up to the large black door bearing a polished brass plate engraved with the word 'Laing'. The ringing of the bell triggers a dog's wild barking and children's voices. Inside, the rooms are large and light. All the doors are open – this is very relaxing – and many tall windows reveal a leafy *back* garden. From the hall an iron spiral staircase descends to the basement. This nether region is also light, being built above the ground, and yet retains the intimate, submarine air of basements everywhere. The main room down here is both businesslike and calm, simply furnished with a few old chairs, and the walls are stacked with academic publications – the words *schizophrenia*, *madness*, *neuro-*, *fear*, *therapy* reverberate horribly among the titles. There is even a couch – Edwardian, brocaded, worn – because this is the room where R. D. Laing receives his patients. He is, despite writing influential books and responding to inter-national invitations and the more frivolous pursuits of celebrity life, also a full-time psychiatric doctor. His approach to the subject is rather informal. For example, in reaction to the question 'What is madness?', he starts to giggle.

'We can give a sociological answer and say that madness is that which does not conform to the prevailing sense of reality in any particular society. We also know that the sages of various civilisations – Buddha, Lao Tsu, Jesus – have said that this ordinary consensus reality is a state of ignorance and delusion. They say that, from the point of view of higher truth, this ordinary state of mind is in itself mad. I agree with both uses of the word "mad".'

So was Hitler mad? 'From the first point of view,' Laing says, 'in terms of his own society, he wasn't. In the meta-sense, he was.'

'What is schizophrenia?'

The doctor starts giggling again and gives his head a rapid scratch. This causes the hair, which is grizzled and thinning on top, to stick out in donnish fashion. 'It can be so many things – let me show you something!' He disappears and returns with a thick book in soft lime-green covers entitled *Diagnostic and Statistical Manual of Mental Disorders, III*. This is 'DSM 3', the bible of the psychiatric profession, a book of working definitions published by the American Psychiatric Association. In it virtually every form of 'interesting' behaviour is stigmatised as schizophrenic or potentially so.

'That's right! Look here – "clairvoyance, telepathy, 6th sense" – what's 6th sense? "superstitiousness, overvalued ideas" – overvalued ideas are not on!' Laing's face is all screwed up with delight and in the centre of his smile a tooth is missing. 'And look, another symptom of mental disorder, it says here, is neologisms, "new words invented by the subject". In fact Carl Jung diagnosed James Joyce as schizophrenic and as a result Joyce's allowance, which he'd been receiving from a rich American lady, was stopped. "Or distortions of standard words to which the subjects has given new, highly idiosyncratic meanng." You're not allowed to do that! Here is DSM 3's example of a mad sentence: "They had an insinuating machine next door".'

'But the use of the word "insinuating" there, it's very clever. A whole situation can be inferred from it, the whole bad neighbour syndrome.'

'Exactly!' rollocks Dr Laing. 'But this is the sort of thing one has to battle against, people who think a sentence like that is insane.'

'What is the purpose of the sense of humour?'

'I certainly couldn't have survived my life so far without

mine – there is something absolutely necessary about a sense of humour. DSM 3 has something to say on the subject – it tries to include everything. It says that one of the symptoms of a mental disorder is "flattened affect" which means not laughing or crying enough. Or "inappropriate affect" which means you laugh and cry in the wrong places – you mustn't *do* that!'

Laing is gleeful – and then something else occurs to him. He rubs his eyes, into which a weariness has suddenly seeped, and says 'But regardless of the endless argument over definitions, the bottom line on madness of course is that there are many people who are just suffering in states of complete misery and confusion.'

Perhaps more than anyone else, Laing has softened up psychiatry, which is a branch of clinical medicine, by applying to it what has often turned out to be hardly more than the etiquette of human communication: proper attention and mutual respect. The hard psychiatry which posed as an exact science and whose tools were straitjackets, padded cells, insulin comas, electric shocks, was not only unattractive – its cure-rate was unimpressive too. In fact Laing says that psychiatrists can't cure people at all. They can only guide the individual through a self-healing process. 'On the other hand I don't want just to insult psychiatry. For example, I'm not against the use of drugs *per se*. Lithium Largactil, Stelazine, these things help people to live a life which is far and away preferable to a frantic or desolate existence in the back ward of a mental hospital.'

So how would he formulate his underlying idea, his particular contribution? '. . . The transformation of perception and experience according to the intention you bring to them – this I've tried to explore and it is something you don't find in conventional psychiatric thinking at all. You do find it however in Thomas Aquinas, for example.'

And what has been his biggest mistake? . . . . . Long pause. He puffs on a tiny cigar. There are plenty of long pauses. '. . . . . A certain naïveté . . . in thinking that other psychiatrists would welcome what I had to say. In fact they presented me with a brick wall . . . Funnily enough, many psychiatrists completely agree with me now – at least they do in the bar after the conference. But they don't like me giving the game away in public, they don't like me being familiar with the lower ranks.'

'We hear a great deal about the abuse of psychiatry in Communist countries . . .'

'I only have word-of-mouth experience of that. One thing has struck me – the psychiatrists in Russia seem to be sincere. They really do believe that free thoughts are symptoms of psychotic behaviour.'

'If you had to go mad, which country would you prefer to go mad in?'

'Britain is not bad. Like everything else in this country, it's hit or miss whether you get a good psychiatrist. But on the whole they do try to do the decent thing here.'

In a country like Italy, where emotional exchange between people is supposedly more free than say among the British, Americans or French, one could imagine there to be less incidence of schizophrenia – is this borne out by the statistics?

'Well, in 1978 the Italian parliament passed a law to phase out all mental hospitals. From 1978 there were to be no more admissions. In the area round Verona for example, there has since been diagnosed only one case of schizophrenia. This is because the system which demands a constant supply of schizophrenics has largely been dismantled. But it looks as though for various political reasons they might be bringing back mental hospitals in Italy.' Despite what one might have expected, Laing himself is not politically involved. Indeed he has never even voted for a political party – 'so far', although a list of his heroes does have some political overtones: Kierkegaard, Nietzsche, Camus, Sartre, Foucault.

'What is the most bizarre mental case you've encountered?'

'So many bizarre ones . . . A woman came to me because she saw penises everywhere, showering down from the ceiling, sprouting up from the floor like mushrooms. And all she wanted was a quiet life. So I said to her, do you think this could have anything to do with sex? She thought a long time and then she said "No . . ." She was a woman who'd married, had children, she'd had a sex life. She came back to see me again some time later and I asked "Are you still seeing showers of penises?" She replied "Sanitary towels are growing out of my knees . . ." '

'What sort of sanitary towels? Used ones?'

'I don't know about that, I didn't have the presence of mind to ask. But she did say "Doctor, you know, I've been thinking about what you said, whether this had anything to do with sex, and I think maybe it has." This was a pretty bizarre case. Eventually it resolved itself.'

But Laing is careful not to ascribe all unusual phenomena to 'delusion'. He believes in the paranormal and by the paranormal he understands 'Clairvoyance, telepathy, distant vision – but I don't want to limit the possibilities.'

'What is the most difficult thing about being a psychiatrist? I mean, why are there more suicides among psychiatrists than in any other profession?'

'You spend your life dealing with human misery, terror, confusion. It's not the kind of work from which you can draw much encouragement about the human lot. Music is very important to me as a release.'

'Have you ever felt yourself to be going mad?'

'. . . I have sometimes felt that, er, the mind I have is a particularly taxing one.'

'But you haven't ever gone over the edge?'

'If I had, I don't think I'd be sitting here talking to you now as a professional psychiatrist. And I've never tried to commit suicide.'

'But you do get depressed.'

'Yeah . . . yeah, that's the band of things I find most unpleasant. I don't know that I'd call it clinical depression but it's a state of not getting pleasure out of things, not seeing the point in anything, losing zest, no glow. When this happens I try to keep up a reasonably ordered life, even though I don't feel like it at all. I make a special point of shaving in the morning, of making sure my trousers are creased when perhaps I wouldn't bother, of getting up instead of lying in bed for hours. If I have a mixture of depression and exhaustion however and feel I'm really getting to the end of my rope, I will crash out . . .' He also has 2 families in 2 cities which he finds very useful for his states of mind, a first wife living in Glasgow whom he still sees along with 4 grown-up children from that marriage, and a second wife and 3 young children living in London.

'Do you have a particular hang-up or problem?'

'. . . . . The drugs that give one a temporary euphoria or oblivion, these I'm tremendously drawn to. Especially alcohol. I've really got to watch my drinking – especially as I get older.'

'Have you tried heroin?'

'Only once. I felt I was the still absolute centre of a spinning gyroscope. It was an *extremely* pleasurable feeling and I felt a very great temptation to take it again.'

'What is the best way to avoid mental illness?'

'If you mean how does one avoid falling into undesirable states of mind, I do wish I could put that into a simple formula. But I don't know – except that one should avoid "asking for it".'

And finally the future – as in 'hope for'. Casting one's eyes across the planet, where are the healthy societies to be found?

'I'm a great believer in small is beautiful. It's not necessary to go with the anthropologists in search of Amazonian indians. I see it for example when I go on holidays in the Western Highlands – small, fairly self-sufficient communities, very successful at the human level. One of the extraordinary things about hypnotism, on which I did a lot of work years ago, is how very simple it is to remove a man's survival apparatus, i.e. the evidence of his senses. You'd think it would be very difficult to remove something like that, but it isn't. And this is because our strategy for survival is twofold. One is of course the evidence of our senses, an individual experience which hypnotism can wipe out. But the other is our capacity for social solidity. Our capacity to act all one way, in a crisis for example, is highly developed, perhaps even genetic, and this is what the hypnotist uses, the suspension of individual judgement. So a healthy society – and a sane individual – needs to balance both. It would be impossible to live in a total anarchy of individuals. On the other hand we don't want to be lambs going blindly to the slaughter, do we?'

(1985)

40

THE BLACK RINSE

JAMES BROWN

'I'VE GOT YOU in the middle of my coiffure,' says Mr Brown in his suite at the Hilton Hotel, 'but I thought it wouldn't make much difference.'

His voice is rich and gravelly, a tough man's voice, but a tough man of experience – the tone is self-possessed, not resentful. His burly assistant Mr Stallings – to-day everyone is being referred to as Mr This or Mr That (there are no women up here) – Mr Stallings is mashing black goo into Mr Brown's hair. Some of it escapes and thin rivulets of pitch black juice run down the brown forehead and, if they aren't dabbed away in time, which usually they are, run over the closed eyelids and on down the deep creases in his cheeks each side of nose and mouth. Below the chin Mr Brown is wrapped in a barber's gown of black and white vertical stripes which vibrate dizzyingly like an op art painting.

'Do you always put black on your hair?'

'No, no, I have about 20 grey hairs on my head, but when I'm performing dust and smoke get in it and it gets dull and brittle, so I have it done for every performance. The show at Hammersmith last night was unbelievable – we made not just a video out of it but a *world* video. Most artists are famous in one place but me, I'm one of the few, along with Louis Armstrong, people like that, who is worldwide.'

He speaks with a heavy accent of the southern USA, delivering words slowly and quickly but rarely in between, in lots of little curves of expression, and sometimes they drawl out or swoop together and the ends are lost.

41

'I was born in South Carolina, raised in Georgia. Kind of dual situation there.' Born 1933. He is still going strong – so what about the much reported heart trouble? 'I did have it but I went past that. Didn't have time to have a bad heart. I was kind of restored – with implants in my mouth. I can still get a broken heart though, ha! And I've had my toenails removed, which affected my equilibrium for a while.'

'Toenails removed?'

'Yeah. The big toenails. Some infection there.'

'Do they put new ones on?'

'No, they don't put anything on. They take em off – and that's it. You soon learn your balance again.'

'Do you remember World War II? Were there a lot of black soldiers in the army?'

'What we're trying to do now,' he says, closing his eyes as he senses a drop of black juice running towards one of them (Mr Stallings catches it just in time), 'is get away from the words black and white and make it just humanity. But I know that's the way you have to identify me, as black.'

'No, it's not that. I'm just interested.'

'Well, the Afro-Americans have always been in all the wars, but I guess that World War II was really the breakthrough for ethnic people. The war made a lot of money for them. I remember my father before the war made 4½ dollars a week. When the war started he got 18 dollars a week. And just before he went into the Service he was making 35 dollars a week.' (James Brown's father was also a singer but made his living doing odd jobs, working in factories, petrol stations and so on.)

'And as a boy, who were your heroes?'

'Joe Louis. Bing Crosby. Louis Armstrong. Count Basie. Duke Ellington. Louis Jordan was the one I really liked. He played saxophone and sang and had a fantastic band – the Tenpenny Five – they kicked their legs, they moved, they did everything. And Louis Jordan did lots of other things, he made a lot of movies too, and that I liked because men of my origin, they don't have a lot of em that goes *all* the way. Even Nat King Cole – and it's not knocking him – I think he was allowed to do just 10% of what I'm doing.'

'You go all the way, do you?'

'Yes. I've been lucky. I've had brothers like Mr White here [Cliff White, head of Charly Records, one of the James Brown scholars] who've stayed in there with me. Being uneducated probably gave me a boost in one respect – because I didn't know what had never been done before, I had no reason to *fear* anything. For example, I was at Midem, the Cannes Music Festival, I walked on the stage in a cowboy hat and a jump suit and big high boots – really against the grain – and they *loooooooked* at me!'

James Brown is extremely popular in France and crops up regularly on all French pop music stations and in all the discothèques.

'Yeah, more popular there I guess than any place in the world. We drew over a million people once, the biggest crowd to attend a show in history – about 26 miles from Paris, an open-air thing called "Humanity". It was done by the Soviet Government.'

'Really? The Russians?'

'It was about 2 years ago. Also I worked all through Italy – and I was promoted there by the Russian Government.'

'Why?'

'Because they bought it from the local promoters. Because everybody's looking for an attraction that can go worldwide. I'm going to Poland and China. I've been to Australia – when I first got there they'd read about some of the things that happened in the 60s and thought I was a revolutionist that was *angry* but I'm a revolutionist trying to bring people together – humanitarian. I *was* aggressive in the 60s but I went out to help. I was able to quell the riots after the assassination of Dr Martin Luther King. I've always been a vehicle for goodness.'

Mr White nods his head sagely, but retains a diplomatic silence as he has done throughout. Likewise Mr Stallings.

'What's the closest you've been to death?'

The noise of Mr Stallings kneeding Mr Brown's head is quite loud and crunchy, like the sound of a man walking through dead leaves.

'Er . . . as close as I am now. You either get killed or you don't get killed. You're never close to death. You're probably

43

closer to death than me – coz I never thought about it!' The glittering white gate of his mouth opens in an enormous smile showing a tongue of startling pink – obviously he doesn't smoke cigarettes. Mr Stallings finishes mashing and with his big black hands delicately fits a plastic shower cap over the soggy heap of hair while the colour takes.

A lot of people in popular music in the 60s died in dramatic ways. A typical but almost forgotten case was that of Little Willie John, the boy with the marvellous voice and much admired by James Brown in the early days – indeed, almost the JB prototype. Willie John was born in Arkansas in 1937; singing with Count Basie at 14; huge hit with 'Fever' in 1956; success brought problems, became paranoid about his short-ness, started to carry a gun and knife; in 1966 stabbed a railworker during a fight, convicted of manslaughter and imprisoned; 1967 James Brown visited him inside and found him sick in a wheelchair; 1968 Little Willie John died in prison leaving a widow and 2 sons.

'Yes, I lost other friends too,' he says. 'Sam Cooke, Otis Redding, later on Elvis Presley. Oh! I'm gonna play baseball for a worthy cause, against hunger of the Ethiopians, and I'm gonna pitch. Really I was supposed to be a baseball player. I don't see how I ever made it as a singer and a musician – because baseball is where I'm good. I was also a fighter. I fought professionally, not a lot, but I did it. Me and Mr Stallings fought the best. Mr Stallings sparred with Ray Robinson. My stamina shows on stage.'

Although the great days of his dancing have passed, James Brown is still capable of exceptional exertion.

'Why then did you choose music?'

'Because I was a juvenile delinquent, see. Getting into sport would've slowed me down. But as I look back, I can see that the Government had this plan all along and really wanted me to do what I'm doing. Brother Cliff don't agree, but now I think I'll go all the way and probably wind up in politics. Because I can do *so* much!'

'Why did you go to prison when you were young?'

'My family was very poor and I was breaking and entering and taking things from automobiles in order to get decent clothes to go to school with. And when I got to prison I did almost 4 years – and then they turned me loose.'

'Did it teach you anything?'

'Yes. It taught me that I don't wanna go back. And I've never been back.'* Black juice begins to run out from beneath the shower cap but Henry Stallings comes across and pats it away before it gets very far. Mr Brown opens his eyes with relief. His eyes are warm and soft, and the slight frown which is often above them gives him a boyish look which disarms his more bombastic statements.

'Do you believe in the American dream?'

'I'm *living* the American dream! That you can start from rags and go to riches and walk with Kings and Queens and Presidents.'

'What do you hate about America?'

'That some poor people didn't get educated. That's not just Afro-Americans but all sorts. A poor Caucasian American is treated worse than a poor Afro-American – because they say the poor Caucasian don't have any excuse to be that way. I think the biggest cross a man can have is for someone to tell him he's better than the other person.'

'What's been the hardest time for you?'

'Um . . . . probably when I was 8 or 9 years old. It's got better since. I had nothing then. But – I think being alone is probably the better part of your life because that's really the only time you get to know yourself. But I remember when I was in prison I'd look out the window and I saw the advantages that anything free had over me – whether it was a bug, a bird, a cow. The worst thing in life is – to be hungry.'

'Do you think you are a free man?'

Certainly to be interviewed while having your hair dyed suggests great freedom of action. It isn't something many American stars could take in their stride. Mr Brown looks a little bizarre in this situation but he's not reduced by it and he doesn't feel obliged to play it for laughs (although while thoroughly enjoying the trappings of stardom, he often seems

* Some years after this – he went back.

45

to be sending them up – and similarly when seeming to send them up, he often isn't).

'I think I'm freer than most people. Because people listen to me. And when you can come in where Mozart, Beethoven, Bach, Strauss, Muddy Waters, Howlin Wolf, the Beatles, Elvis, where they all come in – and people are waiting on you to hear your music, that's more than freedom, that's a Godsend.'

'Are you a religious man?'

'Very religious.'

'Church religious?'

'Baptist. But also I'm religious above my faith. I respect your religion – whatever it is. I believe very strongly there's an eternal life. But I'm not sure what it's like. I think we go through different phases – I believe that living is probably the hardest part of your life. Your body eventually wears out and your soul takes on a new form. My body's OK at the moment. We played 125 concerts in the past year. But that's small. 15 years ago I played 335.'

The inflexions of his singing voice are still wonderful. And his dance music – it has been as influential as rock 'n' roll: that extraordinary sense of levitation in the James Brown sound, the high floating singing drive of even the heaviest rhythm.

'Has it made you rich?'

'Wealthy. Not rich. A wealthy man can get whatever he wants. A rich man is worried by what he gonna lose. But in my business you don't brag about what you got. Naturally, cash is something you don't maintain because governments don't allow you to.'

'And what do you do to relax?'

'When I'm performing that's the most relaxed I am. After that, what I hunger for is good intelligent conversation – and that's a very hard thing to find to-day.'

Mr Stallings is hovering round the shower cap and seems keen to take the hair into some new phase. Before I go, Mr Brown decides to deliver a sermon on world peace and understanding and his own part in it.

'. . . that my aim in life is to try to make people relate to each other more, to help them understand that you are your worst enemy, that it's out there for you if you wanna get it, tell the young kids to get a good education, set your goals high but realise you gotta start somewhere real, to come into a country and let the government know I'm coming to do a service to humanity, not to interfere in their politics, to tell the governments that if at any time they want me to help with their problems, that I'd like to help but I'd like to be called first, that I'd like to see record companies not try to have me exclusive but let me do projects for all of them. I want the small man on the corner, whether he's a beachcomber or derelict, to know that he can talk with me. I want my children to not take their father for granted but to have a sense of responsibility. And last but not least, I'd like to see everyone try to get into a religion they feel comfortable with. I'd like to see the rich nations help the poor nations without doing it for gain or destroying the civilisation – sometimes if you find a group of people deep in the jungle and you can't help their situation, it's better to leave them alone. And my biggest worry is that we won't be able to handle our nuclear weapons properly. I want to think that a man makes a weapon to protect himself. If you've got a weapon and I've got a weapon, we can talk. But if you've got one and I don't have one, *you* can talk – but that's not fair. And I'd like to close by saying I thank God and hope God blesses each and every one of you out there. Thank-you, sir, and I hope you'll bring your kids to the show.'

'I don't have any kids.'

'Bring your wife then.'

'I don't have a wife.'

'Then – oh, let's not get into all that. Bring whoever you're gonna bring and have a good time.'

(1985)

THE QUEEN OF EGYPT

DEPARTURE FROM HEATHROW Airport after heavy anti-terrorist security checks. So unnatural seems the rise of such weight into the air that there is always an uncomfortably prolonged moment, as the aeroplane hurtles down the strip, when one is convinced that it's not going to take off, that a magnetic force holds it to the ground, and one will plunge off the end of the runway into turf and explode! . . . . . Egyptair passengers look an exotic bunch – discover many of them are Pakistanis bound for Karachi where this plane ends up after Cairo – Karachi sounds as appetising as a squashed cockroach. Sunset over the Alps at 31,000 feet – Byron never had that . . . No alcohol is served. But there is beef curry for dinner. Afterwards air stewards pass up and down the gangways with trolleys of duty-free pearls and gold. 2 religious-looking gentlemen disappear into lavatories and come out wiping wet hands. After the ritual ablution, they unroll prayer mats in the small space outside the lavatory doors, kneel and genuflect approximately towards Mecca. Less devout Muslims remain in their seats, nodding sagely, dropping their heads onto their chests as they quietly murmur verses from the Koran. Go to the loo, all the paper has gone, so refrain from defecation.

*

Dropped off at Cairo airport late at night. Met, almost on the tarmac itself, by Samy Habib who whisks me at high speed

48

through all the bureaucratic blocks (the currency controls are ludicrous) which so grievously detain less fortunate visitors. At the luggage carousel, have baggage fear (memories of St Louis Airport where my suitcase came through in a plastic dustbin because a transporter had run over it, reducing the thing to an unseemly pulp of burst shaving-cream, toothpaste etc). Eventually it arrives without mishap, Samy smiles at the Customs men and we rattle out into the hot African night. On the way into town our driver, who is a very old man, says something in Arabic and smacks his lips. Samy says the old boy likes young girls.

The wizened driver nods agreement with more lip-smacking. The City of the Dead slides past on the left, a vast cemetery inhabited by poor people, its many mosques and domed tombs illuminated with lime-green neon strips.

'Why are you here?' asks Samy.

'To see Queen Farida.'

'She is a painter these days. I am a painter too.' He shows me his graduation paper from art school. 'But now I work for travel company. The problem was – I paint like Salvador Dali and Egyptians are not ready for this.'

Bumping and grinding into the centre of town, we pass many atmospheric alleyways and cafés lit up inside where men smoke hookahs. Fanciful figures in robes and a wide variety of headgear are everywhere hanging about unperturbed by the passage of time. Little boys zip in and out of the lights on errands.

Hotel is modern. Samy says eat no salad for a few days and drink bottled water. Sleep.

*

The *muezzin* colours the morning. Phone Queen Farida.

'So you came,' she sighs.

'Of course.'

'Why?'

'Didn't Beris explain?'

'Yes. But I am tired. I need a holiday.'

'Oh dear. When should I call then?'

49

'I don't know, Sunday afternoon?' Another deep sigh.

'What time?'

'I don't know. Ring me on Sunday morning. To make sure I'm not too tired . . .'

'Thank-you, I'll do that.' But I'm uncertain whether she heard. She sort of vaporised at the other end of the line, not that I noticed the phone being put down, but I know the Queen isn't there any more . . .

Go up onto hotel roof for a swim. Hotel is in an area planned in the 1960s, a sea of modern blocks the colour of dried camel dung. Chanting to Allah continues to coil in the air, cut across by carhorns and police whistles – sounds like a composition by John Cage. Stretching my head over the parapet, I look left, and manage to descry poking up in the dusty distance the Pyramids! The thrill is unexpectedly *intense*. Cairo is hot, on the edge of the desert which frequently blows into town, and even from this height is full of advertisements for Camel and Marlboro cigarettes. Unpack with TV on (black and white dubbed Latin American soap opera). Gazing at the world map in my diary, discover that Peking is further south than Istanbul.

Taxi to the Egyptian Museum. After much haggling get the fare down to E£2 which is the magic figure that will take you to most destinations around the centre, but it's still way over the official rate. In Egypt, as in all Third World countries, you can get more or less whatever you want wherever you are. This is because everything is done through people, not through systems. The taxi fare for example is a product of one's relationship with the taxi driver, not an abstract amount fixed by central authority. Because of the prime importance of personal relationships over abstract concepts, the Third World means 'corruption' – which also means a constipating bureaucracy which attempts to minimise this. But it also means intimacy and freedom. Get in front with the driver.

Cairo, like so many cities now, is shattered – a mass of bits laced together with roads. The interstices become traffic islands onto which are crowded gasping populations. Policemen in white uniforms (black in winter) and black berets shuffle around town in groups, machine-guns held loosely in their hands – they are all young and thin. As we cross the Nile the driver points out the American skyscraper hotels – Rameses Hilton, Cairo Sheraton, Gezira Sheraton: this gruesome litany is repeated by every single taxi driver. The things which make Cairo itself and not like other cities, they hardly value at all. When you see all this American 'colonisation' you begin to understand the Islamic backlash.

Traversing a flyover, I notice that the flat rooftops of lower buildings are usually of rubble so that it is impossible to determine whether they are collapsing or under construction (most in fact are incomplete because of the Arab saying 'When a house is finished, death walks in'). Plenty of palm trees in Cairo but am surprised by the enormous number of jacaranda trees too.

Cairo Museum, ground floor, Room 14 – New Kingdom – sandstone head of a king (unknown) found at Luxor. This young king is smiling! The 2 things missing from Ancient Egyptian art are sex (apparently the god Min is ithyphallic but have seen no examples of this) and smiling. So to chance upon this smiling pharaoh is an astonishment of great beauty. The declivity of the smile, the tilt forward of it, suggests both sweetness and irony, a generosity of spirit which is at the same time implacable. There is intelligence here in the composed alertness of expression, and wistfulness as if he would rather be in some more playful condition, and even a hint of that melancholy which comes with the solitude of greatness. The smile presents 2 profiles. On its right side self-satisfaction curves in a smirk which on a good day might become impishness and on a bad day petulance. On the left side the curve is animal-like, Pan-like, the mesmerising smile of a sexual predator. This difference comes about because the head, like every handmade or naturally made object, including man, cannot be precisely symmetrical. A minute's pause in front of it and one can distinguish a great range of passive and active qualities, from resignation to voracious pride, but few of the negative qualities. Fear and fury are not here. Really this must be one of the world's 3 great smiles (the others being the *Mona Lisa*'s and the Buddha's). For me he is the most wonderful exhibit in a museum largely devoted to the ornaments of death – because he is so alive, he is with us. And yet there is no postcard of him in the shop by the entrance, no citation in any guidebook.

By contrast his only rival is hugely celebrated: Tutankhamun, as evidenced by the face on the gold burial mask, first floor, room 4. The window of this room is open and through it skyscrapers climb into the dusty bluish heat while carhorns blare up without cease from the street below. Tutankhamun is almost smiling – but in fact is not. He stares into outer space towards some point way beyond. He is not with us. He is beautiful too – but dead.

*

Breakfast late on the roof in sunshine among traffic noise. Although Cairo waitresses for the most part wear European dress, they also wear extra-thick modesty stockings.

In many Third World cities, the harsh option between the modern international credit card ghetto and the native dust and mosquitoes is moderated by recourse to crumbling colonial establishments where you can be close to a place without plunging headlong into the mire. But in Egypt, unlike India, very little of this bridging ground remains (the Victoria Hotel is the nearest Cairo comes to it). A large part of old European Cairo was burnt out on Black Saturday, January 26th, 1952, including the original Shepheard's Hotel. The Opera House, built for *Aida*, was burnt down in 1979. The rest is disappearing in a storm of towerblocks. The British Embassy, the largest embassy in Cairo, a gorgeous mansion in a huge garden in the heart of the redevelopment area, supplies a sublimely nonchalant counterblast, but it is almost alone. With only a few days to spend it is not easy breaking out of the prophylactic of air-conditioned tourism-business. And a few days mean impressions, fragments. You cannot grasp the ever-distending, ever-rupturing corpus of the place even if you go up Cairo Tower. Occasionally one registers unexpected flashes of the Pyramids, far off between modern blocks, and this recognition relocates the psyche. The world's most absolute buildings are not easily defeated – but how much longer can they hold out against the explosion of junk?

Examine my notes on Queen Farida; a strange, unfortunate woman. She was born in Alexandria in 1921. Her mother was lady-in-waiting to Queen Nazli. She married King Farouk, King of Egypt, Sovereign of Nubia, of the Sudan, of Kordofan and of Darfur, in 1938 when she was 16 and he was 17 (he'd been on the throne since 1936). She had 3 daughters by him but, having failed to produce an heir, the couple were divorced in 1948. Farouk married again in 1951 but he was rapidly losing control of affairs and was forced to abdicate in 1952 in favour of his baby son by his second marriage (which was dissolved in 1954) and a Council of Regency. This lasted for a year until June 1953 when Nasser proclaimed a republic. Farouk died at Rome in 1965.

To the Nile Hilton where Americans wear jeans and T-shirts and Egyptians wear very smart clothes. This is the earliest and most beautiful of the modern hotels, memorable for its blue tiles. Through the glossy foyer to the health club below. Here a monstrously fat Egyptian covered in long scars and with heavily bloodshot eyes pads across the wet marble floor from steam room to plunge pool to sauna and back again, fiddling with his genitals under the apron of his vast sagging stomach. A number of the Egyptian clients have shaved pubic hair and, being of Islam, all are circumcised. Afterwards, tip the attendant, tip the masseur (even though he short-timed me), tip everyone in this country. About tipping: not too much, not too little – and very important, don't be self-conscious, don't be pedantic, keep it in round amounts, and recognise that what you are doing is reasonable not condescending. Nonetheless I grow faintly irritated by the constant air of expectation hovering round my pockets. Buy the *Egyptian Gazette* which is printed in English (established 1880). *Guardian* and *Daily Telegraph* widely available in Cairo for those who can stomach News from Home in faraway places, but haven't seen a single copy of *The Times* on sale.

By and large Egyptians are very friendly. Despite the poverty and overpopulation one still senses the influence of an ancient and courteous culture. There is nothing here like, for example, the predatory violence sensed in Palermo where a true savagery has taken root. There is an argument for assessing the cultural status of a system by the extent to which it prevents members of a community from hurting each other. In this sense Cairo and Moscow* are infinitely more civilised than Palermo or New York. In Moscow and Cairo they are unlikely to mug you – but in Cairo they will swindle you. Swindling is a sport here.

Mind wandering. Listlessness. Roll on Sunday. It is no accident that the prosperous parts of the planet are temperate and the Third World is HOT. Local tap water tastes like swimming-pool water, as it does in Calcutta. Tea and coffee are both appalling in Cairo and taste like hot swimming-pool water.

Tourist tip: the smart place to stay is Mena House, owned by Oberoi. The Windsor Hotel is amusingly decrepid. Also the Manyal Palace which is half hotel and half museum where you can find a table made from elephants' ears and an hermaphrodite goat. I am at the Atlas Zamelek. My room is large and when the TV is off there is nothing whatsoever in it to suggest that one is in Egypt. In this room I invent the concluding 5 pages of my novel *The Underbelly*.

*

Sunday afternoon. Queen Farida lives in a suburb south of Cairo called Maahdi where live many foreign residents and groups of policemen hang around in the leafy streets – it used to be smart. There are no smart areas now. But it's safe. As in other upper middle-class enclaves the world over, the large villas have often been demolished to be replaced by blocks of flats.

She lives in a new brown and white block of flats on Road 14 among trees. A white-robed porter in white turban wafts me towards the lift. I rise to Queen Farida's level – third floor – and a servant girl lets me into a medium-size flat, not at all fancy, with a bohemian atmosphere in which the venerable

---

* Both cities have since degenerated alarmingly in this respect.

and the nondescript intermingle. A table carries several ranks of photographs, including official royal ones. Lamps give out a cosy light. Queen Farida, slim and sweet-faced with a soft voice and gentle smile, welcomes me – her clothes are couture casual: black and acid yellow. Her hair is tied back. As I put the microphone on a small table beside her, she sighs deeply and an expression of distaste passes over her features. 'This is my first interview in 25 years.' Her English is fluent and idiomatic.

'What did your father do?'

'Alexandria was very cosmopolitan. It was a Mediterranean city. There was a Jewish community, an Italian community, a Greek community, French people, English people. And we had a special court for strangers – my father was in charge of that. Now all the strangers have gone. Cairo was always more African.'

'Did you grow up in the European style?'

'Oh yes. I went to a very nice French convent in Alexandria. Many Muslim and Jewish girls went there. They didn't try to make you a Catholic. Also, around the time I was born, was the liberation of the Egyptian woman. A very great lady called Hoda Sharawi went into the streets to ask England for Egyptian independence. All the women followed her and threw off their veils. Now the contrary is happening.'

'Cairo seems a free and easy town – I don't sense a lot of violence.'

'Egypt as a whole is a very free country. The Egyptian – I don't know about the new generation, I can't make them out yet – but the old Egyptian is the kindest, friendliest of all the Moslem world. They don't like violence, they don't attack tourists. Of course occasionally it happens – because there is poverty, the heat and pollution are terrible, people's nerves are on edge. Egypt is trying to live the modern life but the population isn't really up to it.'

'Did you travel abroad as a child?'

'Well, yes, because when you live in Egypt you have to go to the mountains because the blood cells get anaemia. Too much heat and sun drains you away. So when we were small – my 2 brothers and me – our parents would take us to Switzerland for a month in the summer. But when we were older we refused to go, we wanted to stay in Egypt at the seaside.'

'Did your family have English friends?'

'The English kept rather aloof from everyone when they were in charge here. The colonial spirit!' She laughs. 'The Gezira Sporting Club in Cairo – Egyptians could not be members.'

'You were very young when you married King Farouk – was that normal?'

'It was normal for a girl. Because it was said that if a girl marries young, her parents choose the husband. Whereas if she marries older, she chooses her husband – and maybe makes not such a good choice as the parents. Boys didn't get married so young. But he had come to the throne very early and was overwhelmed and felt he needed companionship.'

'Did you see him much beforehand?'

'Yes. We travelled with his sisters and his mother and my mother for 6 months' tour of Europe – we were in England for the Coronation of King George VI. And as soon as he took his constitutional oath and wasn't under a Council of Regency any more, he could do what he wanted and we were engaged, then married.'

'Why were you chosen?'

'I wasn't chosen. He chose. We chose each other. The voyage was intended for us to get to know each other, to find out. His mother didn't think we would fall in love so soon. She thought it would take more time.'

'What did you find attractive about him?'

'He had a lot of charm. He could be very very sweet. But he was also stubborn. He was so . . . I felt he was very lonely. I was drawn to that.'

'What sort of wedding was it?'

'It was a huge thing in Egypt. It lasted for a week throughout the country. Because he was *extremely* popular. He was adored by the people. But for us it was just the marriage contract in the morning. And then in the afternoon there was a tea party for the royal family. After that we had receptions. We had to receive for 3 days. We received the whole country! I received the women on my side and he received the men on his side. And then we went off for our honeymoon.'

'What does the ceremony of marriage involve here?'

'Now it's changed – I see that now the boys and girls are together when the *sheikh* makes the contract – it's a signed contract made before the *sheikh*. And you read the *fatiha* which is the opening of the Koran and that's about all. But in my time it was my father who signed the contract for me. I did not witness it.'

'Where did you go for your honeymoon?'

'We went to one of the King's properties. At Inshass. All the big palaces were governmental, belonged to the country, not to the family. So in the revolution, when they thought they were taking something from the King, they weren't, the palaces were already theirs. But where we went for our honeymoon was a private house of the King.'

Inshass subsequently became a casino – then an atomic research centre.

'What were your thoughts at this time, becoming Queen of Egypt at the age of 16?'

'I thought nothing of it. Just automatic. Just like any other marriage – but with lots of bother. Not being able to do what you like. Having to see lots of people. And the honeymoon was very short, a few days – then back to work. My duties were mostly to receive people. And some official outings like the opening of Parliament, opening exhibitions, hospitals, this sort of thing.'

'Where did your clothes come from?'

'Paris. And Egypt.'

'Where did you live mostly?'

'6 months in Cairo at the Abdin Palace – it's now government offices, although sometimes they have banquets there. There are 2 big palaces in Cairo – the Abdin in the middle of town, and Quba on the outskirts which the President now uses – well, it used to be on the outskirts, surrounded by fields, but it isn't any more. And then we'd live 6 months at Alexandria at the Montazah Palace. There were 2 palaces at Alexandria too – Montazah at the east end which has become a famous beach resort now, and Ras El-Tin at the west end where Rabin of Israel was received. We had a few bombs on Montazah during the war because the British Air Force base was very near Aboukir, but it was nothing like the bombing in Europe.'

'Did you have a fairly separate existence with your own budget and household and apartments?'

'Yes. Absolutely.'

'What were the high points of life for you at this time?'

'My children, my 3 daughters. They were my greatest joy.'

'What did you do in the evenings?'

'Sometimes I went out with the King privately.'

'What was bad about King Farouk?'

She sighs and a knot appears in the side of her mouth. '. . . You know, he was very young. Consider a youngster to-day of 17 or 18 – he had all the qualities and defects of such a youngster. Except he had very heavy responsibilities. He looked older than his age – in fact because of the responsibilities neither of us felt our age. We couldn't behave like people of our age *should* behave.'

Farouk was an intelligent man but he developed increasingly obsessional behaviour. He seems to have been tortured by a sense of sexual inadequacy (Barbara Skelton, who was his mistress, has written that his penis was undersized) and this may have contributed to his excesses: compulsive eating, many brief unrewarding sexual encounters, heavy gambling, collecting mania (everything from Fabergé eggs to razor-blades, cigarette cards and empty toothpaste tubes). He also became increasingly reliant upon the services of an Italian, Antonio Pulli, in arranging the gratification of these wants. When Farouk was 9 years old, Pulli had been the youth who turned up to repair the Prince's electric trainset and from that moment the Italian was a rising star. By the end of Farouk's reign Pulli was one of the most influential men in Egypt and the only man the King trusted. After the revolution Pulli was imprisoned but released 2 years later and opened a cake shop in Heliopolis – he could well be selling cakes to this day.

'Can you tell me something about Pulli?'

'He was an Italian who worked in the Palace. He became my husband's . . . homme à tout faire. What is that in English? Factotum!'

'But what was he like?'

'He started as an electrician in the Palace. He was very

clever, as all Italians are, you know. They know how to do everything.'

'When do you think Farouk started to lose control of the stituation?'

'This is politics. I'd rather not answer that.'

'Can't you talk about the bad side of Farouk's conduct?'

'I prefer not to. I haven't yet gone deeply into it. I do think Farouk was double-crossed by everybody.'

'But you kept away from the politics?'

'I didn't keep away. But I didn't meddle. I've always been very interested in politics and I followed everything.'

'You were divorced from the King in 1948.'

'Yes. End of '48. November.'

'That period – after the War, before the divorce – must've been a very difficult period for you.'

'Yes, it was. Painful.'

'How did you cope with that?'

'. . . They were very very unhappy days. *Very* unhappy days, very miserable. And I . . . just *couldn't cope* with it! I was sick, I was ill. It was only much later, when I left Egypt, started to paint and all that, that I started to feel better.'

'So you had this divorce in 1948. Why? Just because there was no male heir?'

She gives a delicate shrug which nonetheless reveals all the facets of her character – passion, fragility, intelligence, charm, nervousness, tact. But most of all she's full of a barely concealed anger, unable to release it, trying for noble resignation yet full of the fury and ghastly despair of a young woman who lost everything.

'Huh . . . well, we'd drifted apart, you know. People pulled him on one side, pulled me on another, intrigues, everything done to destroy the image of a happy family, and once it begins you're involved but you don't know what's happening to you. You're young, your feelings are uppermost, and you can't reason any more. The people around you are older, wiser, cleverer and . . . you fall into a trap.'

'Is Islamic divorce a simple affair?'

'It's simple for the man. Not as simple for the woman. A man can divorce very easily just by saying in front of 2 witnesses that he wishes to divorce his wife. The woman can have the same right if it's put in her marriage contract – but very few men allow this. Our religion is very well built. But, you know, it's been adapted – since we live in a man's world, the men apply it the way they want. For instance, the Prophet said in the Koran that a man can have 3 wives as long as you treat them *exactly* the same, with same feelings, same money, same position. And that a woman should have the same position after her divorce as before. But they don't do it! 3 wives is the maximum at any one time. If a man wants another he has to divorce one first.'

'So in fact the King need not have divorced you. He could just have married a second wife.'

'Exactly.' As she says this her voice falls in a steep slant across the word.

'But he chose to do it in this particular way?'

'Yes.'

'That must've been hard.'

'Yes. And especially because of the children. The 2 older girls I was not allowed to have. They were kept at the Palace. The little one I had for a short time – then she was taken by the Palace too. Then . . . but the revolution was soon after, in 1952. There wasn't much longer left for any of it.'

'After the divorce, what did you do next?'

'Ooo . . . nothing really . . . I tried to adapt but . . . it was a mess.'

'You stayed on in Egypt?'

'Yes. And it was a *miserable* life! I don't know how I survived . . . I just *don't know how I survived*! I was in a very very bad physical and nervous state . . .'

'Did you see Farouk again?'

'I saw him again, yes . . . He had to leave Egypt in 1952. The 26th of July. I saw him once more. I left Egypt in 1963 and I saw him after that, in Switzerland. It was a strange meeting.'

'Had he changed?'

'He'd changed outwardly. You know, he seldom showed his feelings. And he didn't talk a lot, didn't open up. I spent a little time with him, just an afternoon in Switzerland. And that was the last time I saw him – alive. A year or 2 later he died in

Rome. He was still young. I went there to view the body. The funeral was in Italy and the remains were brought back to Cairo – he's buried here.'

Farida did not marry again.

'The '52 revolution – was there much bloodshed?'

'None. What was unpleasant was the filth, you know. The filth in the newspapers. All the things they brought out about the King, his private life.'

Farouk was accused of every depravity – but the erotica collection proved very tame indeed when the army opened it. More unappealing were the revelations of the King's general vulgarity at nightclubs and gambling tables and his passion for outright theft (he was an expert pick-pocket).

'It was terrible for me and the children,' continues the Queen. 'It made us *hate* the Press and the newspapermen. Because lots of it was very unfair. A few true things, but it was *filthy* in the way it was put. Every morning waking up and seeing these terrible headlines in the paper about the King – it was enough to make you collapse. Would you like something to drink?'

'Do you have any orange juice?'

She shouts to the maid who is ironing in another part of the flat beyond a *mashrabiyya* screen. The girl eventually appears with a glass of orange juice on a saucer. Queen Farida has nothing but says something gentle to the girl in Arabic.

'Your English is fantastically good. Why is that?'

'In all our families the girls went to French schools and we had English nannies at home. Later I picked up Italian and a little bit of Spanish.'

'Did you meet Nasser?'

'No. I met Sadat. There was a fashion at the time he was assassinated for saying he wasn't a great man. But that has passed – although the Nasserites still disapprove of him. He did that extraordinary thing of going to Jerusalem, breaking the vicious circle.'

'And he gave shelter to the Shah of Persia at the end. Was that wise?'

'It wasn't a question of being wise. The 2 gestures came not from the brain but from the heart, from understanding. Sadat

61

was a revolutionary when he was young but he learned an awful lot. He became a saintly man. He was at first too free perhaps, he let everyone do what they want. But he told me he'd seen terrible things under Nasser, people tortured, people blown up with air until they burst, and he didn't want anything to do with that. So he went to the opposite, although he had to tighten the reins later on. And something else – he had a great sense of humour.'

'So in 1963 you left Egypt. What was the immediate reason for that?'

'I'd had enough. I wanted to see my children who were abroad. But I hadn't been able to get an exit visa before. They were hard to get. But my life was senseless. I was going to search for something.'

'On this search, where was your first port of call?'

'Lebanon. I had a very good friend who was going there too. We went together. If I had gone straightaway to Europe I would have been completely destroyed.'

'Why?'

'Didn't have the strength for it. Life in Western Europe is very hard and cruel.'

'Do you think so?'

'Yes, it is – if you have no money. And I had no money. Nasser confiscated everything I had, money, jewellery, everything. But I still have my royal robes, the cloak – most of the fur's come off it. Would you like to see?'

She disappears into a bedroom, calls out something to the maid, eventually comes back in.

'We can't find it. Another time maybe.'

'Did you find anything in Lebanon?'

'I found lots of friends. They were great people. It's a terrible tragedy what's happened since. Then from Lebanon I went to Switzerland where my daughters lived. I painted there. I'd started painting in Egypt in – it must have been '54, after the confiscation in '53. But Switzerland wasn't right for me. So I went to Paris. I'd tried lots of things but only painting gave me any relief. I was away from Egypt until 1974 – I travelled to America and Russia and so on.'

'Do you have friends in America?'

'Yes. The thing I like about Americans is the way they . . . cross-examine themselves. They seem confident – in an outward way. But I don't think Americans really are confident. They are confident in that they have a way of living which they think is great and they would like everybody else to live the same way. And they don't take account of people's different mentality or that other people just don't want to live the American way. This is a fault in them. But what I like about Americans is they are not afraid to face a problem.'

'And Russia, do you have friends there?'

'No, it was impossible to meet people in Russia. I just went there as a tourist.'

'And Egyptians – what are they like?'

'The Egyptian character has changed. The Egyptian was gay and witty, the girls liked to laugh. They were kind, human. All this is disappearing.'

'No, I've found a lot of that here, I was surprised. I've never been to an Arab country before, except Turkey which I loved.'

'But we are not Arabs! Neither are Turks. Upper Egypt is more African and Nubian and Ethiopian. The Delta is very mixed. Now many Egyptians marry Arabs since the revolution – this was not so before. It has made another race. When older Egyptians talk among themselves, we say we don't recognise the new Egyptians, they have changed physically. And the younger generation, they just want one thing – quick money. But this isn't really the way of the Egyptian so it upsets him. He runs after money but he feels he's lacking something, he wants to cling to something.'

'So he clings to Islam?'

'That's not the right way to do Islam. Fanaticism is destruction. Islam is not fanatical but they are making it a fanatical religion which is very sad.'

'What do you hate?'

'I hate liars. It's very difficult in Egypt to get people to be honest with you.'

'So . . . at what point did you begin to feel that life was less terrible?'

'I think for me – I have a queer destiny. Life has always been terrible. Except the time in Lebanon. And maybe now it's a little bit easier here in Egypt.'

'Is that because you are accepting more? Or because your life has improved externally?'

'I have detached myself from lots of things.'

'Are you a religious person, a mystical person?'

'I am a mystical person.'

'As a Sufi or in some more general way?'

'A mixture of both. I had an exhibition in which all my paintings contained the name of God written in Arabic and some Sufis came to that exhibition and they asked "Are you a Sufi?" and I said "No, I'm not, I'd like to be, but I know nothing about Sufism". And I don't think I want to study it now because . . . I don't want to be led by anyone any more. I'm not scared of death.'

'Meanwhile you paint.'

'Yes. Come into my studio. I want to show you my technique.'

We enter the small studio, hardly more than a boxroom. She paints Egyptian scenes, not from life, but in a dreamy style, as if the whole of Egyptian culture is fading into a dream. She uses a dimmer-lamp and a mirror as she paints so that different effects are produced at different light strengths. Some of these effects can be unexpectedly strange – as if a light glowed out of the canvas.

'Look in the mirror,' she says. 'It looks better in the mirror.' But I don't understand what she means by this. 'When I'm painting I get almost into a trance. I don't know what I'm going to paint before I start. And if I'm interrupted when I'm painting, I get very shaken and people don't understand. I go down inside myself. I find a lot of comfort in it.'

'You said you've got an exhibition coming up in Saudi Arabia.'

'Yes, but I don't want to talk about that now. Not until it's over. About certain things I am *very* superstitious.'

'What does your name Farida mean?'

'It means "unique".'

I am given a lift back to Cairo by an adept of Sufism who introduces me to some of its mysteries in the traffic jam.

*

Yes, the great discovery in Cairo is the Egyptians. They are stylish and civilised and intelligent and lazy and gentle. Their sense of humour is laconic and silly by turns. Like Sicily, Britain and Brazil, Egypt is a racial mix. Here Africa, the Middle East, and the West overlap. Egyptians of either sex often have strikingly beautiful faces, though their bodies can lack refinement due to bad diet or fashion. A great belly hanging over a belt is considered a sexy thing for a man to have. Many women have thick ankles. Traditional costume is fortunately still widespread, especially among the lower class, but I didn't see a fez (upper class wear). The labourers who erect the new towerblocks often wear turbans or caps and, despite the obvious danger on high scaffolding, the swirling full-length *galabiyya*. On the other hand the history of Egypt, like Turkey's, is intimately connected with that of Europe, and a heavily veiled woman is unlikely to be an Egyptian. Who is this tippling along for example? An oil princess perhaps? A woman walks down the dusty street completely enveloped in a cloud of black silk. There is something about the way she moves within the billowing cloud which suggests she is young and supple. Beneath this total costume, one now and again catches glimpses of a pair of turquoise high-heeled shoes with small leather bows on the back.

*

To the Café Groppi for tea and cake, the standard Egyptian cake which is a long Madeira with a few raisins scattered through. An Egyptian strikes up a conversation with me – where am I from? Do I like Cairo? Am I married? etc. He is called Ahmed, about 50 years old, short, fat, balding. I ask him a question: 'Do you know a hammam, a real one, not the Nile Hilton Sauna, but a beautiful old hammam?'

'Ah!' he says with a glare, pulling one side of his moustache. 'You mean Turkish bath?'

'Yes.'

'This is no good for you. Maybe dangerous.'

'Why?'

He draws a little closer and says conspiratorially 'Because hammam is for man like go with man.'

'Oh. Really?'

'Yes. What I tell you is in secret, you understand?'

'Oh. Certainly. But do you know of a hammam?'

'There are many. You like go with man?'

I notice a metallic glitter in his eye and say 'Not at the moment. What I'd love is a steam bath. I'm very hot and sticky.'

'Hot and sticky?' He pulls the other side of his moustache.

'Mm, yes.'

'Because if you like go with man, I come to your hotel room now.'

'What?'

'Because hammam is dangerous for you. Maybe they even rape you.'

'Thanks a lot but – '

'Hammam are dirty. Hammam boys are dirty. I am clean man. You don't like go with me?'

'I can see you are clean.'

'Man very good sometimes. You should try everything.'

'Of course. I have tried everything, well, I haven't tried a rhinoceros but listen, I thought the City of the Dead looked very interesting.'

'I'll take you there and show you my family tomb.'

At the City of the Dead, Ahmed shows me his family tomb, a small mud-coloured mausoleum with several dead snakes inside, and he says 'I shall finish here. And my wife. And my 3 sons. Can I come to your hotel room? I have big machine.'

'No, I have to buy some plain white Egyptian cotton sheets. It's one of the things I most want to do here. Buy these sheets.'

'I know special place in bazaar.'

We take a taxi to the Khan-el-Khalili bazaar opposite Al Azhar University, but all the sheets are embroidered with a coloured pattern – no plain white. Al Azhar claims to be 'the oldest university in the world'. It is the home of classic Arabic, just as Siena is said to be the home of classic Italian and Oxford of classic English. We wait in the street for our driver to reappear – taxi drivers stick to clients like glue, often for days on end – and an Egyptian woman of breathtaking obesity waddles past with a bag of shopping hanging off the end of each arm.

'See that woman?' says Ahmed out of the side of his mouth. The woman's massive buttocks are a-tremble beneath the thin flowerprint cotton of her pantaloons. 'See what she is doing with her hips? That mean she like it up the back.'

'In England we call that the Italian way.'

'In Egypt we say like the Greeks.'

'She's very fat.'

'We like big hips, big woman.'

'Egyptian men like everything.'

'Yes – and British man too. I notice this. German no, American no, but British man when he comes to Cairo he wants girl, he wants boy, he wants to do different things. Life is very short. A man must taste everything. What you like doing? What you do first?'

'After kissing, you mean? You're very curious.'

'Maybe I learn something.'

He wants me to be lascivious – what the hell.

'Licking . . .' I say. A dreamy look comes over his sweating face. 'And what do you like?'

'I like licking too!' he exclaims. 'Girls are not so easy to find in Egypt so boys are very popular. Prostitutes are not a good idea in Cairo. There are many diseases and some which never go away. We go to your hotel now?'

The street is thronged with people. He notices that 2 men are standing adjacent to us and says 'Shh, come over here so others can't hear what we say, and don't talk of this in the taxi – the driver knows some English.'

We shuffle closer to a shop selling jute sacks, piles and piles of them, all identical. The shopkeeper raises 2 desultory eyes above a hookah, pulls the mouthpiece out, but Ahmed waves no, and the mouthpiece goes back in and the eyes sink again. Then Ahmed spots our taxi battling towards us in the traffic. We jump in and head for some larger sheet shops around Talat Haarb. No white sheets anywhere. All have some coloured embroidery on them somewhere.

'I have an idea,' he says.

'You know a better sheet shop?'

'No. I come to your room. You feel my machine. If you don't like, I go. If you like, I don't go. I have big machine.'

'Yes, you said.'

'Machine – what is, in English?'

'Cock.'

'I have big – cock. You have big cock?'

'Certainly. What is cock in Egyptian?'

'Zoop!'

'And the woman's?'

'Koos . . . In Egypt we have saying "You have big cock, you fuck donkey; you like big cock, donkey fuck you".'

'Donkey?'

'Yes. Many men like play with donkey. You like to try donkey?'

'Yes I would.'

'You would?'

'Why not?'

'When you leaving Egypt?'

'To-morrow.'

He alternately stamps both feet in exasperation. 'This is very bad. Donkey out out, not in centre of Cairo. It best to go out. To village. My friend in village – he has beautiful donkey. But not possible to-day. He is not there to-day.'

'What a shame.'

'I am sad. Next time you come to Cairo I promise we make something with donkey.'

'That's very kind of you, Ahmed. Thank-you.'

*

As the sun sets on the world, speed west along the King Faisal Road to the son et lumière show at the Pyramids. The King Faisal Road is not beautiful even at sunset. A few years ago this was all fields. Now it is a district of colossal towerblock accommodation thrown up in response to the emergency of overpopulation. The horrific mania of over-population, which makes nonsense of all human efforts to create a better world, really hits you here: humanity as the Earth's skin cancer.

Arrive at gate, buy ticket, pass through garden, and suddenly there are the Pyramids. As the sun sinks into the desert it sends up a fervent glow behind them – from a minaret in a nearby settlement floats the ribbonlike chant of the *muezzin*. It is warm. It seems unreal. The outline of the Sphinx becomes apparent in the dusky foreground. Its beard, a New Kingdom addition, fell off in ancient times and shattered. There was a plan recently to reassemble it and for this purpose the Egyptian Antiquities Organisation had requested a permanent loan from the British Museum of the 2 feet high fragment which resides there. But the whole idea has now been dropped because of fears that it may disturb the stability of the head which is already very battered (the Turks used it for cannon target practice).

There are 4 pyramids in a row, grading from the largest on the right to the smallest on the left where a moon in its second day and a star beneath have just come out. The sun has gone and taken its gorgeous light with it and the sky is navy blue velvet. The long silhouette on the horizon, of the pyramids, palm trees and sand dunes, shows, against a deep blackness – the clichés take on a magnificent vitality as when one falls in love. Music strikes up, floodlights flash across the flanks of these immense structures, a fruity British voice reverberates across the site speaking of the marvels of the ancient world . . .

After the show, visit a perfume emporium, Al Amir Palace Perfumes, Giza, attar or roses, heliotrope, black narcissus, musk, frankincense. They also make amber cigarettes.

*

Army Day. Of the many wars with Israel, Egypt has won only 1 – in 1973. This is now celebrated annually with razzamatazz. It is also the anniversary of the day Sadat was assassinated – unfortunate coincidence. But Queen Farida is in favour of Army Day. She says it is important to have something to fire up the people. At night as part of the celebrations they show *The Dambusters* on television – they don't dub it so there's Arabic scrawled across the screen (reading from right to left). The only love interest in this film is supplied by Richard Todd's relationship with his dog Nigger – wouldn't get away with a name like that now. Recall driving to Cornwall, early 1986, when the engagement of Sarah Ferguson and Prince Andrew was announced. The BBC did an on-the-spot radio interview with her father Major Ferguson at home in Hampshire for immediate broadcast. The interviewer asked him if Sarah liked horses. 'Oh yes,' said the Major blithely, 'I remember her first pony was called Nigger.' This was eliminated from all subsequent broadcasts of the interview.

Call on the BBC's man in Cairo, Bob Jobbins. He is very phlegmatic.

'What's the nastiest thing that ever happened to you here?' I ask.

'A man broke into my son's bedroom and tried to knife him.'

'Why was that?'

'Oh, there was some anti-press feeling at the time.'

*

Departure. Drag self out of bed at 5.45am after a few hours sleep. Samy to collect me from hotel at 6.30am for early flight. At 7am I grow jittery – he's not arrived, what's happened? So decide to take taxi to airport, but something is wrong with the old crock's gear shift – we grind pathetically through the rush hour in fits and starts and eventually break down outside a derelict mansion of bizarre architecture in Heliopolis one mile from the airport. Miss flight. The next is not until to-morrow so book into Novotel Cairo Airport and phone travel company in a fury. Apparently Samy was in a car crash – his driver, the old man who likes young girls, is still in hospital. Blank zen day at characterless Novotel, spaced out on insufficient sleep. Sit round the swimming-pool in mushy sunshine through steamy cloud but can't relax for flies constantly settling on me. Look in souvenir shop and buy Nefertiti oven glove. In the evening Samy turns up to apologise and demonstrate arm in plaster. I sleep fitfully for a few hours then Samy reappears at 6am looking grey but determined I shouldn't miss another flight. A squirm in the bowels. Go quickly to the loo in the Departure Lounge and tip attendant E£1. Have E£4 remaining. One is not supposed to take *any* Egyptian currency out of the country but I can't even spend it on coffee because they only accept foreign currency in this part of the building. Take-off at 8.30am after heavy anti-terrorist security checks and the broadcast of a verse from the Koran . . . Notice that the vomit bags on Egyptair are made in Switzerland. I've never ever seen anybody use one on a flight . . . After breakfast in the sky, hit the loo again. Notice too late that someone's swiped all the paper! Go all hot & cold. What to do, what to do? Look desperately about. Then my eyes happen to drop and alight on the 4 remaining Egyptian pounds in the breast pocket of my shirt.

(1986)

FELINE

THE QUENNELLS ON PRIMROSE HILL

THE QUENNELLS LIVE in a cul-de-sac off Regent's Park Road in a part of London that is sensuously pretty – pastel-painted terraces and stucco squares overflowing with trees and flowers, cobbled mews only partly gentrified, a long row of Victorian shops with no chain stores, and up the side of Primrose Hill (weirdly, for anyone living closer to the centre than this) *no* parking restrictions.

A woman in her 50s opens the door. She's extremely thin and alert, in a plaid skirt pulled tightly at the waist with a belt and a small scarlet scarf tied over her hair and under her chin with a bow – a slash of lipstick is the same colour. She scrutinises me with a coquettish smirk and says 'Come into the garden for a mo.'

'Are you Peter Quennell's daughter?'

'You *are* kind.' She's his current wife.

The house is interestingly untidy and through the back door a Burmese cat called Maximilian lies in the sun. 'It's everso nice round 'ere,' says Mrs Quennell in mock Cockney, 'but I preferred Chelsea. I had a Queen Anne house in Cheyne Row next door to the Carlyle Museum – had to sell it a couple of years ago.'

She talks a lot through clenched teeth and in that upper class way (the smart one, not the horsey one) which is both familiar and astringent, explaining that she's née Kerr from Jedburgh in the Scottish border country. At the same time she gives me a subtle grilling before showing me up to her husband whose study occupies the small first floor drawing-room.

72

Peter Quennell was born in 1905, the son of an architect, and of all the literary figures at Oxford in the 1920s he is perhaps the least known and most enduring. He published his first book (poems) in 1922, before university, and his most recent, *The Pursuit of Happiness* (an extended essay with pictures), in 1988. Between these have been further poems, biography, autobiography, criticism, essays. He's probably received and accepted more invitations than any man alive and his chief gift as a writer is the polished clarity of his prose. Tap his books and they ring like bells. Only his autobiographies are unsatisfactory, flawed by an exaggerated sense of discretion which is not so much good manners as social insecurity.

He rises in greeting, tall, smoking, thinner even than his wife, and the moment he smiles about 60 of his 84 years disappear – a disconcerting effect. Navy blue suit – jacket hanging off shoulders due to the narrowness of his frame. Navy blue tie with white spots.

'Oh, darling, thank-you so much,' he breathes as his wife brings him a glass of white wine. 11am. Early drinking. When she's gone I ask how often he's been married. 'Well, 5 times, but we don't underline that.' And apparently it's been alimony every time.

At Oxford he was famously heterosexual in a rather homosexual era and was rusticated for sleeping with a woman at Maidenhead.

'It was at the beginning of my third year. I could've returned later but I was unrepentant and my father was very good-natured about it and allowed me to travel with the Sitwells to Amalfi. I was very fond of the Sitwells when I wasn't quarrelling with them.'

'Quarrelling about what?'

'God knows! Nobody knows what one quarrels with the Sitwells about. A quarrel occurs. After the Sitwells I went to Ravenna and in the hotel dining-room there I saw a small man with a red beard wedged between 2 large middle-aged English ladies. Being alone, I eavesdropped on their conversation – it was D. H. Lawrence and he was saying in a faintly north country voice how he disliked all those Virgins in the mosaics

73

because they seemed to be like flatfish with 2 eyes on the same side of the face.'

Quennell grew up in Berkhamstead and went to the school there where Graham Greene's father was headmaster. I ask if he thinks this business of Graham Greene playing Russian roulette with himself as a boy is true or cooked-up. PQ drapes his long thin limbs in and around a chair, lights another cigarette with the stub of the previous one, and says 'I don't know, probably true, but the troubles he describes in his autobiography were completely unapparent to me. I had no idea that he had a nervous breakdown and found him a very agreeable companion. Other friends of ours were the sons and daughters of W. W. Jacobs, the short-storyteller. And it was at their house on the outskirts of Berkhamstead that I first met Evelyn Waugh. His elder brother Alec became engaged to W. W. Jacobs' eldest daughter and one day Alec brought along this very dashing, dandified younger brother in a grey suit and bright yellow waistcoat. This was before Oxford, by the way. It was Hugh Lygon's family who assisted Evelyn in his subsequent attempts to become a member of the upper classes. He took to riding under their direction. Dorothy Lygon told me that he was one of the bravest men she'd ever seen in the hunting field – and one of the worst riders. He was always falling off but gallantly remounting.'

There's a voice ululating up the stairs. 'Peter, tu veux encore du vin?'

'Oui, s'il vous plait, darling.'

'And what about you?' she asks me, flitting in.

'Un peu du thé? A teabag'll do, Mrs Quennell.'

'Oh God, call me Marilyn. It'll have to be Earl Grey – in a *mug*,' she says through the clenched teeth as if the very idea of tea after 10am is disgusting. She is a curious mixture of hostility and affection.

'To go back to Evelyn for a moment,' says PQ, 'there's one thing which is worth putting on record. During the war he was a very unpopular soldier and his commanding officer said he couldn't be sent on certain expeditions because his men would shoot him in the back. But Bob Laycock, who was a sort of general, told me that Evelyn was without doubt one of the bravest men he'd ever seen. And he described how during the disastrous retreat from Crete, Bob saw Evelyn walking across the field of fire, his soldier servant behind him shivering with terror, and Evelyn not taking cover or anything, just walking straight across in a ridiculous little overcoat.'

'After the war he became increasingly difficult.'

'Well, he got so enraged about everything, especially when drunk. He was *furious* because I became a member of White's – because I wasn't an Etonian or something. I like White's. It's a refuge – and convenient for the London Library, but the food's not good one must admit.'

Maximilian sidles into the room, and so does Marilyn with tea and more wine. PQ plays with the animal, then asks 'Darling, has she had any lunch?'

'Darling, it's a bit early for lunch – and it's a him.'

'He was having an awful row in my bedroom this morning with Suki, darling.' (Separate bedrooms?)

'Darling, she provokes him. Do you know,' says Marilyn turning to me, drinking from PQ's glass, 'Suki's had 14 stitches. We don't know what happened. We think it was her son Maximilian.'

'Who's a lovely Maxi, who's a lovely Maxi,' purrs PQ. 'Oh Marilyn, don't drink my wine!' he whimpers.

'Just a *sip*.' She hits him with her elbow. The atmosphere hereabouts is noticeably feline.

'You see that picture there above my desk? I have it to remind me of the Connollys' lemurs.'

'Cyril Connolly was so amusing and anguished,' I venture. 'Do you suffer from anguish?'

'Occasionally. And I used to have the most terrible irrational anxieties and panics which took the rather undignified form of feeling physically sick.'

An entry in Evelyn Waugh's Diary just after the Second World War reads: '*On Sunday night Quennell had palpitations of the heart brought on by sexual excess*.' And Harold Acton in his second book of memoirs describes how PQ became ill in a country house when chancing upon Acton's first book of memoirs and reading there how fine a poet Quennell was in his youth.

'It is perfectly true, alas, that the poetic impulse abandoned me in Tokyo,' (where he was briefly a professor of English in the early 1930s – his first marriage came to grief there too), 'and I *did* become ill in that house – but from completely different reasons. The illness was of a sentimental kind. Somebody was staying in the house too – with her husband. I think like most people I occasionally feel dotty.'

'Oh, you're *totally* dotty, dear!' howls Marilyn in mock Cockney.

'Look here, darling, we don't want too much from you.'

'Is the tea all right?' she asks me, retying the bow under her chin.

'Now, darling, *please* – I'm answering questions.'

'I'm asking *him* if the tea's all right!'

'The tea's sensational, Mrs Qu – Marilyn. Why did Cyril Connolly have these lemurs?'

PQ's blue eyes follow his wife out of the room and when she's gone he reassumes his standard position in the chair: legs crossed, wrists hanging off the ends of the chair arms, cigarette wedged between 2 downward fingers.

'They do make delightful pets. His were slightly incontinent – but not as badly as their coati-mondi which was *very* incontinent and rather a nuisance in that respect. In the forests of Madagascar the lemurs go into the sunshine at the top of the trees, for pleasure. For the same reason the Connollys' lemurs used to sit in front of the gas fire at Rottingdean, with their palms towards it, warming their very human-looking hands. I remember seeing Cyril and Jean eating in the gallery of the Café Royal and a lemur's head coming out of the front of Cyril's jacket. The lemurs loved him. He had what the French call the terrible gift of intimacy.'

As he talks, the beauty of PQ's voice is almost mesmerising. It is produced at the front of the mouth and has a richness and balance of expression reminiscent of Sacheverell Sitwell's. He is altogether a most elegant, insouciant figure – even his handwriting and fine black socks are elegant – and it is obvious why he has proven so attractive to women.

'You introduced Cyril Connolly to his second wife, didn't you?'

'Oh my God, Barbara Skelton! Is her new book coming out? I didn't like the many references to myself in the last one.' (She describes him as, among other things, *drunk*, *lively*, *violent*, *wheedling*, *amusing*.)

'I used to sleep with her and that had its agreeable side – but she could be painful too. I first met her at the end of the Second War when she was living with De Gaulle's intelligence officer in Mayfair, a Monsieur Boris. Another girl took me to a flat in Shepherd's Market and there was this attractive little creature sitting on the edge of the bed – at that moment a bomb exploded in the immediate vicinity which cheered us all up and Barbara opened a bottle of champagne.'

PQ's amatory and mobile life kept him short of money. 'At one period I was obliged to join an advertising firm' – though fortunately he's had only 2 children (Marilyn is the mother of his son, Alexander, 22 years old, currently at Sandhurst; there is also a daughter, Sarah, by an earlier marriage). During the war he worked in a succession of government ministries and for a while shared lodgings with Arthur Koestler 'who reproached me for telling people he went to bed wearing a hairnet. He said he only wore one in the bath'.

After the war he edited the *Cornhill* magazine, then *History Today*, and between marriages shared a house in Regent's Park with George Weidenfeld.

'I came home one Saturday night and found George looking pale and shaken and he said that during my absence the bell had rung and there on the doorstep was a healthy baby neatly packed in a basket. What did you do, George? My dear, I decided I better not become involved and sent for the police.' The phone rings. 'Oh fuck . . . Hullo. Who wants her?' Marilyn, who's been hovering on the stairs, takes it in here.

'Oh *hullo*, curator dear.'

'That's very typical of her. Curator dear,' he observes.

'Shut *up*,' she hisses, smacking his leg.

After a long talk about plants she rings off and asks 'You're not going on much longer, are you? Then we can go to the pub for a sandwich.'

'Darling, I do hope there's a little bit more to drink. We're getting awfully thirsty here – at least, I am. Betjeman I knew

77

quite well. When he was working for the *Architectural Review* I went to his office room which was very untidy. Betj wasn't there but on his pad in neat gothic capitals were the immortal lines: I sometimes think that I should like/To be the saddle of a bike.' Marilyn flits in with a refill for PQ.

'What is your working day?'

'Keep pouring, darling. I'm not systematic but I usually try to start around 10am. And I write longhand, with a pencil. I can't type. When I edited *History Today* I had a series of excellent secretaries to type for me, but now I have to send things to a lady near Wimbledon Common.'

Marilyn says 'I do think it's time for lunch, don't you?'

Peter hisses at her and goes off for a pee and she says to me 'Let me show you the house. For background.'

Yes, they do have separate bedrooms. Marilyn seems quite proud of hers.

On the stairs we pass Suki who is in the most appalling state, having been mauled almost to death by her son.

'Poor poor poor poor Suki;' pouts Marilyn.

We straggle off round the corner and in the pub she asks me 'What have you written?'

At once PQ's eyes fly up to the ceiling. 'Oh God, don't – the *boredom* of it!'

She glares and pulls a tight mouth. Attempting to fill the busy silence, I say 'I hear Kingsley Amis is a neighbour of yours.'

'Yes, but in fact – '

'Oh, she'll go on and on about Kingsley Amis now!' he addresses the ceiling. 'Reams of boredom!'

'What *can* we talk about, DEAR? The inside of pubs? Your teeth? How fascinating.' Her own teeth are now clenched as if by lockjaw.

'Reams and *reams* of boredom!' mutters PQ.

'Yes, dear, we heard the first time,' miaows his wife.

PQ gazes silently into the distance, chewing his beef sandwich.

(1989)

OUT AT THE BEACH

CHRISTOPHER ISHERWOOD IN SANTA MONICA

TO LOOK AT, Christopher is a short, trim, middle-aged man with greyish hair cut in the Prussian style and just beginning to get thin on top.

'. . . I'm not into the idea of fiction any more and never really was. I'm much more interested now in keeping a diary. What interests me is commenting on facts, trying to see what they mean. I'm not against fiction but for me personally I'm much more interested in just looking at life as I know it.'

Christopher is 80 years old in August next year. The grand old man is not him at all.

'Will you publish these diaries, or leave it for later?'

'I wouldn't much care either way. At the moment I'm reading Noël Coward's Diaries. Anything like that I like. Personal things. Autobiographical. I'm very much drawn to Coward whom I didn't know well but thought was charming.'

'I gather he was much less bitchy than people imagine. Do you find the literary world very bitchy?'

'I really have no idea what the literary world thinks. That sounds rather an affected remark . . . I don't know what the literary world thinks of me – I think probably not much – they think I'm a sort of has-bin or something.'

He wears a blue denim jacket, blue cord trousers, brown slip-on shoes, and spectacles with clear plastic frames which give him a squirrelish air. He is very schoolboyish. He doesn't cross his legs but puts the shoe of one up on the knee of the other.

'You look very young – do you feel old?'

'I see signs of it. But a great deal is, I think, exploiting my predicament. It is sometimes extremely convenient to become very, very old. The awful truth in my view is that what keeps one person going longer than another is favourable heredity. Longevity runs in my family.'

'Graham Greene is another extraordinarily unold – '

'He is my cousin, did you know? I don't think he's as miserable as everyone says. I think he has a fine old time underneath.'

'One can assist death, of course.'

'Oh yes, I used to smoke like there was no to-morrow, then I became disgusted with it . . . all the nicotine on my fingers I didn't like.'

'What else don't you like? What don't you like in yourself?'

'I'm lazy . . . and there have been occasions when I've behaved in what I consider a cowardly manner. Cowardice of course is only deplorable when it gets other people into trouble.' And he adds curiously 'That's something for you to know and others to find out.'

His voice has a sharp mid-Atlantic edge with a lilting fadeout and often long pauses between sentences. He and his American partner, Don Bachardy, sound almost identical on the telephone.

'What makes you afraid?'

'. . . . . yes . . . I'm bothered by heights.'

'That's why you live on the edge of this precipice, I expect.'

'I have a fairly good head, but I get scared nonetheless. And thinking of heights makes me think of Yosemite National Park – I can get really quite breathless with a kind of fear near to a very big waterfall. The feeling of the tremendous mass of water overwhelms me – if you stand real close to a big fall.'

The house in Santa Monica is one of the oldest in Los Angeles, built in 1926. It is small and bright and stuck limpetlike to the side of a wide gulley running inland from the beach. The Pacific Ocean starts in the middle distance and fills out beyond, a hazy blue under a hazy blue sky. This is a suburb-on-sea.

Inside: books, paintings, bits of ethnic stuff, a head of this, some mythological creature there, furniture comfortable in an

80

unemphatic modern way. The atmosphere is almost colonial –
indoors it could be Ceylon, Sydney, Durban. Mr Isherwood is
an expatriate. 'Which goes very deep. It goes to the feeling that
I wanted to be a sort of wanderer. I wanted to have a life with
all kinds of adventures roaming about the place.'

'But you stopped roaming when you were 35 – you never felt
like moving on from California?'

'I've usually been nudged along by events into doing things. I
lived in the Berlin area for 3 years and was blissfully happy
until the Nazi thing started up.'

'The implication is that there are few provocative events
hereabouts.'

'Of course when you live at home, there is so much life going
on in the mind. Auden was a great part of my movements . . .'

'He returned to England.'

'He had much more roots in England than I did. He would
say very often that really what he wanted to do was eventually
go back to England. I'm not like that – my home is here. It's not
that I dislike England – I like going over there very much – so
does Don – my goodness, he got a scholarship to the Slade
School of Art and studied in England. We go back and forth
. . . England seems very, ugh, near to me all the time.'

Isherwood met Don Bachardy in 1953. There is a photograph of them taken in that year when Bachardy was an 18
year old art student. They both look fantastically happy and
fit. It might be a propaganda shot for the Gay Life, in the style
of those blooming Soviet peasant pictures or the 'young &
covered' newlywed photos put out by American insurance
companies. Bachardy is the laughing urchin, Isherwood some
Kirk Douglas type with crewcut and tan. Bliss is theirs.

'People in the east USA and Europe have a rather
contemptuous/envious view of the Californian life.'

'Oh I know! I just . . . I'm not terribly – concerned with any
of that. I've met people here who've become among the most
important in my life . . . I suppose it could've happened
anywhere . . . but it didn't. My deep affection for California is
a matter of experience, of having lived here.'

'It's supposed to make you flabby-minded.'

'With all due respect to other people's opinion, it hasn't had that effect on me. In my view I've done much of my best work out here.'

'Aldous Huxley ended up out here too – were you ever in that drug . . . thing?'

'So many came. I knew Huxley very well. I took mescalin on one occasion.'

'Was that a dramatic moment in your life?'

'No, I can't say it was. As a matter of fact . . . I don't particularly dig that kind of thing. It had the conventional sort of effects – lots of paranoia and also feelings of excitement and stimulation. I have a rather convivial sort of character – I like – alcohol – but drinking has . . . never in the least been a problem.'

'Are there any good new American writers?'

'Do you know Calder Willing?'

'No.'

'He wrote a book about an army cadet school called *End As A Man*. You know, the object of the place is finally you'll end up as a man. Big deal. He's very talented, I think. My greatest American writer friend was Tennessee Williams.'

'A very Tennessee Williams ending he had – choking to death on a pill.'

'He was quite a pill-taker. But so many people I know are pill-takers. One day he just turned up and announced himself – this was before he became really famous – and we became the greatest buddies.'

'He strikes me as being a rare kind of American writer in that he didn't make this sort of ra-ra fetish out of optimism.'

'Yes, he quite enjoyed pessimism. He was very pessimistic in an optimistic way. He had the most incredibly infectious laugh – and wasn't at all a wilting, despairing creature, but rather round and solidly built – a *tremendous* swimmer – every day he had to find a pool, everything depended on it, God knows how many lengths, right off. He was a tremendous drinker too of course. I don't know what else he took.'

'Well, I think basically it was the ones to get you up and the ones to put you to sleep. The Judy Garland recipe.'

Some children are shouting in the suburban street. A dog gives out an elegant, expensive-sounding bark, though this is not an especially rich neighbourhood. Mr Isherwood takes off his spectacles and looks dreamily through the window into the warm bluish goldenish mid-day haze and into the Pacific Ocean. He has been breathing the Pacific ozone for over 40 years and looks impishly spaced out on it.

'Isn't Rajnish out here somewhere?'

'Who?'

'You know – Bhagwan, Rajnish, that cult man from Poona – he hopped it with some favourites and left the majority of his disciples behind in a great confusion.'

'Oh, that one. I don't know. There are an enormous number of monks and soi-disant swamis round here. But just because some of these characters are a bit dubious, people are fond of dismissing any religious activity in California as completely fake. Which isn't at all the case.'

(Isherwood studied with the Hollywood-based guru Swami Prabhavananda and published a book about him in 1980.)

'There was a period during the war,' he says, trapping his hands between his knees, 'when I worked with the Quakers outside Philadelphia. I was very drawn to the Quaker way of life. We taught refugees from Central Europe to speak English.'

'Hollywood must have been a weird hothouse sort of place during the war and for a while after – until McCarthyism killed it off. Stravinsky came out here, didn't he?'

'Yes, he was here. Thomas Mann. Brecht for a while. Stravinsky was an adorable person . . . Don! . . . Don!'

Eventually '. . . Yeah? . . .' comes filtering through from somewhere on the other side of the house where Don is busy preparing an exhibition of portraits for a Hollywood gallery.

'Where did the Stravinskys live? It's gone clean out of my head!'

'. . . . on Beverly Drive above the Strip . . .' filters back the answer through the various bungaloid chambers, sliding doors and glass panels.

'That's right – just above the Sunset Strip . . .'

'Did he pine for Russia? Oh, I like your Mickey Mouse socks – I've just noticed them.' They are in bright red wool with Mickey Mouses appliquéd onto them.

'Ha, somebody gave me these. I didn't feel he was pining all that much. He aroused the most tremendously strong protective instincts in one. He was – kinda – little. Perhaps because I'm little I feel very protective towards people who are smaller than I am . . . There was something childlike about him – and trustful – also of course childlikely suspicious at times, probably for good reason. I wouldn't call myself musical because I don't think one is really *into* an art unless one is enormously open to what's going on in it all the time. Musically I'm *terribly* conventional – the Eroica Symphony, the C Sharp Minor quartet – it's all dreadfully impeccable taste.'

'*Cabaret* must have made you more famous.'

'It sure did. I wasn't personally involved in the *Cabaret* film – but I did do a great deal of film work when I first came out here . . . scripts and so on. That's why I chose to come to California. I was very, very film-struck at an early age. American film magazines like *Photoplay* I used to take. I sort of dreamed about Hollywood and the stars – I thought it kinda glamorous – well, I still do – showbiz is always interesting . . .'

'Who is your favourite?'

'Oh, Ingrid Bergman. I think she was the most beautiful creature I ever set eyes on.'

To pause over the use of the word 'creature'. It has a strange androgynous quality. When used of beautiful women it has a distancing effect. It can be a put down. For example, it was a compliment to Tennessee Williams to say that he wasn't 'a wilting, despairing creature'. Virginia Woolf uses it later about Isherwood himself. It is of course dehumanising.

'Did you mix with the Beverly Hills set and go to the outrageous parties? I was surprised to discover that Beverly Hills is flat. I think Bel Air is nicer.'

'I went to a few. I had this job at MGM. But I didn't get deeply involved with any of the stars.'

'Was it decadent in those days?'

'I never quite know what decadent means.'

'Well, it often means enjoyable. But I'm thinking of the Kenneth Anger/*Hollywood Babylon* cliché.'

'It maybe just innocence on my part but I had

extraordinarily little contact with, for example, drugs of any kind.'

Is it innocence or timidity? One imagines Christopher hanging around at parties, smoking against a wall, being 'a camera'. A literary camera in Tinsel Town? That kind of camera is irrelevant in Hollywood which eventually will humiliate a writer into believing that his vision, compared to the Production's, is of little importance. And neither has anyone written in really top gear *about* Hollywood. Fitzgerald? Unfinished. Nathaniel West? Too ponderous. Raymond Chandler? Excellent – but limited. Evelyn Waugh – *The Loved One* – one of his pulpiest novels.

'I never met Evelyn Waugh,' says Christopher with raised shaggy eyebrows (his least boyish feature). 'It's rather weird in a way – I think we would have gotten on quite well together.' The use of the word 'gotten' suggests otherwise.

A character in Isherwood's *Prater Violet* describes Hollywood writers as feeling like married men meeting in a whorehouse. There is an obvious moral here which Isherwood wasn't the first to ignore. Also, no writer worth his salt can be part of a team. Collaborations hardly ever work. Isherwood's with Auden (a travel book and three plays) in the 1930s produced nothing of distinction. In that era of comradely collaborations, Waugh was the only one to point out that the practice was in the nature of things doomed to triviality.

And script-writing isn't writing anyway. It's script-writing. Thomas Mann wrote to his son Klaus from Pacific Palisades, November 12th, 1948: 'The starry-eyed one [ie. Isherwood] seems to have failed – anyone who counts on the movies is throwing himself on Satan's mercies.'

But 'failed' is too decisive a word for Isherwood's situation at this time because his main interest throughout the 1940s had been the pursuit of his aforementioned Hindu devotions with Prabhavananda. They were originally introduced to each other by another English Californian, Gerald Heard, in the summer of 1939 at the Swami's onion-domed ashram off Hollywood Boulevard. The Swami smiled sweetly and chain-smoked.

'When did you actually come to California to live?'

'Er . . . I get very – I didn't really make any plans. This outburst of travel took place because Auden and I decided to go to China which was then involved in being invaded by Japan.' This produced the collaboration *Journey To A War* (1939). 'We just thought we'd go there. And we did. It was fascinating as China and it was exciting and sometimes unpleasant because of the fighting. Not a huge-scale thing but . . . a *war* going on with air raids and trenches and soldiers and bombardments. So we did a bit of that kind of war correspondent stuff. We went to the front and all that. Of course once you get to the front, as you know – '

'I've never been to a front. Unless you count the fall of Laos. I was in Vientiane for that – all the war correspondents playing backgammon and smoking opium. One day the money started to change from Royalist to Communist and you had to sign papers but the dreamiest sort of front, the dreamiest sort of fall . . .'

'Well, an active war front, it's exactly how you imagine. It's noisy and dirty certainly. Whether it's dangerous is a matter of speculation because war is so spotty. You may be out there laughing your heads off in the front lines, chatting away, and then some plane comes over and drops a bomb and you're dead – suddenly you're a war hero who died on the field of honour . . . but we had a great time because Auden and I had been great friends – ever since we were at a little prep school together. Later I was living in London and everybody of course goes through London, so we met again. He was 18. I was 3 years older. To my absolute stupefaction this little boy had become an extraordinary poet. I could see that he was a major talent at 18. On the way back from China we came through the States and were very turned on by New York which now is not at all my dream place.'

'Was there rivalry?'

'No. We were devoted. Occasionally we got on each other's nerves on long train journeys or something – nothing more than that . . . We both had extensive lives that had nothing to do with each other. We each knew all sorts of people whom the other didn't know. But we were very, very . . . allied. And remained so all through our lives.'

'But when did you move to America to live?'

'. . . I get very confused with dates. I was first here in . . . I think it was 1938 that I came out here more or less to live.'

Strange. Because it was 1939. How can he forget the most important year of his life?

1939: *Goodbye to Berlin* is published in London, in which Isherwood famously states his position as a writer. 'I am a camera with its shutter open, quite passive, recording, not thinking.' It is of course also a sexual image. This concise and vivid book (like its 1935 *Mr Norris* predecessor), a very modern reportage novel, was turned into a successful play and film (*I Am A Camera*) and an extremely successful musical play and film (*Cabaret*).

January 1939: Isherwood and Auden sailed to America. This became significant with the declaration of war in September and their decision to stay in the USA, implying a rejection of European civilisation and its fate. But their departure failed to become what Cyril Connolly described – it is poignant to read it now, even bizarre – as 'the most important literary event since the outbreak of the Spanish War.'

Julian Trevelyan gave the pair a going-away party. 'It was a large affair,' says P. N. Furbank, '. . . walls decorated with collage pictures made from lumps of wool and frying-pans . . .'

E. M. Forster later wrote to Isherwood in an auntyish tone: '. . . it is clearly your job to see us sink from a distance, if sink we do.' Like many of Forster's auntyish remarks it contained within itself a ripple of condemnation – if Forster didn't see it, Isherwood surely did.

1939: The Second World War. The two English literary princes at a stroke found themselves in a backwater, upstaged by more visceral human considerations. The timing of their move was such that however you looked at it 'running away from the action' was always the first interpretation (this doesn't particularly mean military action). As Englishmen in America during the war, they contracted into being curiosities. Auden subsequently overcame this deracination by returning to Europe and for me he wrote his best poetry after the war, during the Ischia period. Isherwood remained in the USA and in so doing somehow sealed his work into the 1930s. However, leaving when they did had one decisive consequence – there was no better way of ensuring that neither would become members of the British establishment (it seems impossible to live in England as a success and not end up part of the establishment).

Isherwood became a pacifist as the best way to resolve this profoundly awkward position – not a surprising choice for a man whose father had been killed in the Great War and whose lover had been a German: powerful facts. And indeed how could Auden and Isherwood go to war against a country to which they both owed their personal, emotional liberation? It was Germany in the late 20s and the early 30s which had taught them how to love. Yet at almost 80 years of age there remains part of Isherwood which is not at ease with himself, which cannot quite look the rest of the world in the eye. Perhaps it is constitutional – because Virginia Woolf, ever perceptive, ever bitchy (because she didn't want to believe that she was the only wretched soul in town), noticed this characteristic when describing a party at Sybil Colefax's in a letter to Vanessa Bell, November 2nd, 1938: Christopher Isherwood '. . . seemed all agog with amusement; but is a shifty quicksilver little slip of a creature – very nimble and rather inscrutable and on his guard.'

The expatriate solution to conflict is not inherently wrong. In the case of writers it is only regrettable if it makes their work less interesting, less true. Many writers find they can become more true by working abroad. For the bourgeois English sensitive, abroad is escape from the tight little island, the suffocations of family and class and the endless knowingness of ironical conversation (although abroad for the American or Australian or postwar German is different, is the escape into the third dimension: depth). It is not possible to be anonymous, to get lost and explore, for very long in the British Isles, and for some people this hampers their development. In fact the English have always gone abroad: the Empire for merchants and adventurers, the World for writers and artists. Only recently has it at all seemed necessary to justify this. When John Lennon was asked why he lived in New York City, as if it were mean of him to have absconded, he quoted Winston Churchill to the effect that it was an Englishman's right to live wherever he damn well pleased.

D. H. Lawrence, according to Rebecca West, 'travelled to get a certain Apocalyptic vision of mankind.' Lawrence travelled to sustain himself in the mythological reality. Isherwood originally travelled for a mythological reason too — for sex and for sexual love — which is mythological and physical and dynamic. But it is necessary to distinguish between the expatriate and traveller or nomad. Lawrence wasn't really an expatriate but a traveller. Anthony Burgess, who moves about a lot, is also really a traveller for whom the big thing is this love/hate relationship with his own country. Burgess has said 'Exile is a negative state. You're not in exile anywhere, you're just in exile full stop. Once free of England, the tendency is to drift.'

So the wonder is not that Isherwood went to California but that at the very early age of 35 he came to a stop there. Perhaps he found happiness too soon, or something akin, but maybe not that greater happiness which is a kind of noble exhaustion. There is in the air about him a fine vapour of — what is it? Not disappointment exactly. Perhaps that timidity again which had once used Auden to help it connect up with the dangerous stuff of life. His earlier remark about cowardice being deplorable only when it gets others into trouble: cannot cowardice hurt oneself? 'I am a camera' — what does it mean? 'I am wood' or 'I am insensible' or 'I must pretend to have no heart'. Isherwood is a cold writer and you can only get so far without heat. He is never less than intelligent reading but the chutzpah disappears in Santa Monica, the little door closes which once said let's go to China, all right, yes, let's go now!

Christopher Bradshaw-Isherwood. Born 26 August 1904 in Cheshire. Educated: Repton and Cambridge. Thereafter studied medicine briefly but gave it up to teach English in Germany and to write. In 1946 he became an American citizen.

'When were you up at Cambridge?'

'Oh . . . I'm so bad at dates . . . Oh, it must have been before the 30s, mustn't it? The 20s.'

'Was it fun? The 20s always seem to be Oxford.'

'No, I don't think Cambridge was particularly very fun . . .'

'What happened to Sally Bowles?'

'I think I heard that she died. I went on seeing her when I came back to London, but then the connection fell away. When you come back to London from some place else, there are so *many* people to see . . . I saw her after the war . . . then I think I heard that she died.'

It's no good – he's fading on me – and it's all so long ago and so far away . . . The sun is somewhat brighter now, the haze thinner, the Pacific Ocean more strongly present. Christopher is having a little grin and thinking about lunch.

(1983)

TWINKLING AS HE COMES

KRISHNAMURTI

THE THEOSOPHICAL SOCIETY, founded in the USA in 1875 by the Russian Madame Blavatsky and by Colonel Olcott, a veteran of the American Civil War who was interested in spiritualism, was to be concerned with comparative religion, the unexplained laws of nature and the development of man's latent powers. Olcott was its first president. But Madame Blavatsky, claiming esoteric wisdom derived directly from adepts living in Tibet, became the society's characteristic personality and was responsible for its increasingly occultist preoccupations. In 1882 the society moved headquarters to Adyar, Madras, in India and from there conducted a very modish operation. The Theosophical Society is still based in Adyar, although its present is rather less vivid than its past.

In 1909 Jiddu Narianiah, a widower and retired Indian civil servant in the British administration, went to work for the society. He lived just outside the compound at Adyar with his 4 sons. Madame Blavatsky had died in 1891 and Olcott in 1907. By the time Narianiah arrived, a vigorous Englishwoman, Annie Besant, had become the society's president. She welcomed the new family (the boys were in poor health) and soon after went off on a 7 month tour of Europe and America.

Mrs Besant's closest colleague was another distinctive character, Charles Leadbeater. He arrived in India just before her departure, and while she was away, he observed the sons of Narianiah. One of them in particular, Krishnamurti, struck him as having a very remarkable aura. On her return Mrs Besant agreed. The Theosophists proclaimed Krishnamurti to

91

be the latest incarnation of Lord Maitreya, the World Teacher, who showed himself in human form every 2,000 years or so. His previous incarnation had been as Jesus and in the sublime hierarchy Lord Maitreya was only a little below the Buddha. In 1911 the Order of the Star in the East was founded with Krishnamurti, aged 15, at its head.

To groom him for his glorious future Mrs Besant decided to take Krishnamurti and his younger brother Nitya into legal guardianship and eventually bring them to Europe to be educated. The father agreed, then recanted and Mrs Besant, a determined woman, was only able to carry out her plan after a protracted lawsuit. In England, Krishnamurti failed all his exams (while his brother passed with flying colours) but nonetheless continued to be subjected to various forms of instruction.

Krishnamurti's fame grew steadily and he travelled to many parts of the world making public appearances, although his natural shyness made this an ordeal for him. In 1922 he underwent a strange physical experience, the exact nature of which remains obscure but which is said to have transformed his life. In the same year he made his first visit to the Ojai Valley in California where later 450 acres were purchased for a study centre (it still prospers).

In 1929 a gathering of the Order took place at Ommen in Holland, at Castle Eerde which had been given to the Order by Baron van Pallandt. Several thousand people were there, including Mrs Besant who had interrupted her work on the Home Rule League for India to attend. Krishnamurti was 34. He stood up and dissolved the order which had been built around him, saying 'I do not want to belong to any organisation of a spiritual kind . . . I do not want followers and I mean this. The moment you follow someone you cease to follow truth.'

Since then he has pursued a more practical, less fanciful life, although his purpose has remained the same: to set men psychologically free. He continues to travel and to talk and he has founded schools in England, the USA, and India. These are not esoteric centres but schools for young people providing an all-round education according to Krishnamurti's principles of good living.

*

Krishnamurti is 90 this year. He is visiting the Brockwood school in Hampshire, a white Georgian house set in a park planted with many beautiful trees including a mass of copper beeches and a rare handkerchief tree. He is tiny and fragile and squeaky clean and walks at a slow pace into the large pale drawing-room, picking up his feet like a small wading bird, twinkling as he comes. He is dressed in blue jeans, soft slip-on shoes and a greenish blue shirt open at the neck, and he sits on a hard straight-backed chair because he doesn't like to sit on soft ones. The only vanity he betrays is in contriving to overcome his baldness, resulting in a most extraordinary hairdo. In old photographs Krishnamurti's hair was always the most luxuriant aspect of his appearance. Now it is swept up on either side from the ears and, with the help of a fixative, interlocks over the crown like the tips of fingers in prayer. Thus he retains that touch of dandyism, one of his youthful traits, which in the past extended to Huntsman suits and Lobb shoes and sometimes aroused scorn or derision.

His voice too is tiny but carries and impresses itself very clearly on the magnetic tape (sometimes bigger voices fail to do this, for no clear reason). He doesn't drawl but speaks precisely, clipping many words – 'Sir' is 'suh!' and 'No' is 'noh!' He also giggles and laughs a great deal. Generally his talk is not smooth but full of gaps, switches, exclamations, changes of tempo. He uses his body a lot and has a number of characteristic gestures: the eyes roll up into the head showing their whites when he is thinking or embarking upon a long statement; when horrified (by the bomb, by overpopulation for example) he throws his hands up to his face and throws his body forward; and constantly he is grabbing one's elbow or shaking one's knee to emphasise a point.

Krishnamurti's conversation does not follow the strict rules, laid down by grammar, for the expression of the ego in its relationships with the surrounding world. That is, sometimes when speaking of himself he speaks in the third person; and sometimes when speaking in the first person he is not speaking

93

of himself. Nor is he always strictly biographical. For example, when he says he's never been depressed he is speaking from the position of the mature Krishnamurti in the eternal present, whereas we know from Mary Lutyens' excellent 3-volume biography of him that he has known depression and unhappiness, especially in his early life.

Though not effeminate, he is androgynous – androgyny is something many evolved people possess. But not only of manner or temperament – photographs of him in middle years on the beach show a thin, undeveloped body with curious, feminine breasts. Alternatively, though he was usually clean-shaven, photographs do exist showing him with full beard. And evolved, yes – but childlike too. A paradoxical human being.

F: Are you surprised to have lived so long?
K: . . . no!
F: Is your health good?
K: Very!
F: What does surprise you?
K: . . . . . Human behaviour.
F: Where's home for you?
K: Come and sit a bit nearer. Then you can be more comfortable. Ecco.
F: You have an Indian passport.
K: That's correct.
F: But where are your headquarters?
K: Wherever I am.
F: You like to travel light?
K: Yes. But I don't like to travel. Airports are so noisy. But I travel an enormous amount.
F: You never spend more than a few months in one place.
K: Yes. I spend 4 months in India. 4 months in America. 4 months in Europe. Every year. Before the Second World War I was all over the place. Now the travel is getting a bit much. Not because of age. But you know, I'm a strict vegetarian, it becomes rather difficult . . .
F: I hear you used to love driving.

K: I still drive. In California. My eyesight is very good.

F: To what do you attribute your remarkable well-being?

K: I don't know really [*chuckles*]. The family in which I was born were Brahmins and for generations they've never eaten meat or fish or foul, never smoked, no alcohol.

F: Is vegetarianism something you advocate for others?

K: Oh I don't advocate things!

F: But for generations my family has eaten meat. If I were to become a vegetarian, wouldn't there be a drop in my energy?

K: No, no, not if you do it properly and have a balanced diet. I know many Indians who've never eaten meat, they have only one meal a day, poor coolies you know, poor people, and yet they have tremendous energy.

F: What was it about you which first attracted the attention of the Theosophists?

K: Dr Besant first. She was an extraordinary person. She was the first woman to talk freely about divorce, birth control. She was an atheist – in the Victorian age. And she was the first woman to lead a strike. She was a Fabian, a great friend of Bernard Shaw and all that crowd. She had no religious belief and I think she went to India in search of some kind of . . . religious business. And so got involved with Hinduism and – do you want to know all this?

F: What I particularly want to know was what they actually saw in you?

K: I'll tell you in a minute. My father was one of these brahmins helping with the Theosophical Society in Madras. And some people noticed these 2 boys, my brother and myself, and they said 'That's the boy you've been looking for'.

F: But what did they –

K: I'll tell you. They felt that boy to be, if I may put it humbly, to be without a *self* – without the egotistic outlook on life. And that made them adopt the boy.

F: Leadbeater was the first to spot you – what sort of man was he?

K: I had very little contact with him. It was Dr Besant who adopted us. Our father objected – naturally – poor chap [*chuckles*]. He objected to his boys being deified. There was a court case and Dr Besant took us to England to be educated privately, to France, Italy – I speak Italian and French.

F: What went through your head as this deification process began to wind round you?

K: Sir, I was much too vague. I was slightly moronish. I just accepted it. It didn't mean much.

F: You didn't think, oh this is rather exciting?

K: No. You see, I was . . . absent-minded. Rather aloof from all this. Very shy. Eventually there was a tremendous organisation round me. Friends in Holland gave me 5,000 acres – in Holland – you know what 5,000 acres means in Holland? And a castle and everything. We had a gathering there for 3–4,000 people and I said – I must have found the courage to say 'Look. This is all nonsense.' I said worshipping me was nonsense. I said all the religions are meaningless. We dissolved the organisation, returned all the properties, and that was the end of that period.

F: But earlier, in 1922, you had this strange sort of physical transformation. Could you describe what happened?

K: I've no recollection of it. Forgive me, I really mean it. I have no *direct* memory of it. People around me saw it and wrote about it. Yes, there were subsequent occurrences . . . You can look at it as self-hypnosis. Or as some kind of induced illusions. Or, as the Hindus would look at it, as something the physical body had to go through. You've had it in the Christian saints, this physical pain. Also – I must tell you a little bit more . . . As a boy when they found me, I could read people's thoughts. They'd give me sealed letters in envelopes and I would read them. And I used to heal people. Forgive me, you may think this is all tommy-rot –

F: I don't *exactly*, not exactly . . .

K: I used to do all this – I do some things still – never mind all that [*pushing it away*]. You see, sir . . . The body becomes highly refined, sensitive, very alive, and –

F: Uncomfortable?

K: Little bit. Naturally.

F: Do you still have these particular talents?

K: Little bit . . . oh [*places hand on brow*] I don't know how to explain all this to you . . . It is considered, all the miracles one can do, the occult phenomena, extrasensory perception and all that, it's not compatible with total goodness if you understand. It is accepted in the old tradition that you mustn't touch all that.

F: Because it interferes with the order of things?

K: No, no. Because it leads to power, position, self-importance. I've been through all that.

F: All right then . . . Er, are you ever bored?

K: No. Also I like nature immensely. I used to play golf. I was plus 3 or 4.

F: Um . . . look, you've got me terribly fascinated in this occult business now. But I don't quite know how to question you about it. The actual nature of the gift, the process involved . . .

K: Sir, how can I convey it to you?

F: Let me put it crudely.

K: Put it as crudely as you like.

F: If you were to apply this particular gift, could you tell me what the questions are I've written on this piece of paper?

K: Yes.

F: But you choose not to work yourself into that?

K: Because I consider it rather, er, cheap.

F: Déclassé.

K: Déclassé. Precisely!

F: But do you have to work yourself into it – or is it a gift you can turn on and off like a tap?

K: No, you can't . . . just a minute. You may have had a certain incident of this kind. And then you blow it up! You understand?

F: Yes, but in order to blow it up, to inflate it, something has to have taken place originally – otherwise it's just deceit.

K: Once you may have done it. Or twice. Then the story takes hold and you become a great man because you've done it. You know the game.

F: Not this particular game.

K: Oh yes, you do. The dangerous thing is that it involves self-importance.

F: Did you ever meet Alaister Crowley? He was one of those.

K: Who? I don't know the name.

F: An English occultist. He was a heroin addict eventually.

K: You see, that's the danger.

F: Another was Gurdjieff.

K: Oh yes. I never met him. I met lots of his disciples.

F: Now, Christopher Isherwood wrote –

K: I met him. In California. And Aldous Huxley was a great friend.

F: Well, Isherwood wrote that 'Krishnamurti expounded a philosophy of discrimination between the real and the unreal.' Is this a useful way of describing your philosophy?

K: No.

F: Ha! Can you encapsulate your philosophy for me?

K: You see, sir, the moment you label it you pin it down. And you must take the whole thing, right? Not just part of it, saying this is it.

F: Nonetheless, you do write books.

K: I do, unfortunately.

F: Are you happy with your books?

K: No. I never read them afterwards. I've tried going through them but I change everything, so it's . . .

F: Have you ever experienced loneliness?

K: . . . You see, loneliness is part of this estrangement from life, isolation from everything else.

F: What about depression?

K: Ah hup! I've never been depressed . . . Sir, may I go into this a little bit if you're interested? Our brains are conditioned. By education, by nationality, by tradition, by all the religious superstition, right? We are terribly prejudiced people. Historically, I believe, wars have been going on for 5–6,000 years. First a club, then an arrow – ultimately the bomb. Right? But we are not individuals. [*Leans across and grabs the knee*] Just listen to it first, then throw it out if you want to. Every human being goes through psychological suffering, pain, anxiety, depression, loneliness. *Every* human being, whether communist, socialist, capitalist, the Pope, whoever – they all go through it. So – our consciousness is the rest of humanity. You understand? But we are programmed to be this or that – like a computer.

F: So you don't believe in the individual soul?

K: Wait a moment, wait a moment . . . In the Asiatic world they believe in reincarnation. In Christendom they believe in resurrection. This question: what is it that's enduring? Is it memory? What is it?

F: Awareness of some sort.

K: Wait, wait. Go into it a little more . . . We are a bundle of memories. I am a Hindu, a Brahmin, I function with that limitation, I am that limitation, right? And you are a Christian or whatever – and we battle each other. How extraordinary! Why do we *live* like that? After a million years we are still barbarians. Long distance of time from the ape or whatever. Highly civilised now. But inside we are barbarians. We know how to vaporise a million human beings in a few seconds. Highly civilised . . . There is something radically wrong in all this . . . After a million or 2 million years, after the tremendous experience of evolution – what are we?

F: Nothing very brilliant, I must say.

K: Right, sir. And if we don't do something now . . . atom bomb is there.

F: This is a rather exciting time to be alive.

K: Is it? For who?

F: For me.

K: What do you mean by exciting?

F: Circumstances force a change.

K: Are we changing, actually, under this tremendous pressure?

F: We have to.

K: Not have to. *Are* we?

F: I think we will.

K: Ha! Again in the future. We will, we must.

F: If we survive, it presupposes we have changed. That's all I can say.

K: . . . . . There was an article I was just reading in the *New Yorker* which I like very much. In the article he says that the man who presses the button first – first – gets the other fellow, is the winner. And both sides are considering: who will be first?

F: This is very dangerous.

K: Ah hup! . . . Do you realise how serious this is? Nobody seems to pay attention. The average person – does he know all this?

F: I don't know. I've written about it.

K: It's a tremendous thing!

F: That's why I say it's an exciting time to live.

K: . . . With all this destructive activity throughout the world, man has always sought something beyond. I'm born, educated, I send my sons off to be killed, my daughter gets married to some idiot, mm? What's the point of all this? At the end of it man has asked – is there something beyond all this?

F: What answer would you give me to that question?

K: There is something . . . much greater than all this. Not through any organisation, not through any religious structure, because they're all invented by thought. Right?

F: Can you indicate what this 'much greater' might be?

K: . . . I can indicate but it means going into a great many things. Do you want to?

F: That depends. Start to tell me . . .

K: First of all you have to ask if there is such a thing at all. There must first be the quality of doubt, scepticism. Otherwise you can't find out. God exists? What god? I have faith in that figure over there – but what is it really?

F: A piece of marble.

K: Exactly. So the ancient Hindus and the Buddhists said there must be this sense of questioning, demanding, enquiring. Follow? That's *part* of it. But in Christendom that's not allowed.

F: There's a tradition of it in Christendom of course but it's a tradition of rebellion. Papal infallibility –

K: Ah hup! [*Krishnamurti makes another of these choking noises in his throat – they can mean either violent disagreement – or violent agreement*]. In the Catholic Church, if you doubt, the whole structure falls. So . . . what I'm saying is – through doubt and enquiry, you don't belong to any religion, don't belong to any group, national or religious, sectarian or the gurus. Right? . . . It's not outside . . . God isn't over there. If he is it's because I've created a god over there out of my fear. And the moment you say truth is *ours*, you've killed it. So . . . to come to that, you have to meditate, you have to go right into it. But meditation has now become an organised affair. Ha! Is there a meditation which is not deliberate?

F: Sometimes. But one has to be very comfortable for that.

K: Not comfortable. Extraordinarily aware.

F: By comfortable I mean without conflict. And when there is no conflict, there is no reason to question.

K: What do you mean by conflict?

F: Conflict within oneself.

K: That is because I have several desires, pursuits, wishes. This means we have to go into the question of desire. Which involves the question of time – not by the clock. What is time?

F: This suggests another question – how does one prevent detachment from turning into meaninglessness, indifference?

K: Sir . . . you have to understand attachment first. Not detachment.

F: . . . . What makes you angry?

K: It's not in my nature to be angry. Apart from maybe a flash for a few seconds. Then it's gone.

F: Your assistants –

K: No. Wait a moment, sir. [*Krishnamurti's habit of contradiction is sometimes self-generated, as here. Indeed, he's contradicting it even before the point has been put and simply goes off on a tangent of his own. As a result the question – which was 'Your assistants are mostly women whereas Christ's were men: why do you think this is?' – is never put*] I am a poor man. The Foundation is not rich. This school here – just surviving. Someone said to me 'You're getting old. You must have a house on the Riviera to retire to.' They set aside $100,000 for that purpose. So when we started this school, I said to the friend 'I don't want to retire – can we use that money?' That's how we got this place.

F: Have you known sexual love?

101

K: Little bit.

F: But it's not something you've pursued?

K: No.

F: Do you believe in celibacy?

K: No, no, just a minute. You take a vow of celibacy and then you say 'My god, I must stick to it'. Inside you are burning. So – don't take vows – find out about it.

F: Does the Pope strike you as an intelligent man?

K: [*Chuckles*] Sir, just look at it. [*Claps hands*] That's religion, all that.

F: It's belief of some sort.

K: Yes, sir, that's it. A question of belief. Having faith.

F: But this is dangerous?

K: Obviously. Faith in what? In the thing I have created.

F: Well, um . . . I take it from that, that you suggest the Pope is –

K: Ugh, sir, wait a moment. I have no axe to grind.

F: I didn't mean to imply that, but the Pope is the spiritual leader of many millions of people.

K: 810 million people. But do you notice something very odd about this? The Catholic Church, they never say: Stop war.

F: That's because they believe in the individual, material soul.

K: You see! Ugh what! [*almost tongue-tied with exasperation*] . . . Sir, not only in the Christian world, but also in the Muslim world. Look what is happening, Shi-ites, and so on.

F: The Muslim religion is also a warlike religion.

K: Oh *very*. Very. Very, very. They're flogging people, cutting hands off, all the time.

F: How is it that humans can imagine this is er . . . holy behaviour?

K: Because – the book says! Christianity too is based on a book . . . right?

F: It sounds ridiculous when you put it like that.

K: But it *is* that way. Muslims have their book. Christians have their book. Go to India, the Hindus – 100 books! One book leads to all kinds of fanaticism. This is happening in America too – fundamentalism. The word is the truth . . . think about that.

102

F: Communism too – trying to make life correspond to the word. There's a phrase I've often thought about and never understood – perhaps you can help – it's in the Bible: in the beginning was the Word and the word was God. I've looked at it from all sorts of angles – but it always seems just . . . total nonsense.

K: Of course.

F: But somebody somewhere at some time must have thought this meant something intelligent.

K: Just look over there. That's a door. But the word 'door' is not the actual door. The brain is a network of words, a network of thought, but thought is always limited. Knowledge is based on experience, right? Knowledge is always being added to – therefore it is always limited – otherwise nothing could be added to it. Knowledge is memory – and memory is the source of thought.

F: I wouldn't say all knowledge is memory. But that thinking is always limited – I accept that as self-evident. I love words, I work with words every day and the moment you do this you see the limitations of words very clearly because you can see all round them. It's a language. So is music. So is mathematics . . . What is your greatest failure?

K: I don't think in terms of success or failure.

F: Have you any vices?

K: What do you mean? Smoking, drinking, fornicating? Secret urges which are not moral or traditional?

F: I mean – obsessions.

K: I've never thought about it [*chuckles at length*]. But I'm not upset by any blasted thing at all! [*Splutters and chuckles*].

F: What makes you afraid?

K: . . . Sir, listen. What is fear first? Can I be free of it? Or is it natural like circulation of the blood?

F: Fear is the emotional reaction to threat. Tiger in the forest.

K: I once knew a tiger very well and – but I won't go into all that, it's a long story. Fear is fear of death.

F: Or injury.

K: Fear of danger to my physical being – or to my emotional and intellectual being. It's very dangerous to belong to any tribe. You see danger of the tiger – and you do something

103

to protect yourself. You see danger of war – but you do nothing to stop that danger. Why don't people feel the danger of war?

F: I have to assume that something gets into people when they are part of a group – like a drug which numbs them and excites them too. The approach of death can be very exciting.

K: Yes, I know.

F: Switches them on. Life is no longer boring.

K: That's because I no longer have responsibility for myself, because I handed it over.

F: Partly that. Also it has to do with the way the proximity of death can violently stimulate life.

K: What is death? . . . The whole organism collapses at one point. This is frightening, so we have the idea of life after death or in the Asiatic world, reincarnation. This is the avoidance of death. So what is death? Death is the ending of things, attachment to this house, my relation to that person, ending attachment to everything, right?

F: Also ending your attachment to your awareness of yourself?

K: Yes. So then the point is – why should I wait for this? I'm not advocating suicide. I'm saying why can't you live with death all the time? Live a life which is ending every day. Completely see the importance of living, functioning, being healthy. But all your attachments, all your desires – end it! So you are living death all the time. That is real freedom. Not freedom to do just what you like, but real freedom.

F: Death is absolute. But dying is not. It can be very painful. Or the question of injury. Say I'm captured by the police in an unpleasant country – and they torture me –

K: Or – I don't want to kill anybody. But my sister is attacked suppose. What to do? I have to say – wait until she's attacked. I will react then. Don't ask me what I'll do. That is a question that has no value.

F: I think it has value. There are a lot of nasty people around. I think you'd agree that if one is attacked one's entitled to defend oneself. But there are strong and weak people in the

104

world. At what point is one prepared to help people who are being cruelly treated? The amount of torture in the world is – phenomenal! The war against Hitler – it was justified?

K: Mao Tse Tung in China killed 30 million or more people. Stalin killed a similar number. Why didn't we say look, stop it, this is terrible!

F: Because it was within their own tribe.

K: Eccolo! Eccolo! Unless it touches us, we are indifferent. Touch my house or me, I am enflamed.

F: What do you find most attractive about life now?

K: . . . Have you considered what is going to happen when the computer can do almost everything we can do? I said almost.

F: It could detach us from obsessional thought.

K: Either the entertainment industry, including the so-called religions, is going to capture me – football hooliganism is an example. Or I turn inward. I know I've contributed to the entertainment industry. I've talked to thousands of people in India, in California, they are all there, lying under the trees hugging and kissing, it's a day out, it's a circus, a holiday. I'm not disappointed. I say – here's good food cooked for you. Eat it if you want to. If you don't, it's all right. But I don't want to be part of the circus, so where do I draw the line?

F: You become a hermit.

K: I had a friend who said he wouldn't even write a letter because a postage stamp would be helping the government. He wouldn't travel because it would be helping the travel companies. So many things he wouldn't do. So he drove himself into a corner. Then he said – I'm stuck here.

F: This is the central question. Detachment degenerating into isolation. You can't work it quite like that.

K: But why should I belong to something which I think is totally insane?

F: You have to shelter, have to eat.

K: That's it. I have to clothe myself. So I've drawn the line.

F: Your friend made an obsession of his idea – and so got stuck in a corner.

K: Exactly. That's what the pacifists are doing. Throw away all weapons – but they know the other people are preparing for war. Draw the line . . . but what is important is the operation of intelligence in the highest sense.

F: This er . . . 'much greater' we referred to.

K: Yes . . . What is it? What is timeless. Not thought. Well, this is your life. You have to live and try and find out – not just accept somebody, something or other and trot along . . . We have made life into a problem. Think of the tragedy of this. Is there a possibility for a very quiet mind? . . . Absolutely still, apart from the blood moving through it . . .

F: But there are terrible problems in the world. There are far too many people for example.

K: Oh God yes, I know, sir. And in India – they'll be a billion presently. Oh . . .

F: That is a problem – one worth tackling.

K: And you can't solve it with a brain full of problems!

Krishnamurti says that we are all barbarians. Yes. But there are degrees of barbarism. There are completely amoral people who would slit one's throat for a few coins – and intensely moral people who would slit one's throat for an idea. The coins and the ideas one may forego but the throat is essential: how does one best protect it? Institutions arise so that man can protect himself from his own bestiality. Where is the line between aggression and self-defence? The conflict between individual and collective consciousness? On the whole Krishnamurti prefers the individual because it is sensitive, as opposed to the collective which is ruthless. Also he is a great believer in common sense – stop extrapolating general principles from specific events. In his rejection of all spiritual and theoretical authority, Krishnamurti would not like to be called an anarchist. The brochure for the Brockwood Park school says 'What has to be made clear is that the kind of authority that is destructive is the one that arbitrarily imposes a certain set of beliefs, or certain ways of thinking and feeling. Such authority interferes with the art of learning, whether it comes from outside or from one's own likes and dislikes, prejudices, or desires for status and security. On the other hand the authority needed for the orderly functioning of a community, far from being harmful, is actually necessary for true freedom.' In the same way, when Krishnamurti attacks time, memory, thought, knowledge, he's attacking them because of the way we allow ourselves to be distorted by them instead of keeping them dependent on us (they are after all our creations) – because he has always addressed himself to the possibility of psychological change in the individual. For example, when he says knowledge is bad he doesn't mean the knowledge required to build a beautiful building or to grow food successfully. He means the Pavlovian prison of automatic reactions and judgements.

*

A few months later I visited Krishnamurti again at Brockwood Park and had the opportunity to follow up some of these questions, especially the nature of ESP and clairvoyance. He said that it was fairly simple and it's absurd to have a mystique about this which would make people gullible. 'If you are married or have a close friend you know immediately what they feel, what they think, because you are sensitive to each other – without a word being said or a gesture made. That's also extrasensory perception. That's the beginning of it. As a young man I used to read people's thoughts. But I found it terrible, so I stopped. It was embarrassing. What it demands is sensitivity. If one is *very* sensitive, one can do most things. Not just an emotional sensitivity. Clairvoyance is to see clearly what others don't see.' He illustrated this by positing a river flowing left to right in a great curve. And 2 boats are coming along in opposite directions. If you watch carefully, you will be able to tell at what point they are going to meet. How? By getting far enough above it. 'And that means no personality enters into the observation, no egotism, no self-interest. Otherwise it's impossible. Otherwise you're another boat on the river.'

On the question of healing, which he doesn't usually

practise himself, he said that anybody could understand faith healing and that most healers relied heavily on faith. The healer has renown and that helps him. Or if I have faith in you that you can do something, that helps. This is Lourdes and so on. It requires tradition, knowledge, background. But faith is a very dangerous thing. It's like propaganda. Faith commits you to living in a dream. But, he said, there was also a healing which had no background, was not dependent on faith, and this healing is totally different. It doesn't involve any background or gullibility. It simply takes place. And he has done this. 'Now you're asking – what takes place actually? There's a first class doctor I know in America and I was talking to him about these things and he said that there is in the brain the pituitary gland which can be influenced, and that if it is stimulated . . . well, that's one of the possibilities.'

Then he said 'There is a very very very old tradition . . .' and asked me to switch off the tape-recorder 'because some things should not be recorded and written up in that way but must be reflected on and explored for themselves alone'. And he told me stranger things about knowledge, intelligence, magic etc. These I shall not divulge – in order that the reader may be mystified.

(1985)

DIVINE

DIVINE (NÉ GLEN Milstead), monstrous star of John Waters' bad taste films of the late 60s and 70s (*Eat Your Make-Up*, *Mondo Trasho*, *Multiple Maniacs*, *Pink Flamingos*, *Female Trouble* etc), says 'On Thursday I flew to Munich to do a video for my new record which just came out and it's like, well, all my records are the same, heavy disco beat, then my voice comes in which is a terrible voice, but I love to sing.' Divine's speaking voice is soft but definite, unlike his stage voice which is like a raucous drunken navvy's.

To-day he is dressed in a dark banker suit (Tommy Nutter) and striped shirt. 'Well, I was on a big chat show in the States and he said "You're a transvestite", and I said "I'm not, I'm an actor and entertainer", and he said "So if you're not a transvestite, why are you sitting here in a cocktail dress?", and I thought, well, he's got a very good point there. It was the last time I made an appearance in drag that wasn't my own show. And that whole Divine look – it was designed by a friend of mine, Van Smith, who is still my personal art director – it takes hours to put on and no one takes you seriously, they just think you're another drag queen.'

The banking image is modified by shaved eyebrows and bleached balding hair cut close to the scalp and 'Is that a diamond in your ear?'

'Yes.'

'Have you got lots?'

'Not lots.'

'But there are lots more holes in your ear.'

'That's from my hippy days, multiple earrings – the holes just don't close up again.'

'The world does seem a lot more proper these days – but I suppose one can't fall about on Mandrax for ever and what with these horrible new diseases . . .'

Divine nods deeply and scratches a point behind his ear with the tip of a fingernail. 'I've cleaned up quite a bit myself, though I'm not Doris Day yet. I've had quite a few friends die from AIDS. And I just lost over 100 lbs. You may not realise it because sitting down like this with my stomach hanging out is not my best position. But I was 387lbs and I jump up and down a lot in my show and I got worried I was going to drop dead on stage. I'd come off and it would take an hour to get my breathing back to normal.'

'Were you always big?'

'Yes – and I was spoilt when young – I was an only child, born in Baltimore, Maryland, into what in America would be considered an upper middle-class family. Daddy played golf, Mother shopped a lot. I hated school. I never knew what was going to happen, if I'd be beaten up. It got to the point where I had to have a police escort to school. Avocado green was the big colour then but I didn't look good in avocado green and I'd wear red or something – so I was this fat outcast in red with a police escort. I was a lot more effeminate then than I am now and I just wasn't appreciated by fellow classmates.'

'How did you discover the facts of life?'

'I asked my father and he told me just about everything. Then I asked him about homosexuals and he said when he was at school he and his friends used to beat up those guys, so I never went into it with my parents after that. I was engaged to a girl once in High School, then I met this guy and it all changed.'

'Were you called Divine at school?'

'No. I was called Divine on Sundays. That was when John Waters had his Super 8 camera and we started to make those films like *Mondo Trasho* on Sundays when we were still at school. John said to me "I think you're divine and that'll be your name". We were all teenagers in Baltimore together. Then on the Wednesday or Thursday of the following week we'd have a Coca Cola party and potato chips and popcorn and sit around and watch ourselves on the screen and eat food. I'm now under 300 lbs for the first time in 6 years. I love to eat – and I love to eat the wrong things.'

'I know. Did you really eat dog shit in *Pink Flamingos*?'

'Goodness, I didn't swallow it! I just put it in my mouth and pushed it around.'

'Did you rehearse it?'

'No. John Waters said "In this film you're playing the Filthiest Person Alive, so let's really give it to them – it would be fabulous if you did something like eating dog shit". And I said "No problem, John, anything for a good film", and then I forgot all about it. When we came to the last day's shooting he was very vague about it which isn't like John because he likes everything written down but for the last day nothing was written down. I'll never forget Van, who was doing my make-up and became hysterical and had to sit down. I said "Van, what is it?" and he said "I don't know why I'm bothering with all this lipstick when all you're gonna do is eat shit to-day". And I said "Come on, John's not serious, they're gonna give me something fake". When we got on the set John was strangely excited and said "We've been feeding the dog and it's been locked in the house for days – ".'

'What did they feed it on?'

Divine scratches that point again behind his ear with the tip of the fingernail. 'Steak. Sirloin. He ate better than I did that week. People seem to think it was a poodle but it was a Hungarian er, I can't remember the name, but a kind of Hungarian . . . something. Anyway, he belonged to friends of mine and was very well house-trained and wouldn't go in the house and had been locked in for about 3 days. And John said "Now, the dog is going to come out. And when it squats down and does its number, I want you to jump down, scoop it up, bite it off, throw the excess away, and give me a big shitty grin. Don't even think about it." Really it didn't hit me. We followed that dog around for 3 hours and the dog wouldn't go. So they took it back in the house and gave it an enema and when they brought it out again, the dog didn't just shit, it shit all *over* the place, and John said "Go on, now, hit it, quick!" So

I jumped at it because the cameras were going and I scooped it up, threw it in my mouth, and I thought "What *am* I doing?" But my head was spinning and John's screaming "You wanna be famous, you wanna be famous, don't you?!", and I thought "But do I want to be famous as a shit eater?". I gagged a bit but then I gave him this big shitty grin and poked my tongue out.'

'I remember your tongue all smeared with brown. It was revolting.'

'Yeah, then I spat it all out and went home and had 3 bottles of Listerine mouthwash. John said "It'll either make you world famous – or we'll never hear of you again". For 2 years John showed *Pink Flamingos* to every distributor and they wouldn't touch it with gloves. It was confiscated and burnt when it came to London the first time. Then it became very popular on the college circuit and the Elgin Theatre in New York booked it for a try-out midnight show – it was packed, they had to turn people away. At the time I was living in California in Santa Monica. They called me from New York and said you're a *huge* hit!'

'How did your parents swallow it?'

'They didn't. We didn't speak for 9 years. Then I heard my father was very ill and they were always wonderful parents – I always had everything I wanted, and even things I didn't want were still thrown at me – so we started talking again.' (At this point 'Glen' comes fully out, the persecuted fatty at school, with sweet eau de Nil eyes and a gentle nature, Divine's opposite number.)

'You see, John worked hard for 2 years on *Pink Flamingos* before we even started shooting. It was supposed to be bad taste in every way. That's why we made *Polyester* because the critics always said John's movies stink, so he said well here's one that does. It had the Odorama cards which you scratched and sniffed when certain numbers came up. The smells were horrid, dirty tennis shoes, farts, dirty underwear, you name it. The card was numbered 1 to 10. Number 1 was a rose, then it went downhill completely. 2 was a fart. I can't remember what 10 was. Something unbelievable. Because you see the whole idea of Divine is to be very bold, like those women do exist who've been in prison, running around with gangsters. The

112

word "fuck" comes very naturally to them, they don't sit around talking about crochet. But Divine is also very likeable. Even the terrible things she's done, like murdering people, it's always for a decent cause like helping her family.'

'But she chained up her daughter in *Female Trouble*.'

'The child was rebellious but, yes, that wasn't my favourite thing to do.'

'Were you rebellious?'

'I chose to look different, shaving my hairline back, doing the eyes, then I was fat, then on top of that I did drag. 3 strikes – you're out of the ball game.'

'James Baldwin said he was black, communist, homosexual, ugly, a writer – 5 times alienated.'

'Oh my God, he should've done drag too – it might've helped him.'

'He went to live in France.'

'It's always a bit easier away from home base. And the more popular I am in Europe, then the more popular I become in America. In the States I'm an import item – if it's imported, it's considered better.'

'What did you do before you were famous?'

'I was a hair stylist – until I ran out of there screaming. Then I had a shop called Divine Trash in Baltimore. Then the movies started taking off and it turned into show business. I'm just coming into my own. I've been doing a slow build for 22 years. It would be terrible to be an overnight success at 21 – it's downhill for the next 60 years. To come to it slowly gives you the strength to sustain yourself in the business. I play all over the world now. I just did a fantastic season in Hong Kong and Sydney where they had to turn people away. But my favourite place is London. Most of my friends are here. I think I'm going to move here,' says Divine, brushing a non-existent lock of hair from his hard-working brow.

(1985)

N.B. Divine is also the name of the transvestite hero of Genet's *Notre Dame des Fleurs*. Glen Milstead died from a heart attack on March 7th, 1988, aged 42.

ELEVENSES

LADY SOAMES IN KNIGHTSBRIDGE

WITH THE PUBLICATION of her various Churchill books, Lady Soames (otherwise Mary, wife of Christopher, mother of Nicholas, Emma, Jeremy, Charlotte, Rupert, but always, inescapably the daughter of Winston Churchill and invariably referred to as his only 'normal' child) continues her upward drift as a woman of letters. She is very pretty with beautiful blue eyes and fine skin. There is nothing slight about her – the phrase which comes to mind is 'lacrosse captain'. Her voice sounds like Queen Elizabeth II but hyper-stimulated, very nearly out of control, and frequently leaves her short of breath. Somehow she manages to keep 3, 4, even 5 sentences on the go simultaneously, by dashing from one to another like a Chinaman spinning plates. She is a great giver. The heart comes pouring out and when it reaches you it is warm.

For a long time Mary Soames didn't consider herself in the least writerly. 'In fact I'm not really tempted to write any book at all,' she gasps. 'It just you know – would you like coffee? yes? biscuits? – sort of seems to happen.'

Her first book was *Clementine Churchill*, the biography of her mother which won 2 literary prizes. She found writing it a very moving experience.

'Did I say that in an interview or something? How very odd. Well, no, yes, no, you see I'd never written anything before, talk about fools rush in, and as for my father I was rather unanalytical about him, I loved him and had a good relationship with him. He was very bound up with his career and destiny but I think that a lot of people who are egotistical tend

114

to be rather cold and he certainly wasn't, he was very warm and loving and ... oh dear, that's something I've inherited from him, the ability to cry easily. And another thing I've inherited is his wonderful constitution touch wood but I'm *deeply* allergic to sport, I can't bear playing games.' Lacrosse captain was misleading. 'Except Scrabble, which reminds me, I must get this new Scrabble dictionary that's come out. I always wear Father round my neck, I can't think why I haven't got it on now, it's just a Churchill crown you know that were minted after he died, I've had it dipped and wear it as my lucky talisman, not that I'm superstitious but still. Being his child, er, this is always more difficult for men, certainly for my brother Randolph it was very difficult, also in a way it's quite difficult for my nephew Winston, Randolph's son. On reflection my father was not a wise father to Randolph and over-indulged Randolph in his own opinion of himself. This is why my mother had such a difficult relationship with Randolph because right from the beginning she thought my father overdid it with him, but you see my father's father Lord Randolph Churchill was cold and beastly to Papa who adored, hero-worshipped him and Lord Randolph treated him with, um, really *chilling* contempt, so Papa went right the other way with *his* son.' She fiddles with her necklace of big sensible pearly beads and since I'm just nodding my head, Lady Soames launches out anew.

'As for the girls, I've never had a career or sort of independent ambition – awfully tame, isn't it. I'm not at all exceptional or eccentric, no, really I'm not, oh yes, well, all right, I smoke cigars but I never smoke a big one unless (a) I'm offered one, (b) I've got the time, gossiping after dinner, 2 a week of the big ones would be a lot. But really I don't think that's eccentric. I'm not – but then I suddenly see my children looking awfully embarrassed by something and sometimes they scream at me for God's sake Mummy! So nice. Very good for one. And my sister Sarah certainly, you know, whether that, again, maybe she got auditions because, anyhow she was a talented actress, well, the last bit was a bit sad but, um, if you look at my parents' personalities and breeding, if they, if we were rabbits or racehorses you might well expect us to be rather sort of jumpy, excitable ones, it must work a bit with humans as well. Sarah and I used to see each other or speak about once a fortnight. And Diana was a worrier who got very tired through nervous strain. But I've had a happy life. It is so much the luck of the draw.

'We are now in this anti-hero knocking stage. Somebody said about my father the other day that he was paralytically drunk throughout the war, oh some obliging person, people do write the most extraordinary balderdash, so I'm always very glad when people say he didn't get paralytically drunk all the time, didn't offer up Coventry as sort of, um, bait, did you see the other day all that about poison gas and all that? I could've answered but I can't always be, because frankly I've got my own life to get through from dawn to dusk, dear God, sorry, we've strayed away, I started rattling on, but in my biography of my mother I wanted to tell the truth but I didn't want to lay around me with a hatchet and if you say my parents used to have awful rows before you know where you are people are saying the awful rowing Churchills, and they *did* have awful rows but their marriage was a very happy and, er, people who have long and happy marriages, I doubt if any would put up a paw and say they'd, you know hands up who's never had a tiff. One of my father's great virtues he was *tremendously* forgiving and now that I've said it somebody will say he was the most dreadful unforgiving man, but if my mother had gone to bed early after a row because you know she used to get tired, she hadn't night stamina, he'd put a little note under her door saying "Wow, I'm sorry" or something. He was capable of getting very angry but not capable of harbouring a grudge and was tremendously natural and unhypocritical and uncontrived, tremendously really not a different person in public to what he was in private. Several people have said that he was a *terribly* bad liar. And he was magnanimous in victory – I had lunch with him the day after VE Day – I found it in my diary recently. He was talking about how the Germans had to be got back into the European family.'

'Did your parents explain the facts of life to you?'

'Agh! Oh, no, absolutely not! They were awful about that. I wouldn't have expected, looking back, Mummy was very

116

backward about that, I think she was *deeply* shy about it and she'd had a very unhappy childhood which I won't weary you with now, she still came from the generation that, I don't know how she, I think she was *deeply* relieved when she discovered I knew – oh Maria, that's wonderful, thank-you so much, I'll have the coffee here and we'll give Mr Fallowell that table and the biscuits. My mother I don't think she had a tremendous capacity for enjoyment. She always thought she was going to enjoy things much more than she did. Which is rather sad. She was a nervous person and a perfectionist and I don't think perfectionists find it easy to, um, because everything falls short of their you know. She had much more energy than stamina – do you see the difference? She always said she conked out in the third set. But she had this iron determination and could *make* herself do anything.'

'What other great men from the past do you admire?'

Mary Soames kicks off her shoes, jumps up on the sofa and tucks her legs beneath her with a neat all-in-one movement, throws off her cardigan, snatches off her spectacles, pulls her skirt over her knees, twists frantically various gold rings and gold bracelets (she wears lots of gold), blinks the gorgeous blue eyes in the wide open face, and says 'I'm not really . . . um very well read, um.'

Then let us move from greatness to goodness.

'What do you think is the difference between a great man and a good man?'

'Oh dear, how do you define goodness? Um, um, help! I find his goodness part of his greatness. But I don't think of Papa being good as you think Saint Francis of Assisi is.'

'Are you religious?'

'I'm a straightforward Anglican. And I'm rather left of middle or a very wobbly, wet Conservative, but I don't think one should go round assuming *everybody* is the walking sick needing help. What I really think is bad for us in this country is if talent and get-up-and-go and cleverness are somehow made to be slightly off side. In France the thing that is very interesting, well it interested me, I think it is true to say that when you've lived in France a little bit it's very marked how what an amazing fabric of work is done by voluntary work in

England. One remembers all one's cousins and aunts doing meals on wheels, our social services are underpinned the whole way by this voluntary tradition, but I tell you what in France a terrific unifier is – food. Entertainments laid on by the French are nearly always wonderful but I suppose they're a much richer country, aren't they. They drive like maniacs so I'm WERRGHHH!!! and my daughter Emma says of course you're going to get hooted at in France Mummy crawling round like that, but it's the Gallic temperament, isn't – but oh God, it's a beautiful country and the most delicious grub. I always think that gardening is to Britain what food is to France. Gardening is very trans-class. My idea of a treat is to spend the whole afternoon gardening. But I do think the French – oh dear, our friend Generalisation – and I don't want to sound anti-French because I'm very pro-French and was brought up to be – De Gaulle and my mother got on very well and after my father died he wrote to her and nearly always wrote to her on the anniversary of my father's death. So I don't want to sound anti-French, but I have really let myself go because I don't see any point otherwise in having an interview like this and I'm rather bad once I get going of holding back as no doubt you've noticed and, um, but, um, what was I saying? Goodness, what an absolute desert my mind's gone to, now I can't think, but my friends thought it *frightfully* funny because when the news came through that Christopher was going to be ambassador to France I had at least 3 telephone calls saying Mary darling you'll have to give *endless* parties because the joke being I'm *deeply* unsocial and *frightfully* lazy and also I'm rather apt to fall asleep rather early in the evening. One of them sent me a lovely present called No-Doze which are keep-awake pills which I've taken ever since to stop me dropping off in the middle of grand dinner parties. I get them in America. You see, we were complete – more coffee? – amateurs, Christopher wasn't a diplomat, but the embassy wives were simply sweet and stopped me putting my great feet in it. When we went to Rhodesia I mean Zimbabwe I didn't take one formal evening dress – I had to have one sent out for Independence!'

'You were in Zimbabwe for 4 months – did you lose weight?'

'I think I stayed static!' Then her face goes, as it often does, from jolly to serious in a split second (and vice versa). This is an aspect of her free and candid spirit, the emotions registering directly on the face. 'I see now there are marauding bands in Matabeleland but I don't think this is the breakdown of the peace. And too many skilled whites are leaving but when you think that the entire white population of Mozambique left in under a fortnight or something, I mean they went WHOOSH like that, um, the Congo was of course a nightmare, but in Rhodesia I was *amazingly* struck by the friendliness of the blacks. It's no good talking about this to somebody whose relations have been slit up the middle but I can only speak like Nanny as I find. Their spontaneity and I mean *instantly* they want to sing and dance and smile. It's quite sort of embarrassing and harrowing going into those refugee African townships just outside Salisbury, Harare as it now is, talk about God how the other half lives, I'd not seen that sort of thing before and it shook me up a bit. It's very good to be shaken up a bit, like the Brixton riots here woke a lot of us up, but I felt also rather abashed walking up to an obviously totally down and out African family sitting against their little hut and saying "Hullo, I'm Mary Soames, I'm the Governor's wife, I've come to say hullo". It makes me embarrassed just sort of recounting it to you but the reaction was oh how nice and how are *you* and great dignity and courtesy with which the woman would show me this really unbelievable place she was living in but absolute cleanness, all the pans in their place, spotlessly swept up. Goodness knows there was nothing much I could do really. But I tried to get about and be normal. I used to hitch-hike around on helicopters.'

The telephone rings in the hall and Mary Soames slips off the sofa and pops her head outside the room. 'Maria, could you give a message and say I'm not available.' And nips back to the sofa again, hitting the cushions with soft thuds. Off come the spectacles and, er, oh no, they go back on again, no, they're off again – and they stay off. She blinks and smiles.

'We had a lovely black chef at Government House called Madziwa who'd been well trained but hotel trained so I taught him some lovely recipes from home, lovely sort of . . . *eggy* dishes, English fruit puddings, cold haddock. If people were coming out from England I'd ask for smoked haddock so we could have smoked haddock mousse. Bring me haddock! I tell you what was delicious we loved was impala, tastes like roebuck, and fish was difficult except up at Kariba, lovely fresh fish up there, and both Christopher and I are very fond of fish.

'The shops in Salisbury, that is Harare, had marvellous sort of cardboard displays but only 3 bottles of it under the counter and when you ask for your Johnson's Baby Powder – I always use it, yes – it was always "We're getting our consignment next week". There had been a good deal of sanction-busting but not on the Baby Powder front. The bookshops were absolute pathos, empty shelves, and Christopher used to get a lot of very abusive letters from hardcore whites saying we'd betrayed them but I was surprised how few sulky and cross faces we met in restaurants for example because we quite often dined in public. Our party-giving was all squished into the last week. Apart from the big celebration for Prince Charles and Independence, we gave a big multi-racial one on our own account. About 1200 came and we gave them to eat, well, lots of it all made in Government House by Madziwa and his Merry Men, sausage rolls, little lovely um cheese things, lots and lots of beer, and for one of the smaller parties we had Pimm's, a lovely consignment was sent out.

'Government House is a divine house to have a party in, sort of Cape Dutch all on one floor with a colonnade all round thank God because we were there in the rainy season, terrific storms *pouring* down, but I thought there wasn't enough cane furniture, it was mostly good old fake Georgian, with very comfortable sofas and one or two nice pieces given by previous Governors General. The great state dining-room with the great mahogany table and then these wonderful state portraits which have all gone now of course, no not slashed, to the State Museum, and I can quite understand that they don't want to sit there eating with Queen Victoria staring down at them but it's a little sad all the same but I think it was the most moving and wonderful and exciting time of both our lives. When we called on President Mugabe at State House as it now is you would hardly know it was any different, the most wonderful heavenly garden with cranes, but the minute you go in the dreaded huge portrait of Rhodes in the hall is gone of course and a weird combination with um sort of crossed spears and drums put up among it all – what did you say? As you've probably noticed I'm going deaf. The last person to interview me said *she did shout rather* and I was so mortified because he had such a faint voice I was sitting on the floor trying to get what he was saying and when you can't hear you tend to up your own voice rather. I haven't shouted at you, have I? What did you say?'

Mary Soames's cardigan is going on and off her shoulders, the spectacles on and off her face, the rings going round, endless girlish fidgeting, and a kind of involuntary coquetry. A little black dog called Jubilee trots into the pinky, salmony, cluttered drawing-room that is filled with family photographs and Churchill memorabilia. It is not exactly a soothing room but it presents a noticeable contrast to the chaotic, lurid turquoise and crimson wallpaper in the hall – clearly there is a big wild streak in Lady Soames.

'I asked what sort of things make you uncomfortable.'

'Funny question. What do you mean? What makes me uncomfortable, Jubilee? Um, lots of things make me uncomfortable. *Mawkishness*. If I hear my parents overpraised for things that I know aren't you know, oh, my toes turn in with embarrassment.'

'What frightens you about the future?'

'I'm bad at thinking about the future. Life is extremely hectic *now*. I've been doing this album book of family photographs, not that any of us were any good or quick with the old Box Brownie, they come from all over with long and copious captions by yours truly. Then I've got my various committees with children and old people, and the Churchill Memorial Trust – the idea is travelling fellowships, it can be anything, dust collection, wood carving, butterfly collecting. For instance the dustmen went to America to see how they collect their dust over there and you're meant to come back and plough some of it back into the community, it's a sort, of, um, quite a lot of, um, who sort of it's a sort of and they're worth about £1,600 each. Then I do quite a lot with Christopher – we're a notably *unmusical* family, it never entered my head until now because Christopher's got this great new thing about

121

music and when we went to Rhodesia one of the things he took was lots of lovely classical cassettes and we used to play ourselves to sleep after a tense day listening to lovely Mozart and Schubert. We seem to go out to dine quite a lot but now to-night for instance, Thursday, it's the first free night this week and Christopher's out on his own, man's dinner, but I'm actually glad I'm not going out. To-night I'll write letters or look at the telly a bit or whatever.

'When we're not going to dinner parties Christopher likes eating Chinese or we have scrummy dinners, and he's the cook, not me, he cooks scallops beautifully, and if there's just us or we have just 2 friends in we eat in the kitchen. Sometimes I find I have to work at weekends too in the country in Hampshire and I don't participate in village life as I'd like to which is sad, although when we lived in Sussex and the children were small I'd come to London perhaps only one or two nights a week but now they say "Oh, it's no good counting on her, she's only here at week-ends", so I'm always paying guilt money, contributions, and tearing the clothes off my back practically for jumble sales – where do I get what? My clothes? Jaeger. Marks and Spencer. Sometimes I treat myself to something at Hardy Amies or Chatelaine in Chelsea Manor Street. I find after an exhausting week in London I don't want particularly to do good works around the village at weekends. Anyhow we haven't got a cook or anything so it's all hands to the pump. I bottle mint. I'm a rather good mint bottler, but rather haphazard about bottling other things. On the other hand I sometimes wonder what I've done that's taken me all day to do it. I don't have a maid but I do have a daily, Maria, who's the best shirt washer and ironer in the world thank God. By the way, would you like a drink? I'm having this.'

'Do you always drink pastis at lunchtimes?'

'It's not pastis! It's grapefruit juice! I hate pastis, not that I'm a teetotaller, far from it. Would you like gin & tonic? Whisky & soda? Some vod? Do you want to go to the loo or anything? I don't know why I should say that like Nanny – most probably because I rather want to go myself.'

(1982)

122

BETWEEN PRESIDENTS

GABRIEL GARCIA MARQUEZ IN MEXICO CITY

MEXICO CITY IS a weird dump, lovely at night seen from an aeroplane, an immense cartwheel of lights below, turning, turning, tilting . . . In the morning from a high hotel window, the place looks ravaged by smallpox, pitted and eaten away, limitless miles of dusty buildings either half built or half falling down, impossible to tell which, except that if it is old and beautiful it will be coming down to make way for another cardboard skyscraper. The most beautiful building in Mexico City however is the new Cuban Embassy, perfect proportions of white stone and dark glass, overwhelming restraint floating in its symmetrical compound, seen through vertical rods of iron, a gift of friendship from the people of Mexico.

But a dump of 15 million people cannot be a bore, even though it is pitched up high where the oxygen is thin and the air anyway the most polluted city air in the world, filled with traffic exhaust, industrial waste, gritty acids, dust. The streets are taut with traffic, in a perpetual crossfire of hysterical car-horns and police whistles – then the lights change and the metal shoots forward as if from cannons. In Chapultepec Park dark-faced women, wearing powder two or three shades too pale, which gives their faces the quality of cakes dusted with sugar, walk beside the artificial lake created by the Empress Carlota during the momentary imperium.*

The reduction in air pressure forces the blood out. The gums bleed, the nose bleeds, the eyes become blooshot, the vessels in

*   The women of Mexico City develop magnificent chests for breathing at a high altitude.

123

legs and arms inflate. Everybody coughs in the thin sunshine and even from a high hotel window you cannot see through the lemon smog to the snow-capped volcanoes which ring the city, which form a perfect bowl in which to contain the ever-thickening pall of poisons.

Beware, in Mexican hotels of every grade, of non-flushing lavatories. Or lavatories that flush in reverse and send a maelstrom of enchillada excrement spiralling up and over-flowing into the bathroom. In a house near the hotel the occupying family keeps half a dozen turkeys on the roof. The turkeys gobble among the washing which dries up there. A boy sits on a parapet swinging his legs, hour after hour, day after day.

This is the world's greatest Spanish-speaking city, so where else, though he is Colombian, should the world's most successful Spanish-writing writer live? (for not only has Señor Marquez won the Nobel prize, he has for some time now been selling more books than anybody else in his language: he is rich, with the texture of richness).

'It intrigues me that every time I come across a tranquil and solitary landscape,' he says in Spanish but soon falling into uneven but perfectly clear English,* 'whether coast or mountains, the person with me will always say "Look, what a good place to write," and I think that they are completely wrong. Why should they think it a good place to write when it is obviously a good place to rest? Writing is very hard work which shouldn't be done in places of rest but in places of work. For me the ideal place to work is Mexico City. During the day I need peace and quiet, this house, but as soon as I finish writing I need the huge city, friends, I need life. That's why I get very bored writing in the country or on a desert island, because when I've finished writing I still have no contact with life.'

Ah, life. *Life!* Mexico is certainly strong on life. Or to be more accurate, on death. The bloodiness of Spain with its

---

* When he discovered that I couldn't speak Spanish, he suggested I put my questions in English, he would reply in Spanish, and later I could have the tape translated. But our desire for direct communication soon overrode this – his English was excellent and only occasionally did he need to drop back into Spanish. When the tape was translated, his English answers were much sharper than his often too florid Spanish ones.

bullfights and purgatorial religion amplifies the bloodiness of native Aztec Mexico with its pyramids of human sacrifice – the Mayans, less bloodthirsty that the Aztecs, nonetheless had Ix Tab, god of suicides. The result is a vehement baroque mentality, the epitome of all Latin America, of Virgin Marys and Crucifixions drenched in blood, crocodiles, jaguars and plumed serpents, decrepit cultures floating in the heat, cracking, flaking . . . the hiss of malignant swamps to the south, or the dry hiss of rocky eagle-starred landscapes periodically reconstituted by earthquakes and eruptions of lava, and hanging over all this great country (considerably greater from its top to its tail than is the distance between London and Istanbul), forever impending – the world's biggest foreign debt.

There is a joke they make about themselves with naughty machismo pride. There was a competition to see which was the most corrupt country in the world. Mexico came only second. Why? Because they bribed the judges.

Two facts ensure Mexico an interesting future. (1) A recent official survey has shown that 64% of Mexicans suffer from malnutrition. And (2) 78.8% of Mexicans are literate.

'Would you like something to drink?' he asks with that odd look first noticed in the hall, a curious mixture of shyness and scrutiny, a kind of nervous arrogance, but with a wistfulness behind the eyes which in memory seem to have been grey but surely they were brown?

(In the hall he greeted me not by looking into my face but by first looking at my shoes, then letting his stare travel slowly up, absorbing information on the way, until he reached my head, whereupon our eyes met and we shook hands.)

'Thank-you, just a glass of water please.'

'Is that all? Are you sure? Wouldn't you like some coffee?'

Marquez, friend of Mitterand and Fidel Castro, is a supporter of left wing causes. 'I am not a communist,' he says from within the sumptuous billows of a creamy sofa, 'and I have never belonged to a communist party. The problem is that in to-day's world we Latin Americans don't agree with the position of the United States so they automatically say we are communists. That is why they won't give me a visa for United States.'

'Have you been to Russia?'

'Twice. The first was 30 years ago to the Festival of . . . the Youngs.'

'What?'

The Festival of . . . er, what is it? Youth! And the second, three years ago for the movie festival. Never for a political reason.'

'You are connected with the M–19 Revolutionaries in Colombia . . .'

'Yes, I have many friends in that group. They believe it's possible to find our own system without following either United States or Soviet Union. They are looking for our identity. I do think that Latin America needs a form of socialism, but it needs its own form based on our historical, political, and social conditions – very special conditions which need a particular system invented just for us.'

'Have you read Solzhenitsyn?'

The young maid appears, with her black and slightly slanted eyes, her large unfocused eyes, and hair tied back in a knot, silently opening doors, silently bringing a glass of iced water, silently disappearing.

'His novels, yes.'

'Does what he says worry you? That it is impossible to have a communistic system that is human?'

'Solzhenitsyn is a bad example because he is not a politician. He is a mystic. His vision appears to be totally religious. Therefore he is not in to-day's reality.'

'I see. But you are?'

The telephone rings. 'Excuse me . . . Hullo [*in Spanish*], you are coming to lunch? Come around 2. You may have to wait. I am being interviewed by an Englishman. Yes, I'm trying to compose speeches in English. Remind me to give you the 6,000 pesos for . . .'

Yes, remind him because he says, 'I'm very bad about money. I don't know nothing about money. It's the responsibility of my wife. I don't believe in money.'

'Are you a gambler?'

'No, no, no. Oh – maybe, yes. Maybe it is the only thing I do in my life. But not on the table in the casino. I have very bad luck in the casino. And I also have a superstition – that money I win in the casino is no good luck. Is bad money, brings bad luck. I don't know why I feel that. Maybe my Catholic upbringing. I am not religious at all. But my parents are. So culturally my mind is Catholic. I think money has to be difficult to get. When it is difficult, then it is good money, then it is real, and I deserve it.'

Marquez lives in Pedregal de San Angel, Mexico City's most expensive and most recent suburb, built on a vomit of lava. Large modern villas with automatic doors and rifles in the kitchen are here accumulated, their tropical gardens endlessly watered, but the separate parts do not come together and the district has a half-baked seediness, a temporary and random quality, without root or consequence, bits of things somehow just dropped haphazardly among the scrub, despite the fabulous opulence of the lives lived here. The quality of the 'finish' is very poor. In fact 'finish' is something never encountered in Mexico, except in certain ancient sculptures of shocking elegance.

Marquez's is the only house built in a mock colonial style. All the others are mock Le Corbusier. One or two of the most recent are post-modern fantasies – a pile of glass pyramids belongs to a well-known television comedian; another is designed to look like a heap of concrete television sets.

Outside: drivers wait in the dust, chatting to each other across long gloomy American bonnets – Lincoln, Ford, Cadillac – smoking Fiesta cigarettes. Waiting. Which is one of the things Mexicans do very well.

Inside: the Writer's Study: despite its hacienda beams and well-ordered, well-travelled chic, it has a slight redolence of beads and feathers. One end is dominated by a huge colourful erotic painting of a naked women posed in such a way as to reveal both apertures between her legs. In a tiled corner small bottles of water and soda are arranged in tidy blocks, with tidy blocks of glasses nearby, like little phalanxes ready to march on the thirst of choice companions (for Marquez is a connoisseur of humanity). In the other half of the room, away from the sofas and near the desk, is a boiler always turned up to maintain a room temperature of 28°C in the moderate ·

climate of Mexico City. 'The cold is very bad for my mind. I can't think in the cold. My country – Colombia – is 40°C. I need the heat to work like some people need cigarettes.'

'You don't smoke?'

'I smoke till 11 or 12 years ago. Then I stop overnight. Four packets a day. Then I stop dead.'

'Do you write with a pen?'

'No, directly onto the typewriter. Electric typewriter. And now I am going to get a word processor.'

'Do you write every day?'

'Every day. The only day I don't work is to-day. Because now is my work time but you are here.'

'Oh . . .'

'But I am very happy to see you. No problem. No problem.'

The telephone rings. 'Oh dear, excuse me . . . it's long distance, excuse me a moment . . .'

Marquez has lived in many places. Born in 1928 in a small town near the coast of Colombia, he was one of 16 children of the town's telegraph operator. To ease somewhat the compress, he was raised by his maternal grand-parents. He studied law at the National University at Bogotá, then became a journalist. In 1955 he travelled to Europe as correspondent for *El Espectador*. The paper was closed down and he found himself in Paris without a job, without money.

'Did existentialism influence you?'

'My problem was not existentialism. My problem was the difference between Europe and Latin America. Europe is a place that understands nothing about us in Latin America.'

'But you understand Europe?'

'Yes. Normally the centre of a culture is enclosed within itself. But a dependent culture which is on the edge of it can know the central culture very well – but not be known by it. This is the subject of my Nobel Prize speech, why the Europeans don't understand us. For example, Europeans like my books because they think this is a fiction, this is magic fantasy, but it isn't, it's Latin American reality, our every day reality. We don't have a rationalist mind in the way Europe does. We interpret our reality in a way which is very difficult for the rationalist to understand.'

128

'Is Europe rationalist? It is a very peculiar place.'

'Yes, every place is peculiar. That in fact is the meaning of the word peculiar.'

New York: 'In 1960 I worked for 6 months in New York as representative of Prensa Latina, the Cuban News Agency. New York is one of the cities that most interests me in the world. I think it is the greatest phenomenon of the twentieth century. Even the tension and sensation of danger in this city is exciting and very attractive. I like very much United States. My difficulty with it is political, not with the people. I like very much New York – or maybe I detest it and like it at the same time. I care not to be there and I *need* to be there. The only thing is I wouldn't like to live in New York but I have to go every year at least once. Not for business. Just for being there. But I don't have a visa. It's a pity.'

Rome: 'Yes, I was there in 1955 when I did a course in film directing at the Experimental Movie Centre. My grandfather took me to the cinema a lot when I was a boy. In the 60s I wrote some film scripts. Commercial films, very bad. I'm not proud of them.' Marquez has been a judge at the Cannes Film Festival.

'Do you go to the cinema much in Mexico City?'

(The cinemas here are full of incident. A stand-up fight at the Cine Colonial. At the Cine Teresa a young couple quietly and cleverly make love – the whole thing – under a poncho, while immediately behind a family of ten stuffs itself with popcorn and cheers on *Flash Gordon*. The auditoriums are deliberately kept dark. The Mexicans have a healthy casualness about these things.)

'No, not much. I go to Paris every year for about two months and during this time I see all the films for the whole year. Paris is very good for that. I see the best films all together.'

'Are you interested in avant-garde art, experimental literature?'

'No. I don't have time for experiments. I prefer to leave it until the experiments are over, then go straight to the things which worked out. When Bartok and Stravinsky composed their music it was avant-garde. Now they are classical.'

London: 'Yes, I even lived in London. 1970 or 71. For

3 months. I had just finished my novel *The Autumn of the Patriarch* and I needed a place where nobody knew me to work on the final corrections which were very difficult. So I decided to go to London which is a strange city that I like very much, where I know very few people, and where I could be quiet to do this work. But I do have some very good friends in London. At that time Sonia Orwell was there and round her a very interesting group. She later died in Paris.'

'Did you feel foreign in London?'

'It was perhaps the town where I feel myself more a stranger than any other place I have been. That is a very interesting feeling! I think the English are the most different people I know in the world. *Everything* is different. The culture is too far away for me. At the same time the English novel is for me the best in history.'

'Do you know any living English writers?'

'I know Graham Greene. He is my friend. He deserved the Nobel Prize long times ago. I don't understand why he didn't get it. I like his books very much.' ·

'They translate well.'

'He is very good when he writes on Mexico. For us he is a very good Latin American novelist – we get this other view.'

'Why don't you write a novel about the English?'

'Oh! Ha! I read Graham Greene in English. I read English quite easily but I can't speak it very well. I can read Shakespeare. I think the problem with Graham Greene and the Swedish Academy is that they think he is a commercial writer. But me too. I am a commercial writer.'

'But you write . . . less.'

'Ha! OK . . .'

For Marquez, commercial success came abruptly in 1967 with the international reception of *One Hundred Years of Solitude*, extending to the English-speaking world via Gregory Rabassa's beautiful translation. 'He is the only translator who never asks me anything. He does it all. Every other translator in all the other languages send to me a list of questions this long – the questions are nearly always the same. But Rabassa never consults me. I don't know him very well.'

In the same year Marquez moved to Barcelona, dividing his

time between the Old World and the New. So, now, here, in Mexico City, for a writer so deeply involved with his Colombian childhood, is this home or is this exile?

'Good question. The fact is that I've lived in Mexico for 21 years, although I had another foot in Barcelona for part of the time. I never had sensation of being in exile but after a certain time, with age, I begin to feel nostalgia – but with me it's more complicated because when I am in Mexico I feel nostalgia for Colombia and when in Colombia nostalgia for Mexico. So I think that the solution is to live part of the year in each country. I am planning to stay in Mexico for about 6 months while writing literature, then go to Colombia to work on my newspaper for the other half.' Marquez is using his prize money to begin a left wing daily in Bogotá.

'Is it easier to see your own country when you live in a different place?'

'Well, the global perspective that I have of Latin America was obtained in Europe when I went to Paris. It is a more critical view, but it is also more compassionate.'

'In coming to Mexico the thing which surprises me most is how strong the Indian factor is – stronger than the Spanish.'

'The same thing happened to me when I first arrived here. I already knew practically all the rest of Latin America and when I arrived here I was very surprised to see the Indian – in the first row. You don't get it elsewhere in the continent. In Mexico the Indian is to be found at all levels.'

This seems to me not quite exact. It is not the presence of the Indian alongside the Spaniard, but the extent to which the two have intertwined, interbred, so that although the distinct strands may be discerned they arise within the same person, same building, same work of art. This is the New World – but in Mexico it is the New World backed by ancient history. The Indian heritage in Mexico is the strongest in the Americas and therefore it is the least provincial country in the Americas. In the USA there is no sense of history behind things, which can give life there a kind of slippery vertigo, but here history backs everything and in a rather horrible, fanged aspect too. The fundamental stuff is Indian. Indian features fade slowly as you rise through the social classes but even at the grandest

131

assemblies that ancient profile is always there, is often the host's indeed, in the land of Montezuma and his bright green quetzal feathers.

Does Marquez have any Indian blood in him? He thinks not. He is Colombian and the races are more separate there. But this is a continent of mixtures and one cannot be sure. Many people ask him if he has Arab blood because of his looks and temperament.

In Mexicans however the Indian and Spanish are each alive in everyone, though never equally, there is no sense of balance but endless permutation instead, so that, for example, no 2 Mexicans look alike. And inside too it is the same. Suddenly the Indian aspect arises in one previously more or less European and suddenly he is fading away from you, fading into blankness, shooting backwards from you with a fixed lost smile which doesn't spread to the upper half of the face, drifting backwards saying yes, yes, yes, when he means no, no . . . They always say yes. They will, for example, accept an invitation in the full knowledge of being unable to attend – because it is rude to refuse an invitation.

Or street directions: they give the wrong ones if they don't know, rather than no directions at all because that would be rude. Sometimes the Indian world claims them abruptly, especially when faced with an awkward situation. You wonder what you have done. But there is no finding out. They have gone blank on it, clouding themselves with ink like an octopus, hoping the problem will go away. Thus was Cortes able to conquer the Indian Empire.

The Mexican fear of punctuality is the Indian fear of being trapped in the mechanics of time. Then the inevitable paradox: the Aztec Calendar was more accurate than the Europeans'. Cosmic punctuality they venerate, social punctuality no . . . Time is for the priests. Well, writers and artists are the modern priests. Marquez loves to play games with time and has an exact command of its repercussions. So – what is his favourite colour?

'The yellow of the Caribbean Sea in Jamaica – at 3 in the afternoon.'

And favourite bird?

'Duck *à l'orange*.'

Favourite poets?

'Nowadays – Cavafy, Pessoa, and Neruda.'

Pet hate?

'Sundays.'

Who in history does he despise?

'Christopher Columbus.'

Favourite historical figure?

'Julius Caesar, beseiged by omens.'

Favourite occupation?

'Conspiracy.'

Favourite virtue?

'The ability to keep a secret until death.'

Favourite vice?

'Roses. I always have them in my work room.'

Favourite writers?

'Sophocles and Conrad.'

Favourite quality in a woman?

'Indulgence.'

And in a man?

'Tenderness.'

How would he like to die?

'In bed. But in good company.'

There are a great number of records stacked against the wall. 'No, not so many, but more than books. Music is the most important art in my life. All music. Bartok is my favourite composer. Do you know *The Letters of Bela Bartok*? A very, very beautiful book. My copy is in Italian.'

He likes to draw away from the subject of writing, to avoid suffocating it with too much self-consciousness. After all, writing is what he *does*. So he will say that the most important art in his life is music. He will also say 'I believe journalism is my predominant vocation. Journalism has enabled me to keep in contact with reality.' Or his grand remark that he would have preferred to have been a magician instead of a writer (Hermann Hesse, when asked at parties what he did for a living, often replied 'Magician'). What about that remark?

'Well . . . I did not say magician actually – I said prestidigitator. I do believe that writers are magicians and in that sense I have some magician in me. But what I wanted to say was that I write because I like to fascinate the audience and I think that to be able to pull rabbits and doves out of a hat at a party is a much easier way of doing it than writing and that it causes a much quicker impression.'

'Do you like parties?'

'I detest them. But I love to be with a small number of friends, old friends, with whom I always talk about the same things.'

'Do you know Carlos Castaneda?'

'Yes, I met him here in Mexico.'

'Do you feel an affinity with the world of sorcery and witchcraft?'

'He has explored with scientific and medical or chemical resources. Much more advanced than I. I only have intuition.'

'Do you regard Castaneda's books as novels?'

'Very difficult to say. In his work reality and imagination are confused to such a point that it is difficult to know. The same applies to my work.'

Marquez is attracted by the grand gesture. He is also a writer, so it tends to work itself out as the grand remark. There is one about how nothing interesting happened to him after the age of 8.

'I meant that the raw material of my books was completed by then.'

'Have you tried to allow in more raw material?'

'Yes, I've tried . . . Impossible! Now I am writing short stories about Latin Americans in Europe. Looking for the contact point of the cultures. But I'm not sure. I *am* sure however when I write about my life in Colombia, when I was a little boy. I am a little monotonous as far as my subjects are concerned. I live in the big city but I am not submerged in it. I am submerged in my roots. I don't think I could write a novel about the city because it is not in my nature.'

In 1975 he publicly vowed he would stop writing novels until Chile's General Pinochet was deposed, probably Marquez's grandest and least impressive gesture. The pledge was broken with the publication of *Chronicle of a Death Foretold*. The clarity of Marquez's vision is due partly to his being able to refuse to admit certain data. He would call this idealism. In anyone other than a writer or artist, it would be called naïvete or even idiocy, at best innocence, at worst cruelty or injustice. It sometimes gets him into trouble. The last time he had to flee Colombia was as recently as 1981 for fear of arrest by security forces. Since the Nobel Prize however he has become even more the national hero and the new Colombian president, Señor Betancur, would like to be friends.

The telephone rings. 'It is impossible to live in this house! Excuse me, please . . . Yes, how are you? Well, I shall never win this prize again! You see how far things have gone – I have the Englishman here interviewing me in English! He didn't bring an interpreter . . . The Mexican President was yesterday . . . I'll arrange it with you to-morrow. Most of the guests are foreign. Plus the press. Then immediately I'm flying to Cuba. I'm staying with Castro. Are you at your hotel? I'll call you back.'

'Is loneliness ever a problem for you?'

'Personally? Yes. There is a zone of my personality that is always alone. It is impossible not to be alone there. Loneliness is very unhappy. The moment when I am most alone is when I'm writing. It is impossible to ask the help of anybody at this moment. It is very hard.'

'Do you get depressed?'

'No, never. I have a friend who is a very good psychiatrist and he don't believe me because I say never, never in my life have I felt depressed. They say it is terrible to feel it, they say it is a very deep loss of . . . But I am always too occupied for this. Sometimes I feel sad. That is different. What makes me sad – if I have a friend and I discover something that is not good, if I discover that a good friend is not a good friend, it is the biggest catastrophe I can suffer. Because friendship for me is sacred. I have very few friends. All of them very important.'

'Do you fall in love easily?'

'I fall in love once in my life 25 years ago. With my wife.'

Marquez married Mercedes Barcha in 1958. They have two sons. One is at Harvard, the other studying music at the Paris Conservatoire. He laughs a great deal as he imparts this information, laughs at the golden clichés of success. But he is

135

proud of it, of the polyglot jet-setting sons who use their father's achievement to become part of the international deracinated posh . . .

Something, just something in Marquez, far away in the distance, at the centre, remains untouched by all this withering glory; that loneliness and vulnerability surviving the fusillade of flattery, the ooze of unction like a glue which would like to settle on the soul and harden there, paralysing it.

Marquez is an attractive man, given to many small gestures of physical affection, and an attractive writer. He operates by seduction followed up with intoxication. There is very little brute force in him. There is something feminine in him too, in his gait, in his fastidiousness, in certain other movements of the body and facets of temperament.

One hopes it is not too easy a life, despite the elegant backdrop, the classy cabinets, the well-polished vestibules, the pad of trustworthy servants, the family photographs, the *objets* placed just so, the precipitations of euphoria and happiness on every side. Meanwhile people go over the top on his behalf. Carlos Fuentes proclaims 'Marquez has done more for the Spanish language than Cervantes did'. President Mitterand, not to be outdone, opens his mouth and says 'With emotion, I salute the novelist who has captured the imagination of the people of the world'.

When asked by a reporter with which character in *One Hundred Years of Solitude* he most identified, Marquez replied 'The whore. She helped to make the largest number of people happy in the shortest amount of time – and without anybody knowing.' Not that anonymity is very big around here. The telephone rings again.

'I want to try and put happiness back in style,' he told *Newsweek*. They put him on the cover.

'That's unusual for a . . . modern writer. In Europe the modern literary ideas have been nausea, depression, paranoia, absurdity, loss, alienation, fragmentation, extermination, disgust.'

'Yes, but they didn't have any reason to be optimistic. We in Latin America, we have the whole future before us. We are at the beginning of identity.'

'Like Russia in the 19th century . . .' That is, the beginning of self-consciousness, of the mythologising of itself through literature. Now Marquez is going to mythologise *himself*, explicitly. 'You are writing your memoirs . . .'

'I'm going to, 6 or 7 volumes. But not in an academic structure. I want to write in a flow, the flowing reality behind my books. I want to start in about one year's time and write and write and write and write without stopping and every 300 or 400 pages I have a volume and I publish it. I can write every day for the rest of my life like this because it is the moment where my literature and my life become the same thing. Living, writing, living, writing, a combination of diary and memoirs.'

On and on flows the great river of happiness and achievement, optimism and success and honours, positive values, glittering, tugging ideals, presidential invitations, friendship, the memoirs, yes, now the memoirs already, the bending of the waters of experience so that they circle in great phosphorescent arcs about the triumphant ego.

But . . . 'easy life', not exactly. There is the spectre of violence in the *éclat*. For this is Latin America. Marquez has gentleness, charm, effortless courtesy, but how blasé, how ruthless was his dismissal of Solzhenytsin's experience of concentration camps and, well, there is a vehemence in the precision of Marquez's beautifully *pressed* grey wool trousers. And an uncomfortable intensity in the remorseless gloss on his shoes which in mid-day harden into a glare. Such ostentatious propriety is very Latin, very Third World, an overreaction of surface to Mexico City's exorbitance, with so much life leaping and pushing in everywhere. And this Life itself becomes only another surface, another skin, when beneath something atavistic may shift like slippery gears, something alien slipping, sliding constantly beneath the surface, yet breaking out not in curves but in the hard rectilinear zig-zags of the Indian aesthetic which is closer to the markings of reptiles than to anything else, an aesthetic which in the old days induced cross-eyes and cranial deformation.

Latin Americans seem to live half in dream, half in corruption: surrealism's natural home. The effects are beautiful but sinister, as if always slightly touched by the lurid creep of mescalin. An example of such dreaming: in a restaurant the waiter brings a cup of coffee and instead of a teaspoon in the saucer he's placed a fork. This mistake was made several times in different places. The first time is comical. Subsequently it becomes rather weird. Mexican coffee incidentally is terrible but they make delicious pastries for breakfast.

A German count, long fair resigned face, too much brandy, too long posted here: 'Bloody Mexicans! Bloody Latin America! I shan't be sorry to leave – well, that depends where I go next. Mexico City used to be quite safe but it has changed, just in the last 6 months I've noticed it, the unprovoked attacks, the sudden sense of skating on thin ice. It's because they now don't have enough to eat. Somehow they always had just enough to eat before. But now they don't.'

The most dangerous town in Latin America is Bogotá, capital of Colombia, where small boys with flick knives and rows of sharp incisor teeth trail you in daytime packs, waiting for the moment of vulnerability . . .

'Do you enjoy danger?'

'I don't like at all this sense of physical danger. But I can't live without risk, not physical risk, but to be always faced with a challenge, the danger of defeat. If I don't have a challenge I immediately go and look for one, always. Success, fame, makes no difference. One can always go better. Now I am going to Colombia to make a newspaper, a daily newspaper, this is a challenge at my age. It's a very beautiful challenge.'

'What frightens you?'

He has a habit of pulling his mouth into curious shapes, of rolling down the lower lip with a finger as if to burble like a baby. 'Darkness. The dark. When I was a small boy the women of the house told me that if I didn't keep quiet in bed, dead people would come out of every room. Sometimes when I am in hotels sleeping alone, I still wake up with that terror. The thing which makes me afraid the most is any situation that does not permit me to have the *absolute* control of my consciousness. For example, the drug, I don't touch any drug because I have to be quite conscious of everything and be *sure* myself that I have total self-control.'

'Is there a danger here of getting too tight? Inasmuch as the nature of things is to bend. The universe is bent.'

'Yes, I see, but for myself I have to be quite sure that I know everything I'm doing. Why and when and so on. I drink alcohol. But I know alcohol very well and go always only to the exact point in drinking.'

'Do you go to the bullfight?'

'No. It don't touch me.'

'What is the closest you have been to death?'

'Every moment of my life! I am conscious of it always. It is not a fear. It is a very good pressure.'

'Do you believe in a life after death?'

'No. After is the total darkness.'

ACAPULCO: When I arrived in this town, a few days after visiting Marquez, the first thing they said was that a French schoolteacher had recently been shot dead by muggers on the beach at 4 in the afternoon for intervening in an attempt to steal his girlfriend's handbag: broad daylight, on the beach, on holiday. It was hushed up because Acapulco is a great dollar earner. (A girl said to me here with complete emotional honesty 'You have beautiful eyes. They are the colour of dollars'.) So now the police hang around the beach carrying rifles and from time to time an army squad wanders along the sand with machine-guns hanging loosely while fat pink gringos in polyester beachwear and their Mexican imitators disport themselves like pigs in a charnel garden – such people, touring the Third World, suck theft, bullets and death to themselves with the inevitability of vacuums sucking air.

On the second day I joined them. The sun bounced off the sand, slapped one's body, spat in one's eye. I lay in it for 15 minutes – it was like lying in a bath of acid so I retired to the lowrise Bali Hai Motel, the only charming place to stay on that soul-destroying curve of highrise concrete and plastic called the Costera which comprises the new resort town.

When I flew down here from Mexico City, 5 pop music cassettes were stolen from my bag by one of the baggage handlers. My fault – that particular pouch was unlocked. At the Bali Hai I sat beside the pool while the chambermaid cleaned my room. When I returned, some money inadvertently left on a shelf had vanished. I found the chief maid, she had words with the girl, they both came to my room, and the money was miraculously produced from beneath a pillow. 'Señor, it must've slipped down here.' And everyone's face was saved. But my fault again. Tempting them . . .

I like the Bali Hai very much but hate the new town. It is harsh and unnatural, and a sullen resentment is discernible beneath the impassive surface of the Mexicans who work in it. So why stay here? Well, the problem is that the black market exchange rate has given me twice the pesos I expected to have, and the voluminous cash must be stored in a safe-deposit box – and only new town accommodation has this facility.

Sleep however was very difficult at the Bali Hai: the air-conditioning raged and gurgled all night and was one of those systems which cannot be turned off. So, given that I'm peso-rich, I decided to rent a second room, for sleeping in, in the old town – which has what a town is supposed to have, organic vitality and visual appeal (including a picturesque red light district and a mad polychrome cathedral built circa 1930). In the old town boys dive off the harbour wall for coins thrown into the sea and come up grinning with them between their teeth.

The Hotel Añorve is a clean, cheap Mexican lodging-house off the Zocalo and sleep came easier there in a room just below the roof with a view over palm trees and harbour to the sea, window open to catch the breeze, and a few dabs of citronella at ankles, wrists and neck to keep off mosquitoes. Actually I didn't sleep very easily the first few nights because the Virgin of Guadalupe celebrations were coming to their climax with fireworks exploding until dawn, flashing tinsel, torch flares thrown onto impromptu bonfires in the middle of roads. It's illegal to build a bonfire in the middle of a public highway, even in Mexico, so the police turned up to watch.

I felt splendid – rich *and* genuine – maintaining these 2 establishments, sauntering between them, turning a golden brown. And one evening a few days ago I was making my way along the beach from the old town to the new to collect some banknotes from the Bali Hai stash. The sun set gloriously into the sea, and quickly, but the beach is floodlit all night except for a brief rocky patch between El Moro and Condesa (it's typically Mexican to have a black patch for no reason at all). Several steps into this very spot and I became aware of a boy about 15 a little way ahead in the murk. He began to speak urgently and stab at the ground with his finger. I understand little Spanish and was wearing no shoes and for some reason supposed he was kindly warning me not to walk in this place because of seasnakes. I'd never heard of seasnakes and was trying to tell him so when I became aware of a second boy behind me. He was also making urgent noises and held something aloft which glinted in the moonlight. It was a broken bottle. On turning back to the first I saw that he too was brandishing a broken bottle. I went cold, then hot, then cold, and stayed cold. Clearly the stabbing gesture was a demand for me to throw my plastic carrier bag onto the ground. This I immediately did. Normally I'd've run for it, but unshod, over rocks, no, impossible. And they seemed even more anxious than I – a wrong move might have triggered broken bottles into the face. The bag contained very little: 1,000 pesos, towel, espadrilles, 2 pieces of chewing-gum. The second boy picked it up without looking inside.

At this point a third older boy, about 20, came out of the darkness. He was silent, his face held in a caricature of aggression that was no less effective for being actorly. He pulled off my 2 gold rings, both worn on the same finger – one a gift from my sister, the other from the first woman I ever slept with. Then he tore a fine chain from my neck which carried a tiny silver crown, the gift of a Roman Catholic friend who'd had it blessed by Cardinal Heenan as a safety amulet for travellers. The blessing must've worn off.

'Take the t-shirt too,' I said, slipping it over my head. They didn't want it. 'But it's very good, made in Italy!' I threw it at them. One picked it up and all 3 disappeared into the night.

Numb, I jogged at a steady pace into the lights and the half mile or so to the bars at the end of the beach. Here I stopped and the repressed distress burst within me – wild heartbeat, physical tremors, spinning head. One of the barmen gave me a drink of water. As I walked barefoot on tarmac to the Bali Hai the combined sense of humiliation and anger began to grow until it stuck in my throat like a fist and I too became capable of violence.

(1982)

BISHOP SATTERTHWAITE OF GIBRALTAR

IF I WERE in the Church, John Satterthwaite's job is the one I'd like to have.

'Oh no, you wouldn't!' he replies. 'People think it's glamorous but the travel is desperately tiring, I could scream.'

'It's glamorous in that it has perpetual novelty.'

'It's certainly got that,' he agrees, taking a good swig of whisky from a glittering cut glass tumbler. We are sitting in his study in W8, the quaint district of London between Kensington High Street and Notting Hill.

The Right Reverend John Satterthwaite is the Bishop of Gibraltar and responsible for all the Anglican communities in Europe. His diocese extends from the Azores to Moscow, from Helsinki to Casablanca, and in addition to major centres of activity in northern Europe, it includes the delightful little English churches encountered by travellers to Florence, Taormina, Tangier, Menton, etc. Its remotest outpost is Ulan Bator.

'That should belong to the Chinese province but the Chinese hate the Mongolians and vice versa, so I send my priest from Moscow about 4 times a year to the British Embassy there and it's very moving because it's the only Christian service in Mongolia and they come from *all over* central Asia.'

Altogether the diocese encompasses 120 priests and 240 places of worship but, despite being under the jurisdiction of Canterbury, it is obliged to finance itself.

'We don't get a penny from the Church of England!' he declares, with an emphasis which suggests this to be a matter of considerable resentment, 'nor from the Church Commissioners, although they've recently decided to help with the cost of my office in London.'

So the churches overseas are financed largely by the goodwill of their congregations, except where a priest is an official embassy appointment. The stipend of the priest, his housing, medical insurance and travel expenses have to be provided and this comes to a minimum of £15,000 per annum. Some congregations raise far more.

The Bishop spends only about 3 months a year working from his London base. The rest is spent travelling abroad. He has just returned from a pilgrimage to the Holy Land and next week he's off to Vienna. When in London he lives in this pretty white stucco Victorian house in blossomy Brunswick Gardens. It was purchased by his predecessor from the proceeds of selling a vicarage in the South of France, and it goes with the job. The ground floor is filled with rather unappealing reproduction, Draylon upholstered furniture. Ascending to the episcopal study on the first floor, one passes a plate on the stairs inscribed *Prepare to meet thy God*.

So is this a bishop's palace?

'No. There was a huge palace in Malta, in Valetta, but it was sold at the end of the 19th century. As a replacement they acquired a very beautiful manor house in the country at Sliema, which is now an enormous town, and tarted it up with battlements. But the Bishop hasn't lived there for donkey's years, despite the battlements. Our local priest occupies part of it.'

The original cathedral of the Diocese was also erected in Valetta, a magnificent neoclassical structure with a façade of ionic columns, a steeple 200 feet high, and an organ which came from Chester Cathedral. It was built at the expense of the Dowager Queen Adelaide, widow of William IV and a pious Lutheran princess, between 1839 and 1841. The diocese was all set to be 'of Valetta'. But in 1841 the matter was raised in the House of Commons. It was said that since the Catholic Archbishop reigned in Valetta, and Malta was a devoutly Catholic island, this Anglican creation might be the cause of friction. So in 1842 the diocese was established as 'of Gibraltar' and the parish church on the Rock upgraded.

'It's a Moorish building in Gibraltar, very exciting and attractive, spacious and bright,' beams the Bishop, his cheeks and ears now tinged with red. 'When it became the Cathedral, they tarted it up a bit, more chapels, little bishop's thrones, twee things like that.'

The building in Valetta was downgraded to 'Pro-Cathedral' and the pectoral cross was in due course cut from a chunk of the Rock. This was the first time that the Anglican churches overseas had been organised into a diocese. They had previously been under the direct control of the Bishop of London. In the early 17th century left-wing, low-church influences had been infiltrating the overseas chaplaincies. Therefore in 1632 Charles I put all the Anglican clergy outside Britain under the Bishop of London, largely because London was the port and centre of movement and the Bishop of London at that time was the tough high-church William Laud. In 1842 the Bishopric of Gibraltar was constituted under Canterbury and was the diocese of Southern Europe. The Anglican community of Northern Europe, under the Bishopric of Fulham, continued to be responsible to the Bishop of London until 1980 when it was transferred to Canterbury by being incorporated into an enlarged diocese 'of Gibraltar in Europe'. It was Bishop Satterthwaite's job to supervise this reorganisation.

'Then a potty Bishop of London subsequently tried to put the clock back, claiming that Northern Europe at least was the remnant of his erstwhile worldwide responsibilities. Silly bugger. We soon put a stop to that.'

'How often do you go to Gibraltar?'

'Maximum once a year.'

'Is that enough?'

'Ooo, rather! I'd go stark raving crazy if I stayed there longer. It's toytown. But I love them when I go and they always make a fuss of me and they've got a big bunch of very butch tough servers, not fancy boys at all, who work in the dockyard and it's all part of life.'

Will the Spaniards get it eventually?

'They should've had 2 flags there for some time, like Andorra has for example. I could've fixed it long ago. The

145

Gibraltarians, if they go into Spain, still talk about going to enemy territory.'

When I ask about the churches in Morocco, he grins, lifts his eyes up towards the ceiling and places the tips of his fingers together, becoming the very archetype of the lovable Anglican bishop.

'We have a beautiful church in Tangier in the rue d'Angleterre – and the priest gets a very beautiful flat behind the Post Office. But now the resident congregation – I doubt if there are more than 20 left. I've buried 40 of them. We lost a big batch just this year. We keep it open for holidaymakers – and for David Herbert who's my senior churchwarden and who wants to be buried there. There's also a little church in Casablanca.'

For seamen?

'Oh no, not a seaman near it. Seamen are *much* too busy when they come ashore! Casablanca is a vast city with a very big working British community. It's what I call a normal church. The one in Tangier is anything but normal.'

John Satterthwaite was born in Cumberland in 1925, 'a little country boy who went to the local school'. He grew up in Millom, the son of a farm worker who travelled to the USA for a while seeking work during the Depression. His father died when he was 10. John went on to take a degree in history at Leeds University. During the Second World War, 'I was very mixed up. I wanted to go into the RAF but I had to go into hospital for something silly and the RAF wouldn't have me, so I virtually did my war service teaching in Palestine, Arabs and Jews, friends on both sides.'

After the war he was asked to become headmaster of St George's School, Jerusalem, but refused. He loved teaching but also had a strong vocation for the Church. 'Besides, I was already unhappy with the way things were going in Israel then – they would've murdered me by now!'

John trained for the Church with the Community of the Resurrection at Mirfield, was ordained in 1951, and his first appointment was as a curate in Carlisle. Soon after he was appointed to the Church's Council of Foreign Relations.

'18 years in Lambeth Palace – that was fun, as a sort of

Church of England ambassador going all over the world. Terry Waite bless him took over some of the work I used to do – but you didn't have to go and rescue hostages in my day. But I didn't have any financial worries in that job which I do in this one. Then dear Michael Ramsay said he wanted me to put Europe straight.' He was consecrated Bishop of Gibraltar in 1970.

'But I still *love* the Middle East. I go to the Holy Land or Egypt or Turkey every year. And I like Arabs. They suit me.'

'You get on with them?'

'Oh, they can walk all over me!'

There is a surprisingly large number of Anglican churches in Turkey which comes under Bishop Satterthwaite's jurisdiction from the days of the Ottoman Empire.

'You must remember that up until the First World War there were only 5 embassies and Constantinople was one of them. All the others were legations and consulates and so on. Our registers are still for "Her Majesty's Chaplain to the Sublime Porte". Beautiful things which go back to Victoria's day.'

There are 3 churches in Istanbul, one in Ankara, one in Izmir (where there's been an Anglican priest since 1638 without a break) and 2 outside it.

'That's the Levant Company, you see, based around Izmir, Smyrna it used to be called, for apricots and raisins. The present man in Izmir is a great prison visitor. We have lots of people in prison in Turkey for drugs. The kindest man I know – but he's gone local, takes his shoes off as soon as he's inside the door. A Welshman, and before that he was in Guyana and used to lose his congregation because their private parts were bitten off by piranha fish.'

Although the diocese is centred on Europe, it is of course linked to all the other Anglican dioceses which cover the globe, and its Diocesan Gazette, while containing all the necessary business and listings for the Continent, can carry some very exotic passages such as the following:

Our Diocese has collected something in the region of £6,000 for the Diocese of Aipo Rongo in Papua New Guinea, where the Rt. Revd Paul Richardson went to be

Bishop, after serving previously in our chaplaincy and other places in Norway ... This year we hope to devote our Lenten Offerings and Christmas gifts to the needy of Antsiranana in Madagascar.

Closer to home, there has always been a strong presence in the traditional expatriate districts of France and Italy. Once thronged by British residents for reasons of health (especially tuberculosis), sexual tolerance, and a good exchange rate, these districts are now occupied more by holidaymakers than residents proper. But there are still 2 churches in Florence.

'One of them, St James, is American now. We used to have 3 in Florence of our own. The other was huge Holy Trinity which we've given to the Valdese, the Italian protestants. But our present church there is the best property in the diocese.'

This is Machiavelli's one-time palace on the via Maggio. The church itself, St Mark's, is built in the cortile and much of the building is let off as flats. But the magnificent apartments on the piano nobile are retained for occupation by the Anglican incumbent.

'The chaplain, who is an Archdeacon, is a converted soccer player – his language is terrible but he's a very good man on property.'

Rents from flats in church property also play a crucial role in maintaining the Sicilian churches in Palermo and Taormina.

'A whole block of flats next to Holy Cross in Palermo used to be ours. We only have 2 floors left now because the Mafia has tricked us out of it and there's nothing we can do. And Della Chiesa, the Prefect who was assassinated by the Mafia, he had one of our flats and hadn't paid us rent for I don't know how long but we felt so sorry for his widow that we didn't press our claims.'

So his next trip is to Vienna. And after that?

'I have to tour the Archdeaconry of the Riviera. Oh, that Riviera gives me the pip,' he sighs up at the ceiling. 'You put a fire out in one place and it breaks out in another. It's because they haven't enough to do. We've 18 churches there but they're not thriving as they are in Spain and Switzerland.'

Among the more delightful establishments in the diocese he

is especially fond of the fine, Adamesque church in Oporto, the church in Hamburg at the end of the Reeperbahn which goes back to 1648 (present building 1812), and the church on Madeira which retains the traditional liturgy and had 300 communicants when the Bishop visited it in February.

'It's such a pretty spot. I could put my hand out of the loo window in the parsonage there and pick avocadoes – but they've gone and chopped the tree down now.'

What's the difference between a parsonage, a vicarage and a rectory?

'Officially we don't have any rectories or vicarages in Europe because we don't have any territorial claims, you see. Our priests are, to be precise, not vicars or rectors but chaplains to a gathered congregation. That's why we've got on so well with the Catholic and Orthodox churches – we've not been sheep stealing. There is a snag in that. If you're not careful you can have an English club on your hands – this is one of my favourite little sermons and they hate me for it. We've been talking about the fun spots, but it's not all gin & sin in the sun. We have many thriving churches in north France, Germany, the Netherlands. There are huge areas of the diocese which are very hard-working. The whole Paris complex, Brussels, the Hague, Geneva, packed out every Sunday. Rome, Milan, among our busiest. Athens, very busy – the church there was given to us by a grateful Greek government in return for the splendid services of "that holy man Lord Byron"! '

Christ Church in Naples was built on land donated to the British by Garibaldi. 'He did it to spite the Pope.' NATO helps to keep Naples going, as it does the churches in Oslo and Izmir. Then there is what the Bishop calls the Costa Geriatrica in Spain where the Anglicans use 49 Catholic churches in addition to their own. The Bishop consecrated a new church there in February at Los Boliches, Fuengirola, and the priest already has about 300 communicants every Sunday. 'Far more than he'd get in England,' he adds ruefully.

The Bishop is sitting opposite me in a chair. His fingers are interlocked over a purple silk belly and he presents a solid figure. His sense of humour and forthright expressions of opinion are very refreshing in a world in which public figures hide behind half truths, yet although he chuckles a great deal this in no sense undermines his seriousness of purpose. His voice is reassuring: this is a man you can take problems too, a man with a big heart, and perhaps the reason for his approachability is that every once in a while a sadness seems to pass through him, an emotional aliveness which suggests that he is no stranger to personal grief and anxiety. To come across a man at the top of his profession who hasn't developed the customary one-skin-too-many is almost shocking. It is also a reminder that whatever one thinks of the Church's teachings, it is no ordinary profession. I wonder if he gets depressed very often.

'Every so often I do.'

'How do you deal with that?'

'I daren't tell you! But I'm quite resilient underneath because I'm a tough Cumbrian. The real problem at the moment is getting the right manpower. The Church in this country is *so weak*. We don't get the people we ought to be getting, we're scraping the barrel sometimes. But I've got an excellent man at Strasbourg, Barney Milligan. *We* kept him going – the Church of England did damn all! And with the Common Market and the European Parliament at Strasbourg, there's a great *need* for somebody there. But at last we've screwed some money out of the C of E to make him the official Anglican representative at Strasbourg.'

'Do you find Church politics become rather Byzantine and get in the way of your real work?'

'They can do. And I tell you what I've noticed all round Europe, because I call on all the cardinals and bishops wherever I go, that with the present Pope, *every* appointment in the Catholic Church has been more and more conservative than the one it replaced.'

'I was very upset to see the Pope in Latin America preaching to vast crowds of impoverished people about the evils of contraception.'

'I know, it's terrible,' he replies. 'As a result of this Pope, a lot of Catholics are going their own way quietly. But I'm not happy about the Church of England either. Its trendiness has weakened it. I was very unhappy about the Revision of

Services, and now they are going on with other mad things. People are disorientated.'

He explains that for people working abroad loneliness and isolation are recurrent themes, for the priests as well as for their parishioners. Marriages going wrong abroad, and the trapped loneliness in that, is another big problem. Then there are the disasters – earthquakes, aircrashes, and so forth – which demand someone on the spot. He is unmarried, so I ask if he suffers from loneliness too.

'I've been lonely most of my life. But I try to laugh about it – go to bed with my teddy bear. And I have an ancient retainer here, Dennis, the housekeeper. He's a Wykehamist, 2 good degrees, brilliant historian, and he's the best cook I've ever had, cleans the house, does the garden, everything, so I'm very lucky. He was with the Jesuits for 18 years and knows how to serve the Mass for me every morning in the chapel here – it's just a little oratory near the front door.'

When he retires, it will not be abroad. He would like to become the curate of a little country church, as Archbishop Fisher retired to the tiny parish of Trent in Dorset after Canterbury.

'I'm 65, I could retire next year. But I shan't because the diocese is having its 150th anniversary in 1992. We couldn't celebrate our centenary in 1942 because of Hitler.'

'What are your interests when you're not churching?'

'Music. Reading. I don't really write but I have to keep a log. Someone asked "Are you publishing it, Bishop?" and I said "Well, in fact I'm keeping 2 logs. One for His Grace at Canterbury and one for the *News of the World* in case times get hard!".'

He shakes with laughter, the tumbler glitters, and he polishes off the whisky.

(1990)

151

FROM BOXING TO BROWNING
KIRK DOUGLAS

KIRK DOUGLAS IS a surprise. The man who always seemed the 'nasty' to Burt Lancaster's 'nice' turns out to have an almost old-world courtesy. The man whose face was a fatless knot of muscle – tight mouth, tight blue eyes, sharp nose, that dimple – and whose rich punky voice proclaimed his origins in New England's immigrant working-class, and suggested depths of efficient violence, well, he's now grown a benign grey beard, speaks fluent French (his wife is French and he's also an 'Officier de la Légion d'honneur'), and has a collection of thought-out liberal opinions (as the producer of *Spartacus* he was a pioneer in the breaking of the lingering McCarthy blacklist; the same film also had a laconic homosexual scene between Lawrence Olivier and Tony Curtis which was cut by the censors). He is well into his 70s but slips and slides around in a green leather armchair with childlike vitality. I was expecting him to be physically small – they usually are – but he's just average. I was expecting him to be bombastic but he's . . . well, yes, he is slightly bombastic. He answers questions as if addressing a public meeting of some sort – he projects – but how can an actor not love a little the sound of his own voice? However this largeness of tone comes more from enthusiasm than from conceit.

'My wife says – I've been married twice – my first wife Diane said a funny thing to me. She said Kirk, you're working like mad all the *time*, you're like somebody who's trying to become a star – but you *are* a star.' There goes that fruity voice, measured, with dramatic emphases, and quite a few slurs to

152

avoid any stentorian effect – beautifully done. 'But I can't think of myself as a star. It can go away so quickly. So it's like I don't *dare*.'

The biggest surprise is that the star of *Paths of Glory, Lonely Are The Brave, Spartacus, I Walk Alone, The Bad and the Beautiful, The Big Sky, Gunfight at the OK Corral, Lust for Life, The Arrangement*, the passionate guy with the acid streak, is now writing books. A novel, *Dance with the Devil*, is only the first of 3 novels he's contracted to write. Before that, he brought out his autobiography, *The Ragman's Son*, which is one of the most candid autobiographies I've ever read – another surprise, given that show business personalities are notoriously frigid about their private lives and usually find it impossible to say anything more than 'wonderful' about the other celebrities they've worked with.

The Ragman's Son contains, for example, a marvellous story about Douglas's seduction by Joan Crawford. He first sprang to fame in the film *Champion* (1949), playing a boxer. After the premiere, a congratulatory telegram to Hollywood's new male star arrived from Joan Crawford whom he'd never met. He rang to thank her – next thing they had a dinner date. After dinner they went back to her house. She hardly let Douglas get past the front door and had him on the hall carpet. In the middle of their congress she said 'You're so clean. It's wonderful that you shaved your armpits in the film.' He was disconcerted by this since he'd never shaved his armpits. Afterwards they dressed and she took him upstairs to see her 2 children *strapped* into their beds – Kirk fled. Quentin Crisp once met Crawford, describing her as 'incandescent with self-belief'.

'You see, the danger in our profession is to lose the line of demarcation between reality and make-believe. Joan Crawford did not have such a line. I never get completely lost in a part.'

'Van Gogh in *Lust for Life* did get to you.'

'Yes, of all of them, that one got to me.'

After the first private screening of *Lust for Life*, the party went off for dinner at Merle Oberon's where John Wayne said 'Christ, Kirk! How can you play a part like that? There's so goddam few of us left. We got to play strong, tough characters. Not those weak queers.'

Douglas says now 'I had to tell him – John, you're not John Wayne for Chrissake, we're actors, the Pentagon doesn't ring you up when we have a war. He was disturbed by that. If you analysed John Wayne you'd probably find a *mass* of problems.'

'Did you want to write when you were small?'

'No. I always wanted to become an actor because acting was my form of escape. But I was always interested in writing. Ask any actor, it's not the director he's interested in, it's *the script*. On a film, the writer is by far the most important person. And I mean – by far.'

Douglas came from a tough background. He was born 1916 in Amsterdam, a WASP town between the Catskill and Adirondack Mountains in upstate New York, an only son with 6 sisters, children of Russian Jewish immigrants who could neither read nor write. In winter the house was insulated by manure piled round the outside provided by the horse of his father who was a rag and bone man.

'Why didn't you go to your father's funeral?'

'The reason wasn't really that I was too tied in to some other place – because I should've gone. The reason was – it was too painful for me, it was too painful. It was over – over – and I'd never now have the chance to reconcile things that I wanted very much to reconcile. If they made a film of my auto-biography, I'd like to play my father because I'd feel that in playing him I could atone for some of my sins, atone by trying to convey the point of view of an illiterate man who made that fantastic voyage from Russia to America, yet who couldn't cope with making a living, who was probably the strongest man in the town, but who could do nothing really, not even give his son a pat on the back, you know, pathetic, really *pathetic*. When I wrote my autobiography, all that anger I had about not getting any support from him, the amount of my anger, that surprised me. If I were doing it again I think I'd try to be kinder to my father.'

The world Douglas came from, didn't they think it cissy that he wanted to be an actor?

'Oh yes. Rarely would I tell anyone. I kept it under wraps coz they'd think I was crazy. I was always daydreaming about it – and that's what a novel is, the creation of an imaginary world. Although I believe that to be good, a novel has to be based on truth, on things that the author really knows about.'

'What about the homosexual episode in *Dance with the Devil*? Is that in your experience?'

'Ha, ha! First of all – if that was in my experience, you'd be the last person I'm gonna tell it to! Have I had homosexual experiences? Of course I'm not going to tell you that. But I remember reading about a man who was quite a ladies' man, a great sex drive, and he went to prison for about 10 years, and in prison he had many homosexual experiences. Then when he came out he went back to women. And I can understand that. The sex drive is very strong – it doesn't disappear just because you go to prison. A young pretty boy comes in, and in a man's imagination, in dim light, couldn't he start to develop a sexual reaction? Yes, I can see how that happens. And what shocks the protagonist of my novel is that he *enjoys* it – and he can't handle that.'

In fact, the novel – which is about survival, Jewishness, the Holocaust, brutality, an American film director, a Polish refugee – contains a great deal of sex (intercourse roughly every 10 pages) including child sex and incest. His autobiography is sexually frank too – there we learn that in addition to Ms Crawford, he made it with Gene Tierney, Rita Hayworth, Marlene Dietrich, tried and failed to seduce Lauren Bacall.

'I thought a lot about whether I should put all that into my autobiography. And I decided that sex is a very important part of who you are, a very important part of life – but it's only a *part*.'

Well, it's wonderful to be given pretty much the whole picture in a piece of non-fiction. That's terribly rare.

'Why write an autobiography if you don't intend to open up? I was very hard on certain people' (*Stanley Kubrick is a talented shit* is a good representative sentence) 'but I think I was harder on myself.'

As for sex in the novel, Mr Douglas has a well-rehearsed

answer: 'People say there's a lot of raw sex in it – but what other kind of sex is there?' Well, many other kinds, surely? Besides, a novel isn't action but a critique of action.

'What makes you miserable?'

'You mean, what don't I like? I don't like being inactive. That's why writing novels was like a lifesaver.'

'You were in analysis for a few years – what did you get out of it?'

'I was in analysis for 5 years, er . . . What did I get out of it? Very important, very very important. Aside from realising the psychoanalyst was nuts, what I realised was *everybody* has problems. No one is as strong as they seem, and no one generally speaking is as *weak* as very often you *think* they are. That was a comforting thought to me. Sometimes I have feelings of unhappiness and I don't know why, feelings of loneliness and I don't know why. But once you learn that this is not catastrophic, you can deal with it. It would be like – I have a problem, whenever I think of a doorknob it arouses me sexually, what shall I do? Well, a problem is a point of view. Someone else would say, Jesus, I don't have a problem, whenever I'm with a girl I think of a doorknob, and everything works fine. Analysis helped me not to be frightened of my weaknesses and insecurities.'

Loneliness is a big theme of his. *Lonely Are The Brave* is his favourite of his films. He has written 'All Jews are lonely' and 'Actors are lonely people'. Yet he's a big family man, lots of fr – well, don't know, maybe he doesn't have a lot of friends.

'No, I don't have a lot of friends. Loneliness, a lot of it is self-imposed. I don't feel lonely writing a novel – those characters as they develop become real to you. I have always been a maverick. When I came to Hollywood, I didn't belong to a studio, I was an independent, and I felt lonely about it but . . .'

He seems very easy and breezy these days, very capable, not really hiding from anything. So what embarrasses him? What throws him?

'I think . . . compliments embarrass me. At the same time, we never get accustomed to adverse criticisms. You learn how to pretend to handle it – but you don't like it. It's always been essential to me to get a pat on the back.'

What are his virtues?

'I'm extremely hard-working, probably too much so, a workaholic. But that's not a virtue . . . virtues – it sounds so *dull* to have virtues.'

'All right, what are your vices then?'

'I'm quick to anger, I'm impatient, you know, moody, *very* moody. It's easy for me to see things in me I don't like. I'm naïve.'

Naïve?

'Oh yes. I think every actor – every artist for that matter –is naïve, he's childlike. Naïveté is an essential quality for an actor – all children can pretend to be cowboys and indians and really live their fantasies. They're not self-conscious, they're naïve. Acting is the most childlike profession in the world – Burt Lancaster and Kirk Douglas pretending to be cowboys – that's not a job for a grown-up, sophisticated man. People who are too sophisticated have like a wall. Naïveté makes you receptive.'

Why did he develop a reputation for being difficult to work with?

'I liked ideas – and I always insisted on being listened to, which directors didn't like. I didn't insist on my ideas being accepted, just listened to now and again.'

He is a real Hollywood man. He loves it and he hates it – and quotes Tallulah Bankhead's glorious line: 'Who do I have to fuck to get out of this business?' But he surely belongs to it, with a house in Beverly Hills and another out in the desert at Palm Springs and a son, Michael Douglas, who is one of the most successful producers and actors of a younger generation. Does he think Hollywood's gone off?

'What I don't like is the overpowering desire to make the blockbuster. But you can get to a point in life where nothing seems as good as it used to be!'

Which brings us to the subject of age. He's getting somewhat deaf. Apart from that, he seems in good health, preserves a lithe figure – he's the physically proud type who probably has a gymnasium in his home, but I forgot to ask. However I did wonder if growing old upset him.

'I find – not at all. That poem – *Grow old along with me!*

157

The best is yet to be, The last of life, for which the first was made . . . [*Rabbi ben Ezra*, Browning]. I still feel vital, I'd hate to become an invalid, I still feel I have challenges, still feel that *a man's reach should exceed his grasp, Or what's a heaven for?* . . . [*Andrea del Sarto*, Browning]. On the other hand, I think back, oh Christ, I'd hate to have to go through all that again, oh God, struggling to get somewhere, I had so much energy, I was so relentless, I'm tired just thinking of it!'

But God seems to have been on his side. Though born into poverty, he had advantages you can't buy – good looks, robust constitution, an actor's voice. 'Oh really? I just think of it as an ordinary American voice. I think if a voice is too good, it's a disadvantage to an actor.' No, he has a good voice for acting. It has a special timbre which comes across clearly yet sounds entirely unforced. He was also blessed with a rampant, forthright egotism, a ruthless determination to advance his own cause. But subterfuge and deceit weren't his style. He had no need of them. From the word go he was making it – some people have this runaway, all-doors-opening passage to the top. Struggle of course there was. There is in every life. But no real setbacks in his story. He wanted to go to college, so he walked into one, Saint Lawrence University, was accepted, worked his way through, and became the first ever Jewish president of the student body. Then he moves on to the top drama school, the American Academy of Dramatic Arts; becomes the first member of his class there to get a part on Broadway. And so it continues until he ends up starring in films which his own company produces, with 4 successful sons, a long and successful second marriage, but still on good terms with his first wife – does he never fail?

He laughs up at the ceiling, then turns a deadly serious stare on me. 'How about buying a book called *One Flew Over The Cuckoo's Nest*, putting my own money in it, how about paying a writer to do the script, how about putting it on Broadway where it's ignored as a half-arsed thing, how about doing the play for 6 months unpaid on the road, how about going back to Hollywood and trying to make a movie of it for 10 years, not being able to, how about my *son* Michael saying look, Dad, let me try, and he succeeds but not with me but with

Jack Nicholson and it scoops 5 Oscars? Not being in that film was the biggest disappointment of my professional life. So you think everything's gone my way?'

OK. OK. But if this has been his greatest disappointment, his most significant failure, then Kirk Douglas is even luckier than we thought he was. Final verdict, final surprise: he's very charming – without being wet. If he's moody, we caught a good mood – and he had a very positive effect on mine. Afterwards, for some reason, I wanted to go all over Harvey Nichols buying things with my credit card. Fortunately I'd left it at home.

(1990)

FANTASTIC REALISTS

7 Days in Vienna

MONDAY

DESCEND THROUGH MUSHY cloudcover to brand new airport. At last! The city of Benvenuto Cellini's golden salt cellar and Montezuma's crown of feathers! And of Gluck, Haydn, Mozart, Beethoven, Schubert, Brahms, Bruckner, Mahler (and Alma Mahler!), Schönberg, Berg, Webern (plus Lehar and several Strausses but not Richard Strauss), Zemlinsky, Schnitzler, Zweig, Musil, Broch, Canetti (Elias), Mesmer, Freud, Wittgenstein, Sacher-Masoch, Sacher torte, Otto Weininger (who wrote *Sex and Character* and committed suicide at 23 in a room rented for the occasion in the house where Beethoven had died), Otto Wagner, Adolf Loos, Klimt, Schiele, Kokoschka (and the young aggrieved rejected art student Adolf Hitler) and lately of the Fantastic Realist painters (Fuchs, Brauer, Hausner, Hundertwasser, Hutter)!

This list demonstrates several things: that there is no culture of importance in Vienna until the second half of the 18th century (although Marcus Aurelius died there fighting, 180 AD), that it was music which got Vienna going, that it didn't get going in a big way until the 19th century, that this inspired activity hardly survived the end of the Austro-Hungarian Empire in 1918 and the invasion of Hitler in 1938. It did survive these events by going into dreamland (a place which had always claimed a great deal of Vienna's attention), so that now – small, grand, the old baroque town ringed by extravagant buildings, 19th century hypertrophies of historical styles,

160

and dreamily original ones, all disposed as it were in a compound – it has become a strange and intoxicating Disneyland of the High Arts.

Astoria Hotel, very central. Go for a *bummel* and come across the Plague Pillar, masses of sculpted stone rolling up into the sky like a column of boiling mud. The transformation of stone's essential quality, hardness, into softness can go no further. An accordionist outside St Stephen's Cathedral sings a melancholy Balkan song which carries the heart away to Constantinople and beyond. Street singers and students often wear Turkish slippers curling up at the toes. 2 boys talking outside Avocados Bar – 'James Brown . . . James Brown . . .' flashes out of their chunky German. The city does have a wistfulness tinged with bewilderment which is Vienna missing its Emperor. In 1910 the population was 2.1 million; now it is 1.5 million and still falling (despite glass UNO City on an island in the Danube – but where *is* the Danube?). Therefore it is the most wonderfully understressed of the great capitals.

Buy a chocolate-covered banana on the Kärntner Strasse and then come across the hotel where W. H. Auden died. The banana is insufficient. All shops have now closed – it's 6.30pm – walk for over an hour attempting to buy a bar of chocolate in this chocolate town – unsuccessful – but discover that the Austrians must be very fond of stamp collecting because there are many philately shops in key positions . . . The Hofburg, city palace and citadel of the Habsburgs, is like the Austro-Hungarian Empire itself, magnificent and haphazard. In socialist Vienna a main road now runs right through it from the Ring to the Michaelerplatz where is located the Hofburg's 'back door' into the Old Town. The Emperor Franz Joseph refused to use the Michaelerplatz entrance after Adolf Loos built his stark, modern Loos House there in 1910 – on the other hand the Emperor was an opponent of anti-semitism and had granted universal suffrage in 1906, many years before it happened in Britain. Another surprising fact: at the turn of the century over 60% of Vienna's inhabitants were non-German speaking.

Franz Joseph had an extraordinary life. Born 1830. Came to the throne in the Year of Revolutions 1848 after the mob had forced his uncle's abdication. His brother, the Emperor Maximilian of Mexico, was executed by firing squad in 1867. His son Crown Prince Rudolf committed suicide after shooting his female lover at Mayerling in 1889. His wife, Elizabeth of Austria, was stabbed to death on holiday in Switzerland in 1898. His heir Archduke Franz Ferdinand was assassinated at Sarajevo in 1914. The Emperor himself died during the Great War in 1916.

The present atmosphere of Vienna is the least threatening of any major city in Europe and it is perfectly safe to walk at night. But looking at some statistics, it appears to be a myth that Viennese society at the turn of the century was more unstable than now. The average number of homicides (murder and manslaughter) in the city for the years 1901–5 is 19.4 per million of population. The average for the years 1981–3 in Vienna is 30.4 per million (in London the number of homicides in 1982 was 28.7 per million). Traditionally of course the Viennese have been much more interested in suicide than in murder – see Arthur Schnitzler's stories. For the years 1901–8 the average number of suicides in Vienna was 291 per million of population. By 1926 it had jumped to 467 per million. And in 1983 it had levelled back at 282 per million. In London the number of suicides in 1900 was roughly 100 per million – and in 1984 it was slightly under that.

TUESDAY

Hot and sunny.

To Sigmund Freud's flat, now a museum, at 19 Berggasse (looking down the bell panel, current flat owners in this building include the names Bormann and Kafka). Discover that the famous couch is in London where Freud went to escape the Nazis. Many black & white photographs on the walls, subfusc figures long dead peering into the future out of grey damask rooms. Buy several souvenir pens, and into the sunshine again for an ice-cream. The excellence of Viennese ice-cream reminds one that much of North Italy, including Venice, was ruled from here not so long ago.

Bummel along the Ring to the Kunsthistorische Museum to see Cellini's salt cellar. Also here, occupying the 1st floor, is the world's second greatest collection of paintings (the greatest is said to be the National Gallery's in London). Rembrandt, Rubens, Bruegel, Dürer, Giorgione, Titian, Velazquez, enough of lists – note the Seasons by Arcimboldo (1527–93) who started surrealism. Cranach, Altdorfer, von Aachen: with these on display there is no reason to ask why the modern school of Fantastic Realism should have arisen in Vienna – 'fantastic realism' is the central tradition of Germanic painting. Saunter into a sideroom and . . . hit the best picture in town, 'Allegory of the Art of Painting' by Vermeer, the absolute moment, sheer sanity, pure reality: very rare. After this, Cellini's salt cellar, hidden somewhere among the three-dimensional artifacts which occupy the ground floor, must wait for another day.

The Viennese – very difficult to engage except over a shop or ticket counter. They are not hostile or surly, not exactly stupid, and not impolite – there's just this lack of response. They are simply not interested in conversation or rapport with people from elsewhere. But at least they don't beat you up. Unemployment is low in Austria (4.5%) and no evidence of heroin addicts (how unlike Florence in this respect!).

The Austrian male: just as the Italian male knows how to contrive an amorous bulge even in the most shapeless trousers, so the Austrian male, even in the tightest trousers, seems to have found the secret of the concave lap. Where do they put it?

The Austrian female: yes, they do have that milky quality, but it evaporates in the region of their breasts which are usually boxed up in cardboard tailoring. There's no cleavage in Vienna.

To the Konzerthaus where Claudio Abbado conducts the Vienna Philharmonic. Mahler – the Adagio from the unfinished 10th Symphony. The strings are very screechy in the upper registers. Is this Abbado? Or the orchestra? Or did Mahler intend these long, very high sweet elegiac string passages to turn into screams? In the works of Mahler all the 19th century and all the 20th century crashed violently together and fused weirdly. The force of his writing scatters the emotions; its inventive complexity and delicacy attracts and clutches at them again in new combinations; one is both disorientated and moved. The scale of his work means that all precedence finds an echo here and numberless possibilities are suggested. After Mahler this form of growth collapsed in on itself leading via the arbitrary, cleansing rigour of Schoenberg to the cool, almost Japanese economy of Webern's last works. In Bruckner the gap or silence is a moment to wipe one's brow and it is filled with resonance. But the silences of Webern are manifestations of the underlying condition upon which the sounds intrude. To-morrow I go in search of cakes. Read some *Victory* by Conrad.

WEDNESDAY

Hot, sunny, muggy.

Visit Arik Brauer, one of the most important of the Fantastic Realists. The houses in Vienna get smarter the further north you go. Brauer lives middle north, an area of elaborate detached villas built for well-to-do merchants in the 19th century and now rather grand. Brauer is small with long dark hair, a moustache and trim beard; is distant, not cool, but dreamily far off. He is Jewish, born in the city in 1929, and was a child during one of the nastiest periods in its history.

'My father was a shoemaker. Before Hitler we were just poor, living in Ottakring [this traditionally is Vienna's working-class district to the west of the city]. I have a good memory of my childhood, making music, walks in the forest. But it was really 2 lives. Playing in the street with Austrian boys, completely integrated. And on the other hand I went twice a week to the Jewish school to learn religion – another life, another language. I can still speak Yiddish and Hebrew. 2 lives, a funny way to live.'

'When did you first become afraid?'

'In school. All my friends turned their back to me and I was beaten and kicked out of their society. I saw Hitler – 100,000 people cheering him. But Vienna then had almost 2 millions, so where were the others? I remember some weeks before the

Nazis arrived with military, there was a big demonstration against occupation . . . I don't like so much to think about it. I was in a camp and later I lived in hiding. My father did not survive. After the War I was liberated by the Russian Army and with the socialist background from my family I became a Communist. I was very young, a student at the art academy. Later I started to understand that Communism was not my thing – and later on I hated it – but meanwhile I was empty. So at 24 years old I went to Israel for a year and met the woman who later became my wife.'

'Why have the Jews contributed so much to the fame of Vienna in the last hundred years?'

'I think because the Viennese Jews were much more emancipated from their religion, from the ghetto, than other Jews [the Viennese press barons were nearly all Jews, for example]. When I was a boy, 10% of Vienna was Jewish. Now it's nothing, 0.5%. I visited the Kunsthistorische Museum a lot when I was young – the Bruegel and Bosch collections were very important to me. And later Dali. I know he is thought of as kitsch and has turned out lots of junk but for me a painter must be judged by his 10 best paintings. I lived in Paris for a number of years which is good because Vienna is now at the end of Europe and our cultural connections are to the West. But in the past Vienna looked more naturally to the East, to Hungary and Russia – to the West are the mountains. And this school of Fantastic Realism began to grow up here in the 1950s, separate from other art movements which were abstract. Fantastic Realism is no longer new and fashionable – but it is not yet historical movement either. At the moment we are between these 2 things.'

'What is Vienna like to live in?'

'It is good. Soft and easy life, beautiful buildings and parks, not crowded, nice weather. But I don't paint city pictures. I'm strongly attracted to nature. In a way you are right when you say Austrians are neutral – and they are politically neutral too of course. They want to be quiet, don't want to mix. Then there is the side of Sigmund Freud, Stefan Zweig, very strong thinking and turning and worrying. Then ½ my time I live in Israel where we built a house. I have 3 daughters and they all speak Hebrew. So I continue this double life which is for me very comfortable.'

He makes a present of a 3 volume study of his work, then with startling suddenness disappears out of his own front door and off up the road and is gone, leaving me blinking on the carpet.

To the *Traum und Wirklichkeit* (Dream and Reality) exhibition at the Kunstlerhaus: Vienna 1870–1930, with all the great names – Mahler, Kokoschka, Freud, Musil, and so on – surging into each other. Many superb architectural models here – e.g. the Tribune Tower designed by Adolf Loos for the Chicago Tribune and never built; it was a skyscraper in the form of a single doric column on a pedestal (viz post-modernism). Alma Mahler looks interesting – the world's most successful genius-groupie – she went with so many of them. In the *Traumdeutung* room, virtually empty except for ice blue light, a vivacious American tour guide is explaining to her charges that Freud's revolutionary book on the interpreta-tion of dreams was published in 1900 in an edition of 600 and took 8 years to sell out. The Klimt and Schiele rooms are stiflingly hot, saunalike. Schiele survives this much better than Klimt . . . Out into the equally hot air of the Ring – Roumanian gypsy girls approach and start to beg, holding up little pieces of paper worn and faded like old lace hankies, printed texts detailing their history.

Visit Demel's, the best patisserie in the world, and spend a fortune. Sublime confections on the cake buffet, not too sweet and replete with naturalness, all made by hand to traditional recipes in the back room – and a toothsome selection of savouries too. If you don't want to sit at one of the little tables in the rococo tea-room, well, since this is Vienna, *coffee*-room, you should leave with big bags of take-away. Back at hotel, ring room service and ask them to send up a fork, which they do, on a tray. Peer into bags. Blissful interlude . . . Vienna generally is a great town for eating. Turn on the radio which is state controlled. Announcer says that the President of Kenya has arrived to-day for a state visit – but saw no evidence of this on the streets. He was picked up at the airport in the Presidential Limousine, the only car in Austria entitled to travel without a number plate. The radio report (in English) says the Kenyan President will go to the Opera and look at the Wachau but is here to strengthen, even further, the already strong economic ties between Austria and Kenya. That these 2 countries have any ties whatsoever is distinctly surreal. Must be the coffee.

Strike up a conversation with a Chinaman, Mr Ow, who is also staying at the Astoria. He remarks on how difficult it is to strike up conversation with a Viennese. Mr Ow is from Kensington and motoring through Austria with his mother who is on a visit from Singapore.

THURSDAY

Very hot and sticky morning, quite windless, after a similar night of fretful patchy sleep.

To-day is a religious holiday (Corpus Christi). Go for a *bummel* through the glittering groggy atmosphere – sit in Kärntner Strasse and ogle Austrians in an attempt to cause offence and thereby precipitate a remark or something. Fail. But discover in the process that although Vienna until recently was a very mixed capital racially, there is little evidence of intermarriage. In the parks along the Ring you're not permitted to go on the grass so there's nowhere to crash out outside unless you go to the Prater or to Schönbrunn.

Cab to Schönbrunn. It's a woman driver and for some reason she won't allow the rear windows open and has removed the handles to prevent it, so the ride is gruesomely hot. Schönbrunn, the Austrian Windsor but on the edge of town, is overrun with tourists in nylon clothes. The palace is being repainted a brilliant mustard yellow. The garden is flowery and fountainous, and fitted out with statues and beautiful wrought iron lavatories painted green. It is exceedingly hot here which makes one feel very abroad. Some of the darker women wandering about are quite hairy. Would this be the Magyar element? Hideous queues for the Apartments, so drift drippingly over to the Imperial Bath for a swim where there's another hideous queue on this Bank Holiday. Vienna's paradox: underpopulated, but impossible queues for so many things. Cab back to town is driven by boy with one leg and an American accent. He was an exchange student in Pennsylvania, studying Data Processing but prefers to drive. He said Vienna's not normally this hot, that it was 35°C in his sister's back garden at midday. Good God, that's 95°F!

Descend by escalator into one of the many pedestrian underpasses for a *gepinkel*. Approached by a Bulgarian traveller with a suitcase of cigarettes. He's cube-shaped, ruddy face shining with heat, and he speaks shattered English, wants help in some way – but what way? A wad of banknotes shows through the white nylon breast pocket of his shirt, so it can't be money. His thick grey hair is cut short all over and sticks up in a brush – his eyebrows move up and down expressively – he says Bulgaria isn't all bad. Then he asks again but he doesn't know enough English to communicate his need. Is it one's gullible face which attracts? In travelling the 'couple' are hermetically sealed from such encounters. Leave the Bulgarian salesman gesticulating in underpass. Notice flyposting along the Ring to promote new brand of cigarette, Johnny Filter in a denim packet. *Johnny Gross in Fahrt* says the ad. Into the Café Kunterbunt for a beer – not one of the famous Viennese cafés but the beer is cold. Next stop – the Prater to lie on grass some more. Look at the funfair – no entrance fee, no turnstile, just go in and stare up at the Ferris Wheel built by an Englishman . . . On the way back to the hotel, the cab passes an arresting modern building almost completed. Stop the cab and get out for a look. This is an extraordinary edifice of green, blue and gold panels, with massive brick bastions of outlandish design at the corners – a technicolour castle glowing in the evening sunshine. It turns out to be the Ministry of Buildings building. So much for conservatism in high places – they come up with a totally unexpected masterpiece of articulate extravagance, a true peacock addition to the spectacle of the Ring whose north eastern limb it terminates . . . spend fortune at Demel's . . .

Opera. 2 ballets (set to Berg's *Lyric Suite* and Violin Concerto), though recent productions, seem to be perfect pieces of 1935 preserved under glass.

Night . . . distant drunken singing emphasises the silence of deserted lamplit streets . . . enter nightclub, no entrance charge, no dress code, no barriers, just go in and buy a drink. One of the nice things about Vienna is the sense of doors having been unlocked – but inside one seems to have stumbled upon a private family party. The presence of the foreigner causes the Viennese to redouble their interest in each other.

FRIDAY

Hot, muggy, close.

1945 exhibition at the Museum of the 20th century. EIN VOLK, EIN REICH, EIN FUHRER! . . . Old crackly recording of a calmly triumphing British commander who says through loud-hailer 'I hope you will make friends with my soldiers'. Cheers from the conquered. Exhibition ends with the appearance of the Fantastic Realists in the late 40s . . . Street poster announces James Brown doing 3 nights in Vienna next month . . . To Alban Berg exhibition in the Austrian National Library. Berg looks very droll in his army uniform, decidedly Wildean. His face has sensuality, generosity and elegance. Adolf Loos looks like Kirk Douglas. And Schoenberg's whole face is drawn sourly down into the mouth which is small, round and pursed like an anus.

To Ernst Fuchs's house on the edge of town in the Vienna Woods. It is an exquisite white villa designed by Otto Wagner for himself, with friezes and a portico front of 4 ionic pillars. The exterior details are picked out in pale blue, yellow, gold, black; there is much ornamental ironwork; and the house is approached by a grand staircase carrying many urns. Perhaps too many urns and too much ironwork for a refined taste – perhaps not. However the bulbous black Venus by Fuchs in the centre of the façade looks as though she has always spread her arms here. The son comes down the drive and beckons – he is dressed like a teenager but has the harassed face of a 35 year old.

The interior of the house embodies perfect shapes, proportions, ascents and descents, and is filled with Fuchs-designed furniture, his sculpture and paintings. Works in progress stand everywhere on easels. These recent pictures are very brilliantly coloured, almost kitsch compared to his great classic works of the 50s and 60s with their superb detail, finish, invention and iconic power (a number of these earlier pictures hang in the dining-room here). But that sinister Mayan quality, so strong in some of the imagery (especially the so-called 'cherubs'), this remains.

Fuchs ambles in, with a little naked girl trundling after – she has a nasty burn on her bottom and carries handfuls of flower petals. He's very affectionate with her. 'But this one's not mine,' he says. 'It's the daughter of my girlfriend, but I was present when she was born and I take care of her as a father. I have 8 children of my own. It's the nature of the universe to be productive.'

His manner is both jittery and vague. He wears a funny round hat and has prophet whiskers and plays the Jew far more than Brauer. Fuchs was born in Vienna in 1930.

'I'm ½ Jewish, my father was Jewish – he emigrated, but I stayed in Vienna with my mother during the War. Heavy bombing . . . I couldn't go to an ordinary school and my mother had to give up the custody of me. Half-Jews were a separate category. And with the Nuremberg Laws there was another distinction, you know, made between the circumcised and the not circumcised.'

'Were you circumcised?'

'No, I wasn't. Therefore I could have the same ration cards as everybody else, whereas the others had to wear the star – even though they were also half-Jewish – because they were circumcised.'

'I went to the exhibition.'

'*Traum und Wirklichkeit*, I suppose,' he says.

'No. 1945. It starts with the SS uniforms hanging there, black leather ties and so on, skull & crossbones insignia – and ends up with your picture of the Crucifixion.'

'I was an expressionist painter, you know, in that Crucifixion. I became more fantastic and surrealistic in 1946–7.'

'The Late Middle Ages feeling seems to have gone – there's an increasingly 19th century *fin de siècle* atmosphere in your work.'

'I think the 19th century is the greatest century for painting and architecture!'

'Don't you like the Belvedere then?' This is Eugene of Savoy's palace completed 1726, Vienna's most adorable building, total elegance and pleasure. There are smiling stone sphinxes along the terrace and inside the floorboards squeak incredibly loudly as you cross them.

'It's clumsy. They should've spent more money on it. I like the Kunsthistorische Museum. Magnificent! My favourite building in Vienna is my house. It was almost a ruin when I bought it. Nobody *lived* here. A bank owned it and sold it to somebody who didn't know what to do with it. The floors, ceilings, I had to restore everything. I designed all the furniture. I will make a museum here. I will open it. The paintings will remain as a constant collection. In those paintings I'm doing my colours have more and more affinity with the stained glass windows here, by Adolf Böhm, a very famous artist of the Secession, who was commissioned by Otto Wagner to do them.'

'You keep a lot of your pictures?'

'I buy them back now. The people who bought my paintings didn't really know what they were doing, you know. Outsiders – like I am an outsider. Many of them still don't know what they have.'

'Are the Fantastic Realists a conscious group?'

'Yes, of course. We are a kind of brotherhood like the Pre-Raphaelites. I love the Pre-Raphaelites. There are the usual jealousies, you know. When we meet – actually we don't meet very often. We all regret that we have so much to do that we hardly have the time to get together . . . so . . . I have to pick up my mother. She is at the subway station. I'll be back in a minute. Can you wait?'

. . . Walk to the tall French windows and look out. The sky is getting very dark for the time of day. The light filters through the leaves of the Vienna Woods and drifts down a rich green between the columns at the front of the house. It faces the main road and is built on a platform cut into a wooded hill, so the back has no view. Fuchs wants to burrow into the hill behind and make Gaudi-like grottoes. All Otto Wagner's detail is very original without being freakish. The Fuchs furniture is mostly in the *jugendstil* manner. Open a pair of glass doors, down

171

marble steps and into a room containing a gargantuan sofa in lemon velvet and old musical instruments placed round. The ceiling is panels of cobalt blue glass bolted on with golden rosettes. Above the sofa hangs a picture of a gaudy pink nude woman going up in flames while dark figures look on . . .

When Fuchs returns he is much more relaxed and starts sounding off on world politics, the industrial revolution in Britain, all kinds of subjects – he has an opinion on everything. 'The artist should be the architect of culture and society. I believe in something like theocracy but the leading man is the Artist.'

'Oh, I shouldn't want to be governed by an artist!'

'There wouldn't be any government! I'm an anarchist! And philosophically I favour Pre-Socratic Gnosis. I like Parmenides.' There's a brilliant flash of lightning through the tall windows.

'I saw something in a magazine about you and Godiva Chocolates.' Thunder rolls . . .

'Yes. I designed their shop in Vienna. It's a nice little boutique, very precious, in glass, wood, fabric.'

'What's Vienna like these days?'

'It has improved. 10 or 15 years ago it was pretty dead. Very good for work. And I love it anyway. I couldn't care less if it's jumping or not. Anyway the ordinary Viennese character is very . . . ordinary. *Extremely* ordinary! They are afraid to wear colour. But they produce these extraordinary personalities. Because there gotta be somebody to *protest*, you know! But it's not like you in England who honour your great artists in their lifetime, like you give Bacon an exhibition at the Tate. Here I am ignored! It's terrible. Except maybe when someone comes from abroad and asks about me and then they'll say "Oh Fuchs, yes, of *course*, Fuchs, oh yes, great Viennese painter". But they do nothing. But I don't care, I like to be in my house. And I have a feeling that Berlin, Vienna, Budapest will become very important places, something trigger-like in the future culture situation of Europe.'

He then expatiates at length on the history of Europe and the future of the world. Fuchs is currently working on large paintings for a chapel in Salzburg dedicated to St Virgil who came to Salzburg from Ireland and whose cosmological speculations shocked the Pope. The thunderstorm breaks. Delicious rain.

SATURDAY

Cool, drizzle, gorgeous, go for a *bummel*. You can get addicted to Vienna and want to read and discover more and more about it. This is because it is both manageable and deep. Kafka described Vienna in 1914 as 'that decaying mammoth village'. The Austrians themselves do not invade one's imagination which therefore grows long fingers in this place and claims it for itself. Smell of horseshit hits you quite often here – which it would never do in Disneyland. The Natural History Museum, the architectural twin of the Kunsthistorische across Maria Theresa Platz, is a frozen zoo full of dust – but the Human Skull Room should be visited . . . Halfday closing of shops on Saturday, like London in the 50s. Cafés stay open however, so spend a fortune at Demel's. Return with booty to hotel and read more of *Victory* by Conrad.

To the Opera. The Opera House looks like a railway station. It is one of the less successful 19th century Viennese buildings. Inside, after wartime bombing, it has been rebuilt in a bland *luxe* style reminiscent of the posh bits of department stores. Strauss's *Salome* based on Oscar Wilde's play is given a colourful art nouveau/art deco production with some cribbing from the Beardsley illustrations. Salome herself is dumpy and her face is ruddy above a body-stocking of unnatural white. This body-stocking is increasingly exposed as she capers all over the set during the Dance of the 7 Veils. Best performance is from the orchestra conducted by Christof Prick.

Encounter Mr Ow in the foyer afterwards wearing very smart clothes, sort of layers of Chinese silk pyjamas in varying shades of grey. He thought the production was very nice. We go for a Saturday night *bummel*, striking into the streets at random, but despite valiant attempts, we fail to get lost, and so decide to return to the hotel – whereupon we immediately get lost. What a *kunterbunt* world!

SUNDAY

Cool, sunny.

To the Ephesus Museum in the Neue Berg – breathtaking – the classical morning housed in its empyrean twilight. The young Greek athlete in bronze is eyeless and, like the eyeless head of Zeus in the Kunsthistorische Museum, he has the intimacy of infinity. The Neue Berg, the most recent part of the Hofburg, was built in 1881–1913 and not completed inside until 1926. It is the most dramatic building on the Ring and impresses externally as an extravaganza the way the Victor Emmanuel Monument does in Rome or the Victoria Memorial in Calcutta, i.e. with a fabulous unreality deriving from the huge scale of the classical style. Such buildings do not fit in the eye but keep swooning out of it – one must move the head in order to encompass them.

The interior of the Neue Berg is the most astounding in Vienna but clearly not appreciated because, apart from the relics of Ephesus which occupy a corner, it is utterly wasted on an endless clutter of glass cabinets containing old weapons and musical instruments. Groups of colossal columns in grey marble with a hint of lavender establish solidity. There is gilded opulence in the mighty chandeliers. Otherwise the interior is cool and pale, the ribbed and plastered vaults painted a pale wash, the capitals ungilded. Standing in the centre under a dome, on a large podium from which staircases fall away, you experience 2 gigantic corridors on either side, like columniated, barrel-vaulted cathedral transepts. But the genius of this architecture is that these great empty wings bend forward and curve slowly out of sight. You cannot see where they end – and therefore there is an effect of eternity.

The staircases under this soaring, bending space are complex and overlapping and on an equivalently gigantic scale. They go up, you walk along, they go down, and vice versa, and there is no real reason for any of this – it is a game of staircases in vast spaces leading nowhere except perhaps to more staircases – Piranesi come true. As in the Kunsthistorische Museum (by the same architects as the Neue Berg: Hasenauer and Semper – it amazes me that no proper big book

174

has yet been published on the architecture of Semper), the vaults viewed up through balustraded stairwells create space mounted on space mounted on space. The whole, curving both vertically and horizontally, wheels in the cool air and pale light. It is a dream of a building in which the mighty Habsburg dynasty, or indeed any other idea, hovers in our awed contemplation, and fades away in ghostly curves, pillared and chandeliered, drifting very slowly and dreamily round the bend into nowhere . . .

(1985)

LUNCH AT SAN LORENZO WITH QUENTIN CRISP, CAROLINE LANGRISHE AND ARNOLD SCHWARZENEGGER

IN THE LATE morning, I make a bunch of phonecalls, have a very large brandy, smoke lots of cigarettes (accidentally burning several holes in my new lemon shirt), and manage to reach San Lorenzo's Restaurant only 3 minutes before the arrival of my guests – still, time enough for a couple of Buck's Fizzes. Followed by a quick gin.

ARNOLD: Let's put some flowers in your gin glass.

DUNCAN: But this microphone thing's got to go in there. Perhaps we should put some flowers *around* it, to disguise the awful anti-social presence of it.

QUENTIN: As soon as one sees a microphone one's flat ordinary voice suddenly turns into a rich basso profundo —

    zzzgr!ghscrg!!!??ssssssgg!! urgh??!!!

DUNCAN: Oh, shit! I've knocked it off the table.

ARNOLD: Do you do lots of interviews and stuff?

CAROLINE: No.

ARNOLD: Coming to England is always very interesting because they ask completely different questions from the Americans.

DUNCAN: Well, I'm not going to ask any questions at all.

ARNOLD: Oh, then thank you, it was very nice meeting you . . . You know, it's so embarrassing when people come up to you always, like that guy did to me just now, and say 'Hullo, how are you? I met you at so-and-so.'

CAROLINE: And you can't remember who on earth they are.

QUENTIN: It's all right if they say something like 'How is your mother?' or 'Do you still go to Beckenham School of Art?' It's when they rush up with 'Do you remember *me*?', that's so difficult. Miss Baddeley's very good at that trick – she turns the tables. You should see the expression on their face when she goes up to strangers and says 'Well hullo! It's been *ages*!'

DUNCAN: Arnold, did you see the film about Quentin on New York TV? It won a big prize.

QUENTIN: It was an Emmy – whatever that is.

ARNOLD: Oh, an Emmy is *big*. Sally Field just won an Emmy for *Sybil*.

CAROLINE: About that woman who had 16 personalities?

DUNCAN: Gosh, that's an incredible thing to have.

QUENTIN: Oh, please don't expect me to read that menu.

DUNCAN: It's only Italian.

QUENTIN: But I'm appalling at languages. I'll eat what you eat. That salmon over there, that looks nice.

DUNCAN: The Italians are good at liver.

CAROLINE: Chicken livers, you mean?

DUNCAN: Chicken livers? . . . Er, I was thinking of the big flat ones. You know, *liver*.

ARNOLD: I must tell you, Duncan, I am only going to allow you to smoke 4 cigarettes during lunch.

DUNCAN: That's terrible!

ARNOLD: I shall take your cigarettes away and he's going to keep your matches.

DUNCAN: My head'll drop off or something.

ARNOLD: Tell them to bring me the entire menu. Actually, I eat very little because now I want to get the weight down. I eat small meals many times a day which is the secret of balanced weight. And every so often a bowl of ice-cream.

DUNCAN: Does anyone not want poached salmon? Actually, I don't want poached salmon.

ARNOLD: How do you get your hair that colour, Mr Crisp? Blue . . .

QUENTIN: It's powder. You put it into warm water which goes the colour of purple ink. And you just brush it on with a toothbrush which is so much more convenient than all that dividing of the hair into squares.

ARNOLD: Yes, but how do you catch every hair on the whole head?

QUENTIN: If you want to, you can make cupsful of it and pour it over your head. Over and over and over. But the nice thing is you can just touch it up with a toothbrush without any bother. This is a great help. In the days when my hair was red – henna is a real business, it's like mud, and you have to leave it on until it dries. I used to sleep in my henna, then have to dunk the whole thing under water next morning to get the muck out.

DUNCAN: Can we have 4 poached salmon, please?

ARNOLD: I should like some salad.

DUNCAN: Crudités, please.

WAITER: For crudités we have a special sauce.

ARNOLD: I should like an ordinary mixed salad as well.

WAITER: A regular mixed salad *too*?

ARNOLD: Yes. A regular mixed salad.

DUNCAN: In the meantime – crudités . . .

ARNOLD: What does poached salmon come with?

WAITER: It comes with salad.

ARNOLD: Oh . . . but I'll still have a regular mixed salad.

CAROLINE: And could I have some French beans?

WAITER: Vino?

DUNCAN: Have you got any Lambrusco? The fizzy red one. All purple froth.

WAITER: Actually we haven't got.

DUNCAN: Have you got any fizzy white? Fizzy and dry.

WAITER: No, I'm sorry – but we have Frascati.

DUNCAN: Well, if that's what you've got . . . I'm not mad about lunches, are you? They're too early. But this is a nice one.

ARNOLD: The atmosphere here is great. Have you ever been to New York?

QUENTIN: I should love to go but I can't afford it so I am waiting for the paperback publishers to invite me over and give me a ticket.

ARNOLD: I've been doing the same thing all my life. I never paid an airline ticket yet. I wouldn't know where to get one. It's one of the great things that come with the profession.

QUENTIN: This is what I'm hoping for too. A man called Cantor – not Eddie Cantor who sang 'I'm Staying Home To-Night, My Baby and Me' – but a newer one apparently –

CAROLINE: I know Arthur Cantor!

QUENTIN: Aha! We can press you – what's he like?

CAROLINE: Lovely! You might think he was British if you didn't know he was American because he wears herring-bone suits.

QUENTIN: He rang me up. It's the first time anyone has actually rung me up of their own free will.

DUNCAN: But I rang you up of my own free will.

QUENTIN: Then that's 2 people. Mr Cantor said 'Would you go to America?' and I said 'Would you pay my fare?' and there was a long silence.

CAROLINE: Knowing Arthur, there would be.

QUENTIN: And then he said 'You could go on a lecture tour', and I said 'You realise, Mr Cantor, that I don't know anything', and he said 'That doesn't matter', and I said 'What about my sin?', because I should need a visa, you see.

DUNCAN: Your sin?

QUENTIN: Yes, my sin.

DUNCAN: What sin?

QUENTIN: Well, I think I have to undertake not to engage in what they call 'moral turpitude'.

ARNOLD: You do what?

QUENTIN: M-o-r-a-l t-u-r-p-i-t-u-d-e. If being gay is a sin, shall I ever get a visa? I've now got a passport – which has taken a lot of doing. And if Mr Cantor writes me a letter I can hold it up and they might give me a work visa. When George Melly went to America he had the wrong kind of visa and they wouldn't let him do a *thing*. America is full of ladies' guilds, women's societies, the Daughters of the Revulsion. Oscar Wilde went there selling them beauty, so why shouldn't I go there selling them happiness?

DUNCAN: What's this sauce for the crudités?

CAROLINE: It's a dip.

QUENTIN: Mmmmmmmmmm, it's hot, it's salty, it's slightly granular – like being licked by a kitten.

DUNCAN: Funny lumps in it. Don't like the fawny colour.

QUENTIN: How did Mr Schwarzenegger get all that butter?

DUNCAN: Do you want some butter?

QUENTIN: I'd like some of his.

DUNCAN: I don't like this dip very much – as dips go.

CAROLINE: I like it.

DUNCAN: Would you like the lot? Would you like to take it over to your side of the table and keep it there? How long have you been in London, Arnold?

ARNOLD: Er . . . one week.

DUNCAN: It's been all madness, I expect.

ARNOLD: The publicity is very good for *Pumping Iron*. But I won't have more than 3 appointments a day. My agent sets it up.

QUENTIN: Once you have an agent your entire character falls to pieces. Because now when people rush up to me in the street and say 'How are you?' I reply 'I've no idea. You must ask my agent'.

ARNOLD: I've got a very good agent. He's a little agent, which I like.

QUENTIN: I was born helpless. My agent says on such and such a day you will take this train, get out at this station, you will stand there, you will be met. Now if I had to arrange all that myself, I'd never get there.

CAROLINE: I can tell my agent what I want to do now.

DUNCAN: What are you doing now?

CAROLINE: I'm Kitty in *Anna Karenina* on TV.

DUNCAN: I haven't read the book of course.

CAROLINE: It's a wonderful book!

DUNCAN: I know. It's one of the 10 books you read if you can read at all. But I haven't read it.

QUENTIN: The last chapters are absolutely wonderful, when Anna's made up her mind to go to the station and kill herself. You really go there with her.

DUNCAN: That sounds dangerous.

QUENTIN: It was the part Garbo was born to play.

[*Waiter brings on the salmon. Much noise.*]

DUNCAN: This is where I would normally have another

cigarette. Before the fish. I'm sorry about these little holes in my shirt.

ARNOLD: Should one eat the skin of salmon?

DUNCAN: There are lots of minerals in the skin.

ARNOLD: Nobody ever told me about that.

DUNCAN: Nor me. But that must be where they are.

ARNOLD: I was in Austria a few months ago to see my mother and . . . Where are the beans?

[*Arrival of beans.*]

DUNCAN: When you get old will you have to trim off all those extra muscles?

ARNOLD: If you want to be healthy, you have to. Because of the heart.

CAROLINE: I trained as a ballet dancer when I was very young and when you stop, those muscles, they turn to fat so *quickly*.

ARNOLD: Diet is the secret. If you eat the right food the muscle cells won't turn to fat because they can't, they're a different thing. I've lost 25lbs but don't turn fatty. I'm trimming down for my own business which I've had since 1970 – body-building shows we put on, mail-order stuff, some real estate. Now I'm getting into acting, playing this character Conan who's a bit like Superman only much more science fiction. I signed a 5-picture contract with Paramount. We begin next March or April.

DUNCAN: Did you go to this body-building contest in London last night?

ARNOLD: No, but I'm supposed to be presenting the trophy to-day. I'm late already. It's this afternoon. 10 years ago I won my first Mr Universe title right here in London.

QUENTIN: I'm a terrible business man. I haven't the strength of character to direct my own future.

DUNCAN: Oh, you have terrific strength of character.

QUENTIN: But even the public-speaking racket I only did because my agent had taken this little lunchtime theatre and was stuck for somebody to put on and so said to me 'I thought you could go on' and I said 'With what object in mind?' and he said 'You could talk to them' and I said 'Well, what about?' and he said 'It doesn't matter' and then he went off to Spain, so I went on. Now it proves possible to convert my identity into money as well as into a kind of social freedom which I never had before. In times gone by I couldn't have *got into* this restaurant. Somebody would've been on the door to say 'You can't come in, the place is full'. I've remained the same but the times have changed.

DUNCAN: But you are a private Caligula.

QUENTIN: Ha! But the books get written because someone says 'Write a book'.

DUNCAN: You like to be ordered about.

QUENTIN: It can help. When the paperback of *The Naked Civil Servant* came out, I was given a woman who took me to places and said 'Sit here, sign these!' A lot of authors however cannot be treated in this way. It would have been very difficult to get E. M. Forster to run round London in a funny hat like mine. But I love it now because I was waiting to rule the world ever since I was born. When a man called Tom Clarkson asked me years ago 'What do you really want?' I said immediately 'To rule the world'. And he said 'Oh, idiot nonsense, stop going on like that, it's no good talking about it then.' But what else can one want? There's the world. And you want to rule it. And you want people to be pleased to see you. Instead of people saying 'Good God! What's that over there?' and you're trying to look frightfully unconcerned. I now arrive at places and I'm actually welcomed. Now if someone crossed the room and said 'Who the *hell* are you?' one wouldn't think 'Oh God, I wish I'd stayed at home', I would say 'Who would you like me to be?'

DUNCAN: There's a nice story about Noel Coward lunching at the Savoy and Paul Newman came into the restaurant. He eventually spotted Noel Coward and went rushing over and said 'Mr Coward, sir, this is a great honour. My name's Paul Newman.' And Noel Coward said 'Of course it is, dear boy. Now go and finish your lunch.'

ARNOLD: How long ago was that?

DUNCAN: Heaven knows how long ago that was.

ARNOLD: I don't think Paul Newman would rush over to anybody now in that way.

DUNCAN: Really? Oh, that's a shame. That's age.

CAROLINE: The amazing thing about the theatre for me, actually, is that you meet the people who have been your idols. I mean, I see Arnold in this amazing film and now I'm having lunch with him!

ARNOLD: You can have lunch with me any time you like. I've met Jimmy Carter.

DUNCAN: You're giving him body-building lessons, aren't you?

ARNOLD: That's right. And I've met the Kennedys, the top politicians, and they *are* different. They are enormously intelligent. There is a reason why they've got there.

DUNCAN: Really? I'm incredibly cynical about that lot.

ARNOLD: I stayed up in Hyannis Port with the Kennedys this summer and the Shrivers – you know they have their little empires up there – and because they are great themselves, they really appreciate it if someone else achieves something. It doesn't matter if it's a writer or a sportsman or a media person.

QUENTIN: The Kennedys *longed* to be with Sammy Davis Jr. It's quite weird. This I don't understand.

CAROLINE: And Sammy Davis *longed* to meet John Kennedy.

QUENTIN: They must have *rushed* towards one another like planets. I remember Mary Pickford *longed* to shake the hand of Gertrude Stein until she found out that Gertrude Stein *longed* to shake the hand of Mary Pickford.

CAROLINE: More than anything in the world I long to do theatre. I don't want to go inside another television studio for 5 years! Television is like an office job. But you get no money in the theatre of course.

QUENTIN: I only made £350 out of *The Naked Civil Servant* on Thames Television. And out of the showing of it in New York I made 17 pounds 10 shillings.

DUNCAN: 'Langrishe' is a very evocative name. I can see you on a chaise longue, slugging laudanum.

CAROLINE: What is laudanum exactly?

183

DUNCAN: It's very pleasant. 'Schwarzenegger' is a bit of a – it's the opposite of crisp. *Un*crisp.

CAROLINE: Can I have some of that wine?

DUNCAN: Arnold, do you take drugs?

ARNOLD: No.

DUNCAN: I mean steroids.

ARNOLD: Oh them, yes. You have to. Because the other top people do. Maybe it gives you 1% edge – but it ends up the same because the next guy is taking it too.

CAROLINE: What form are they?

ARNOLD: They're pills. It's not known how they work, whether it's physical or psychological. Some university did a test with 2 teams – one team they give steroids to, the other just a white sugar tablet. Both teams gain weight and got stronger at the same rate. But it's all uncertain what they do. Frankly, I don't give a shit so long as it works.

DUNCAN: Have you ever been rolfed?

QUENTIN: Has he ever been what?

ARNOLD: It's that deep deep massage where they make you live your childhood and clear out blocks, yeah, I have that. I think everyone can benefit from rolfing because it goes so deep, the blood flows more freely, the nervous system is refreshed.

DUNCAN: I gather it's rather painful.

ARNOLD: Well, I've loosened my body up quite a bit from training. I already know my body quite well.

CAROLINE: I don't know mine at all.

DUNCAN: Then you must be rolfed. I want to be rolfed.

ARNOLD: I knew a man who was 65 years old and he was into weight-training and yoga and many other kinds of weird exercises which you really couldn't say what they were. He was so amazingly flexible. One of the things he did one morning when I got up was he massaged his own heart. He was moving his heart around – you could see it.

DUNCAN: What about the ribcage?

CAROLINE: Ugh. What good did it do?

ARNOLD: It keeps you alive, I guess.

QUENTIN: There are people who can pass a thin knife behind

184

their windpipe without touching the jugular vein. And they stand there and say 'Shall it bleed?', and when the audience says 'Yes!' the blood flows and when the audience says 'No!' the blood stops and there is no scar.

DUNCAN: I must go to the loo.

CAROLINE: So must I. Can you let me out, Arnold?

ARNOLD: No.

CAROLINE: Oh, Arnold's thighs are so big! Let me out!

DUNCAN: Before I stop, is there anything anyone wants to put on this tape which might actually be an advantage to your various careers rather than a disadvantage?

ARNOLD: I should say that my film *Pumping Iron* is gonna be a big hit in England. It got the greatest reviews in America. And I'm coming out with a book from Simon & Schuster called *Arnold: the Education of a Body-Builder* which will be published here later. Now, Caroline, when is your show coming out?

CAROLINE: It's on television now, *Anna Karenina*, and a lot of it was shot in Budapest and it's a great story if nothing else.

ARNOLD: And 50 million people will look at you and you'll be famous.

CAROLINE: Yes, even though I have a baby. That's what I've been doing to-day, having a baby.

DUNCAN: A baby?

CAROLINE: That's what I've been doing all morning. Having it.

DUNCAN: Er, are you married?

CAROLINE: What? Am I married? No – no, not in real life! I've been having it in the story.

DUNCAN: Ah, I thought maybe you were one of those capable women who let nothing stand in the way of lunch.

ARNOLD: What about you, Quentin? Have you got a show or a book?

QUENTIN: What we are waiting for is to see what they think of the book, *The Naked Civil Servant*, which is coming out in America this minute. And Jack Gold has some idea of making a musical out of it.

CAROLINE: A musical!!?

QUENTIN: That is what we hope. I must say, I would love it. A musical about me.

DUNCAN: Right, well, thanks everyone –

ARNOLD: No, no, wait a minute, you don't get out of it that easy. Now it's your turn. What do you want to sell?

DUNCAN: Oh, I can't – not at my own lunch.

ARNOLD: Sure, you can put it into my mouth if you like. Arnold says this is great and wonderful blah blah blah.

CAROLINE: Mind the glass!! zzrrrrrgghhh?!!!zz z!!!gggrrrr-rszszszsz zzzzzzzzzzzzzz zzzzzzzzzzzzzzzzzz zzzzzzzzzzzzzz zzzzzzzzz!!!!!!!!!!!!!!!!!!

(1978)

TIME, MUSIC & DISEASE
SPECULATIONS WITH SIR FRED HOYLE

SIR FRED HOYLE lives on moorland above Ullswater which is the most beautiful of the lakes in the Lake District, though not the most isolated (it's 20 minutes from a motorway). The fells – the moorland slopes – appear to slide upwards. They slide up the car windows the closer we come until the windows are closed in and the fells lay their large hands on the chest and heart with oppressive strength. Then, on reaching the mountaintop by narrow roads and steep curves – poof! Suddenly it opens out under big clouded sky, fell upon fell receding in waves of dramatic remoteness, lavender and grey and dark green. It is cold and windy up here, with a touch of drizzle, and very bracing. The Hoyles live a little way along on the left.

'The CIA has predicted a corn famine in Russia at the end of the century. Is it possible to predict such a thing?'

'Not at all possible! It's like taking a broker's advice on the Stock Market. If brokers knew the future, they'd be very rich and doing something interesting instead of stock broking.'

'Well, quite a lot of them are – and do.'

'I've got interested in volcanoes. A very large eruption, of which there are one or two every century, will affect the harvests the following year. I discovered that there was a really fantastic eruption in Iceland in 934 – it's plus or minus 2 years because of the ambiguity of the record – they date it from the Greenland ice. Now there's a mysterious thing in British history. In 937 the different groups of Vikings unaccountably came together, and were defeated in battle by the Saxons which was even more surprising because 50 years earlier the Saxons found it hard to cope with even small Viking raids. What this means to me is that the volcano wiped out the food supply in the north, so all the northern peoples, the pagan Vikings and the Christian Vikings and even the northern Celts, joined up and tried to get down south. They were defeated because the Saxons were fed and the Vikings weren't and this put an end to the Viking menace. Historians never say any of this because they are not aware of it.'

*

The Ullswater Hotel, sited on a strand at Glenridding, was opened in 1840 and like so many places is best visited out of season, although at any time it would be a clarifying resort – magical without being sleepy, comfortable without being fashionable (precautionary note: my bedroom is cold).

Dinner time. In the dining-room, which is also the ballroom, the scattered weekending couples often don't talk to each other. The pair at the next table, in their late 30s, both wearing thick navy blue jumpers, don't talk at all – at all – and their faces have soft passive expressions folded down like flaps of uncooked pastry over what they may or may not be feeling. Nor do they look through the French windows to the fell sliding up out of the lake and glowing rich brilliant colours like the particoloured flank of a beast in the setting sun. They don't even look at each other, but gaze at some vacuum hanging motionless in the air between them.

At a table which is several empty tables beyond this couple, a woman talks so much that when she goes to deliver a forkload of food to her mouth, she misses it, and misses not only the mouth but her whole head is missed and the forkload of trout hovers near her ear until she brings it back into her view and starts again and succeeds.

And beyond yet again, on the far side of this white, lightly peopled space, 5 men stand up stiffly and self-consciously and very noisily with screeching of chairs on parquet floor as a woman joins the table. They stand up with a kind of desperation not to do the wrong thing, as if obeying an

188

instruction from boyhood to be on best behaviour in an hotel. The waiters and waitresses too are drilled and at quiet moments during dinner may be seen posted to attention round the room like sentries at a state funeral. But this is not often – the people of Northern England are not cynical or languid – they like their meals served quickly under a bright light – most of the time waiters and waitresses are whizzing round corners at an incline of 60 degrees – and the light blazes from above like imitation sunshine.

Overheard in the Wordsworth Lounge. 'The thing to do is to stop Nigel reacting emotionally.'

'Oh God, that's rich . . . He's no idea what a relationship involves.'

*

Hoyle is eccentric and sometimes dangerous. For a long time he poo-pooed environmental terrors such as the greenhouse effect and the deterioration of the ozone layer. But he usually throws up interesting material in the exercise of his independence. His most recent controversial statement is that life did not arise spontaneously from simple to more complex chemical activity on earth, but was seeded here from outer space. He points out that micro-organisms have the capacity to survive very extreme pressures, temperatures, blasts of radiation, abilities not required on earth but certainly required elsewhere.

'The top of the atmosphere is like a soft cushion, so they land there and work their way down. If it's a bacterium it can fall slowly under gravity – it takes about 3 years to reach the ground. If it's a still smaller particle like a virus it won't fall by itself, but descending air currents can deliver the particle to the region you go up to in a plane where they join up in water. Then it rains or snows.'

'Has influenza been detected in rainwater?'

'No.'

'According to your theory it should be.'

'Yes, but it's so difficult to do, the particles are so microscopic. All sorts of things come and go and are never followed up properly. There was a thing which hit dogs several years ago. It broke out within a few weeks in all parts of the earth. Some said it was due to a wrong vaccine allowed out of the lab, others that it was spread by judges at shows, but no one has any real idea. Then there was a remarkable new venereal disease with horses – it's disappeared now but it was very hard to believe this wasn't something from outside. The historical records are revealing. For instance, whooping cough, which is a disease you can't mistake for anything else. There's no description of whooping cough before 1578AD which is just incredible. Reading the Hippocratic writings of the Greeks, there are some diseases which stand out as absolutely the same as modern diseases. The common cold is clear, mumps is clear, so is TB. But most of the rest you can't make sense of. The obvious interpretation is not that the Greeks couldn't describe things properly, because they could very well, but that these were different diseases.'

Does this mean however that different diseases must come from outer space? Can there not be such a thing as disease evolution within the limits of the earth?

Darwin's achievement was to make the concept of evolution more or less axiomatic, to enable the mind to grasp and manipulate large blocks of time. Where Darwin is more questionable is in believing that the mechanism of evolution is natural selection operating smoothly. The New Darwinists now say that natural selection does not produce smooth changes but abrupt jumps. Hoyle replies that 'the obvious flaw in the New Darwinism is that left to themselves, unaffected from outside, all forms of life are far more likely to change by small steps than by major leaps.'

Is this so? If it is agreed that man inhabits an evolving universe, then all phenomena are subject to pressure. An enclosed system has no need to change, does not want to, but the world about it continues to alter, to evolve. This gives rise to pressure from outside which slowly increases until an adaptation is forced. To an observer this would appear to happen quite abruptly, as a stick when gradually bent suddenly snaps. Growth happens when 'something' enters a system from 'outside' and does not happen otherwise. This applies to all activities, including intellectual ones. Unless

190

periodically breached, the intellect – with all its beliefs – will create a self-limiting circle which is at best anti-growth and may become very destructive.

From the evolutionary point of view, what might be the present pressure on man? It is terrestrialism. Man has outgrown the planet. This pressure can be resolved by nuclear war, disease, famine, or by some form of psychological rather than physical advance. The immediate possibility of nuclear or ecological catastrophe is the specific factor forcing a psychological adaptation or jump.

The capacity for self-destruction is perhaps the mechanism by which the universe localises and eliminates undesirable impulses. If we destroy ourselves, 'stupidity' or 'evil' will have been prevented from further contamination of an evolving universe. This moment will occur in the evolution of every intelligent planet and only the truly intelligent will survive it. Those that do are perforce benign – which means, among other things, that if ever you receive a visitor from outer space you should not be afraid! I have insomnia. But I do not care.

*

'Do you feel, Sir Fred, that theoretical science has reached some kind of limit? Is it possible in physics, for example, to go beyond quantum mechanics without changing disciplines? Perhaps the next step is to connect the quantum universe to the psychological universe and develop unheard-of forms of communication. You have said that communication between the stars is not impossible. You were thinking of technological communication. But just as our DNA is programmed for all sorts of latent characteristics we don't possess or require, so perhaps our brains are already programmed for forms of communication which have yet to come into use. This is often suggested.'

'I think it's very likely. I think we are also programmed with a sense of irritation, of being dissatisfied with things, this sense of curiosity about what the schemes are in the universe, which shows most obviously in mathematics.'

'Have you ever had a supernatural experience?'

'No, I haven't.'

'What is the latest evidence for other intelligent beings in the universe?'

'None. But even if the place was thick with intelligence, how would we know? I don't see how any communication can take place at the level of current human technology. Mind you, the technology in the mid 60s was primitive to what we have now. So doubtless by the next millennium . . .'

'Are there any revolutionary scientific ideas coming out of Russia these days?'

'No, no. All these activities are conditioned by the social background. When a great person occurs he can perhaps break through the restrictions of his own society, in the way that Marlowe broke through into blank verse just by the drive of his own thoughts. But the essence of Russian society is that the State derives its power through the suppression of the individual drive and this is bad for any creative activity. Clearly the Russians have people of high intellectual competence but there is no possibility for a young Russian to think outside set patterns which means that one day Russia will simply run into a stone wall. Conformity is a terrible problem there – and it's becoming a problem in the West too. Government intervention in science is choking it – which is basically, I now see, the reason why I left Cambridge. Science has become a job in which one's prospects are the inverse of what they were when I was young. If you were to succeed in those days, it was by doing something quite *different* from what had gone before. Whereas to-day people tend to get ahead by *claiming* to prove what everybody thinks is already right.'

'Maybe this is to do with the technological skin creeping over the earth. The paradox of technology is that theoretically it liberates the individual from drudgery but in practice it demands a very high degree of standardisation in order to function at all. The great crime of the 21st century will be to murder a machine.'

'But technology,' he says, 'which is tool-making, has been going on for a long time. There's 7 volumes over there called *The History of Technology*. I've often felt this has had more influence on human history than politics or even theoretical ideas. It is amazing how much was discovered technologically before it was understood intellectually.'

Helvellyn is the most remarkable mountain in the district, a narrow spine at 3,000 feet barely the width of a path from which concave slopes drop vertiginously on either side and with tremendous strangeness. To walk along the brow is to walk almost tightrope style along the attenuated apex of a triangular prism. According to the Italian head waiter at the Ullswater Hotel, 'Half a dozen people get killed there every year.'

'How?'

'It's very windy up there and very narrow. They get blown off.'

Notice in St Patrick's Church, Patterdale: *Helvellyn praises God, but please do not bring it into church on your boots.* Both church and churchyard are beautifully kept up. The churchyard is littered with rabbit droppings like heaps of tiny dark chocolate Easter eggs. A sheep is standing on the churchyard wall and stares with those piercing sheep's eyes of which Mervyn Peake wrote in *Boy in Darkness.* The church is plain, swept and polished, designed by Salvin in 1853 after the previous one had been destroyed by a storm.

*

'I'm very unsettled by this fact that because of light years and so on, as you look into space you are looking back in time. This makes the earth the youngest thing in the universe.'

'That's right,' he says.

'But in what sense young?'

'Well, think of it – as you look at galaxies they get younger and younger the further you look. Younger and younger from their own point of view. But from our point of view, back in time, older and older.'

'The earth then is the most highly evolved point in the universe.'

'That's right – if you accept the standard form of cosmology. You can see back in time 10 or 20 billion years, long before the earth came into being.'

'So if you look far enough, you should be able to witness the origin of the universe?'

'That's what some people believe they can see. They feel they are looking at one phenomenon, and going right back to the very beginning they think they arrive at the microwave background, the so-called echo of the original Big Bang. But I'm not so sure that's what it is – this is one of the things I'm working on at the moment.'

'But every system in functioning at all produces an agitation. Why should the microwave background be an echo from the past and not the murmur of the continuous present?'

'Because you can't observe the present, except very locally. That's the whole point. And of course there is a lot of noise around locally.'

'Then the only way out of this observation trap, is to escape from the traditional concept of time.'

'My view is that really the universe is a backdrop, a decor,' he says. 'We are not being controlled by the gross change of the whole universe. So this business about what is young or old doesn't apply. You have a mix of ages in all localities. This is a very different approach to cosmology. But the only piece of evidence for the standard view is the microwave background.'

'You argue for the operation of intelligence in the evolution of the universe. What is intelligence?'

'There are patterns of order to events. Intelligence is the ability to influence the pattern of events.'

'How does this influence exert itself?'

'It must be some sort of overt physical action. The level of intelligence I would define by the degree of complexity of the patterns. Clearly a mouse can affect the patterns to some extent; when we get up to humans we can affect a broader pattern of events; and a higher intelligence a broader pattern still.'

'Intelligence then is different from awareness. Intelligence is active. Intelligence may be said to exert its influence by making the correct choice from a number of options. This implies objective. A choice is correct when it advances some purpose.'

'With purpose one's in a more speculative field,' he replies.

'You've written – *Non-living processes tend to destroy*

194

order. Is this true? Take the example of rain falling on a landscape.'

'The strict statement is that if the environment is enclosed, natural processes always tend to a larger measure of disorder. With rain you bring in a phenomenon that doesn't belong wholly to the earth.'

'Give me an example of a non-living process which destroys order.'

'Drop a cup on a stone floor.'

'That's not a process, that's an event. And if you multiplied the event into a process what you'd eventually get is, well, the soil of the earth which comes about through the action of gravity on the environment.'

'All right,' he says, and thinks. 'What about . . . your car when you drive it gradually wears out.'

'So do clothes. These are objects of artifice. I know what you are proposing – the idea of entropy. Why do I feel there is something preposterous about entropy? As soon as you try to apply it to real situations, it doesn't work. Perhaps this is because it excludes *life*. The creation of order demands a matrix from which to arise and this matrix is created by disorder.'

'An ordered state is indeed one with very few possibilities,' he says. 'And a disordered state has many possibilities. If you take the solar system as your enclosed system, then all the natural processes get more disordered as time goes on.'

'I really do think this is a barmy way of trying to understand things, that the universe is running down into a sort of soup and so forth. Somehow I feel that the concept of entropy is a conceptual error in exactly the way that, say, the concept of phlogiston was wrong, that is, *almost* possible but from hindsight totally naïve. There is also the question of how one defines living and non-living. This is all very arrogant of me, by the way, since I am not a trained scientist.'

'Usually people define living in a somewhat arbitrary way. The material has to be of a certain chemical kind and it has to replicate itself rather precisely.'

*

195

Let us rethink the whole entropy-based outlook. Let us rewrite Hoyle's maxim above: non-living processes tend to produce simplicity from complexity. Then consider the following.

The phenomenal world is not in stasis. 'Enclosed systems' are dubious quantities when considering fundamental laws. Stop the world, I want to get off? Not possible. When you stop the world – it vanishes.

The universe is binary in structure. It exists because of the reciprocity between opposites. At any one moment, a phenomenon is the product of 2 *contradictory* procedures. If something is true, its opposite is also true.

Therefore – living processes tend to produce complexity from simplicity.

These 2 procedures occur simultaneously.

Hence we are subject to 2 streams of time. In physics quantum signals are received from the future. In man all significant decisions are based on future events. All decisions based on past events reduce energy and performance: in physics this is stability sliding into entropy; in human life it is passivity sliding into depression. Universal life is not characterised by decisions based on past events. Certain psychologists say that to reach an objective, one should concentrate on it, plant the attention in the future and let one's situation be slowly absorbed by it. This technique is designed to reduce to a minimum the friction from the present. The role of the conscious will: sometimes it is required, sometimes its absence is required.

The 2 streams of time, acting simultaneously, are:–

(1) Evolution towards simplicity, i.e. from past cause to present effect (the machine wears out).

(2) Evolution towards complexity, i.e. from future cause to present effect (the machine gets built).

That's sorted that out. Sleep like a babe.

*

'How would you define the experience of inspiration?'

'It often happens that adequate information to solve a problem is stored in the brain but that the information is disordered. Inspiration is what happens when we order it. But as Thomas Edison said, invention is 1% inspiration and 99% perspiration – that's about right. What makes one person more talented than another? It's a hard question. Is it luck? I think it comes down to energy. Have you ever considered the effort required merely to copy out the plays of Shakespeare?'

'Oh, very often.'

'Wagner – imagine writing all those operas.'

'But of course what one sees here is not the essential task but the by-product of some more fundamental process.'

'There's also the question of the intensity of the work,' he adds.

'Oh God, yes, the problem of quality . . . Most writers and artists surely have, or aspire to, a work routine whose most desirable characteristic is the absence of external events. This allows the material to flow into orderly structures. But in my experience it's rarely a comfortable process – there's always a battle on. I like writing in different places, not just one place. I fall into routines very easily – so it's important to disturb them.'

'Inspiration is an abnormal ability to work hard. But without the initial level of talent – well, there's no question but that Mozart was something more than a person who spent a lot of time writing music.'

'Oh, hard work does not of itself guarantee anything.'

'I've also met the obverse,' he says. 'People who are clearly very talented but they have about as much energy as a fly. They could manage about one bar of music a day.'

'This may be sloth. It could also be a kind of perfectionism, getting trapped in that, which links up with entropy again and the law of diminishing returns.'

'Genius is always said to have an infinite capacity for taking pains. A good example of that,' he says, 'was when Diabelli sent his little waltz round all the composers of Europe asking if they would write one variation each. A friend of mine has studied the results and tells me that, after Beethoven's, the best are the one by Schubert and the one by Liszt who was 11 at the time. Almost everybody managed one good idea. When Beethoven turned to it however he wrote 33 variations in 2 months, one every 2 days. And if you examine his sketchbooks he wrote each one of these 33 about half a dozen different ways to make sure he'd got it exactly right. He was 54, he was not a fit man, and these are said to be the finest set of dynamic variations ever written. You have something here allied to ability but it implies a measure of concentration on the job which is abnormal.'

'Passion?'

'That's right.'

'What is the function of music in human life?'

'I wouldn't have thought anything,' he says.

'It must have a function otherwise it wouldn't exist – that's my position.' (Which echoes one of Hoyle's statements on quantum mechanics: *the modern idea being not so much to say what a particle is as to specify what it does.*)

'Then it probably has some relation to the larger scale organisation of the brain. We don't know how the brain organises its information but there must be electrical rhythms there.'

'Music of course is always connected with dance, anthropologically.'

'Dance is also connected to the rhythms of the brain,' he says.

'Yes? Pure dance is the only art form in which form and content are identical – Yeats made much of this. To dance is a catharsis.'

'Maybe these things have a function rather like religion, of keeping us orientated the right way.'

*

The Times reports: *Mrs Margaret Hogg, aged 37, whose body was found in Wastwater in the Lake District, died from manual strangulation, an inquest in Whitehaven, Cumbria, was told.*

Mrs Hogg, who disappeared from her house 8 years ago, was found in a 100 feet of water and identified through dental records.

*

'I think Beethoven was about 37 at the time, in his very powerful 5th Symphony days,' says Sir Fred, 'and there was a Russian ambassador to Vienna called Razumovsky who commissioned him to write what became the famous Razumovsky quartets. There is one movement, the adagio of the second quartet, and it's said that Beethoven went out and looked at the stars for over an hour as he worked out that movement. And he's hit it absolutely right, the way a scientist feels, which is not oh, isn't astronomy wonderful, lovely sparkling stars. It's very deep, wonderfully controlled emotions. Do the arts bring an order to extreme feelings? Is the species programmed to be protected by such things from its own destructive emotions? We'll know in the next 20 years or so. The terrible danger is that we've already committed ourselves to the final disaster.'

'An individual attains awareness when he knows he can end his own life – this separates him from the animals. But it doesn't mean that everyone goes round committing suicide.'

'In the 1960s it would have been a question of committing suicide,' he says. 'Not now. Do you drive in mist? I used to think that if I could see 10 cat's-eyes ahead I was OK. When it gets down to 3 or 4 cat's-eyes, I begin to feel uncomfortable, I'd like to get off the road. If you cut the vision down, there's a certain moment at which you can't avoid an accident. It's just a matter of waiting until something happens. And this is what is happening with nuclear arms. The margin for control is getting narrower and narrower. You don't want to have an accident in your car. The political leaders don't want to have a nuclear war. But the mist is closing in on them. Do you realise that to-day the time you have for replying to a first strike is down to 5 minutes? The weight of a first strike is so enormous that it's a huge advantage to make it. The counter-measures are down to a 5 minute window. There just isn't time to consult the politicians. If the politician is in the lavatory – it's over. It's like noughts and crosses. The one who goes first will win.'

'Not win exactly – will shrivel up second. Isn't 5 minutes enough to launch a counter-offensive?'

'It is theoretically, but the point is – you have to check that it's not a false alarm for example, that it's a genuine attack.

Otherwise your counter-offensive will be an accidental first strike – which is a very big danger now. You have to make sure that it's not a false signal, or that it's not some colleague who's gone off his head. You have to make sure all your equipment is working properly. There's a lot to do in 5 minutes. But eventually it will be 4 minutes. Then one minute. In the 1960s it was half an hour. Plenty of time. You could get on the phone to the enemy. Not now . . .'

'Can anything be done to prevent technology forcing us to disaster?'

'The counter-pressures are not negligible. There is fear around. But it's like going to the very brink of the volcano's crater.'

The turn of this conversation has made me nervous (and soon after it, there was Chernobyl – and coming up fast on the outside and possibly overtaking the threat of nuclear catastrophe is the threat of ecological catastrophe). Outside the great fells tilt across each other with smears of brooding colour under an epic sky. It is 1.30pm and the wind has dropped completely. The drizzle has petered out and the air is clear and dry. Mankind is at lunch. The landscape is absolutely silent, as though enthralled by what's going to happen next.

*

Overheard in the Wordsworth Lounge at the Ullswater: a man and woman having brandy after lunch.

'Never. Never. Not after what she said on Boxing Day,' says the woman.

'Don't keep on,' says the man.

'Do you expect me to forget it?'

'Then I should have it out with him.'

'With Nigel? Don't be so bloody stupid.'

'It was a joke.'

'Oh . . .'

(1984)

FROM RUSSIA WITH FREAKS

Slava Tsukerman

LIQUID SKY, A surprising international hit in the weirdness category, is about aliens from outer space who attach themselves to the bisexual world of New York's New Wave/fashion/heroin set, in search of a chemical secreted by humans during orgasm. It stars Anne Carlisle as the model they all want to love or, failing that, rape – she also plays a male model junky and therefore gets a chance to make limp love to herself in the ever shuffling equations of sex, identity, and death. But the dominant performance is the baleful, glittering presence of New York as a physical structure, almost as a breathing electronic organism, against which the characters play like decomposing archetypes. Manhattan has never looked creepier, or more majestic. The film is full of sick humour, explosions of vice, video fun and dazzling sleaze, and like Russ Meyer's *Beyond The Valley Of The Dolls* or Derek Jarman's *Jubilee*, is often at its funniest when at its most deadpan.

'I wanted some Brechtian quality of detachment,' says Slava Tsukerman, the director, in a pub in Waterloo – it is crowded because everyone has been evicted by the police from a dance event by a beat group called Test Department under some big black brick arches nearby. He is happy to find himself surrounded by green spiky hair and the constant squeak and crunch of black leather. His own hair is rather odd, bald on top but with long ringlets flowing out of the neck and over his mackintosh. Mr Tsukerman is given to mirth generally, which is just as well since he is a Russian Jew born in Moscow in 1939, who arrived in New York in 1976 with his Russian wife.

'These New Wave people I use are already extreme people who make a theatre of life, so when you film them it's like double theatre. My feeling is the more ambiguous the film, the better – including the comedy.' His wife is in it too. She plays the fashion editor with cold, lesbian-style chic.

'What's Russian humour like?'

'. . . That's a good question . . .' (mirth).

'An awfully long wait for an answer.'

Mirth. 'I just want to be . . . fair. I don't want to tell you there's no such thing because there is such a thing . . . I just can't think of any examples.' (Mirth).

'Well, I know one Russian joke. What's 10 miles long and eats cabbage? Answer: the Moscow Meat Queue.'

'The British tradition of dry black humour,' says Slava, 'is very like Russian humour. But Russians get very sad. It's a national characteristic.'

Liquid Sky, with its oriental sense of colour and display, is a celebration of his own freedom too. It has at times a quite luxurious obscenity. 'I find decadence very good for showing the problems of society.' If this was his intention, it happily got mislaid along the way.

And 'Why do you call it decadence? I'd have thought these excesses were a result of energetic development.'

'This modern New York world – I don't call it decadent, the Americans do. They love to think of it as decadent. Of course although it is modern world, it isn't necessarily new. Necrophilia which we have in the film for example has been around a long long time.'

This is also his first feature in the West, and by some fluke the first feature film ever made by a Russian emigré in the USA. Eisenstein tried and failed. Where did the money come from?

'A real-estate developer in Pennsylvania. Surprisingly easy it turns out. Like my leaving Russia – for the visa I wait only 1½ months. It was good timing, Nixon's visit or something. Of course the moment you apply for the visa you are outlawed, so you *have* to get it or your life is finished. I leave Russia for Israel April 15th, 1973 – *Liquid Sky* opened in United States April 15th, 1983. Another piece of synchronicity: my Russian film career began with 20 minute short *I Believe In Spring* which won a prize at Montreal Festival in 1962, although the authorities didn't tell me that I won a prize. They were always so mean like that. I had to read it somewhere in a magazine. And my American career begins with the prize for Originality at Montreal 1982.'

'Did you train as a film-maker in Russia?'

'No, as a construction engineer.' Then he registered as an 'amateur film-maker', an official status (and necessary too since you could not buy raw film in Russian shops), and began making science documentaries. 'It's better now than in Stalin's time. In the last year of his life, 1953, only 2 films were made in Russia because Stalin was editing them himself and if he didn't like it you were killed. But comparing it to Krushchev's revolution, which was that short spring I once believed in, 1957–61, it's worse now. If you do anything unofficially, they put you in prison.'

'But Tarkovsky for example can work abroad now.'

'Yes, this is new. When I left it was impossible to imagine any director with Russian passport could make a film outside Russia. Now 2 have done it – Tarkovsky and Konchalovsky. But the most talented Russian film-maker, Paradjanov, who made *The Colour of Pomegranates*, he's only just out of prison.'

Encouraged by Kuleshov, the teacher of Pudovkin, Tsukerman began to develop a genre of his own at the Central Science Film Studio in Moscow, imaginative abstract films on science, philosophy, mathematics. 'It was a good time for this. There was a cult of science in Russia around 1970. A book about quantum mechanics and the theory of relativity was number one bestseller in the country.'

'Do you think we have a good picture of life in Russia?'

Mirth. 'I had breakfast this morning with some young people and one of them said he thought the American press just as controlled by the government as the Russian press. So the first thing I have to explain is that there is no press in Russia, just government clerks releasing certain things. You cannot imagine what it's like to live under *total control*. But nobody believes propaganda any more in Russia, nobody believes in this perfect future society which is an outdated eighteenth century rationalist idea.'

'You mean, the fallacy of all religious or political mania: destroy people today for a better tomorrow.'

'It's ridiculous. But propaganda can still be powerful even when you don't believe it. For example, I expected very much to be homesick. This is one of their big points. If you read books about Rachmaninov or Stravinsky they say they suffered tremendously abroad from homesickness and never create anything after they leave Russia. I knew this was propaganda, I knew that when they say you cannot cross that border, immediately you want to go, I knew that the alternative was to stay, to drink vodka and slowly die, but still I was frightened, sitting in a small restaurant in Moscow a couple of days before I left, feeling really terrible like it's the last time I can ever hear Russian conversation. But in New York there are almost as many Russian restaurants as in Moscow and crowds of people speaking Russian everywhere.'

'The USA and Russia have a lot of surprising parallels.'

'Yes, my first impression of New York is that this is like Moscow, with the crowds running in the street and big square apartment blocks.'

'Say something good about life in Moscow.'

'The greatest Russian specialist in the world is a British person called Dewhurst, the only person who has read everything written in Russian, every book, every newspaper – no Russian would be permitted to do this. He came to Israel to talk with Russian immigrants and his main reaction to us was amusement. How could we do it? How could we leave such a fantastic country with such a high intellectual life? And it's true – the only place you have crowds of people discussing modern poetry going from party to party all through the night is Russia.' This appears to illustrate the principle that intellectual activity increases with physical repression. 'Exactly. They talk because they cannot do anything. If you do anything you go to prison. After years in Israel we had a first letter from our good friend in Moscow. It was a long letter and maybe 90% of it was her describing street buildings – 2 years we don't talk, and when we communicate at last, she is analysing street architecture! It was like getting a letter from a psychiatric hospital. She was terrified of writing anything personal, intimate. So the good thing about Moscow is also the bad thing. And it's the same in America. What's good about it is what's bad. American society is too healthy to have culture. American audience goes to the cinema like going to a restaurant – it wants only to be pleased. If you disturb them, they hate it.'

'Presumably *Liquid Sky* cannot be shown in Russia.'

'Oh, never. They are repressed about everything including sex. All Communist societies are very repressed sexually.'

'Do you know Norman Mailer's remark about an important key to totalitarianism is the fear of orgasm?'

'This is absolutely true. I used to think that Catholic countries are the most restricted, like Italy, but an Italian producer is going to show *Liquid Sky* on Italian television.'

'It would be more the case with Northern Catholicism, Irish or Polish, which are heavily sin-orientated. But from this point of view Italy is more Mediterranean and pagan and physically at ease.'

'We thought the best market was going to be Japan but it is completely impossible to sell the film there because, although they make the world's most violent films, they have the strictest censorship in the world for drugs – you cannot even mention drugs on the screen. But we've had great success in the Philippines. And fantastic success in Australia where it was voted Best Film at the Sydney Festival.'

'Has its success taken you by surprise?'

'Success never takes you by surprise. You always expect more.' Mirth. The pub closes. Green hair and black leather diffuse into the wintry night.

LOADED

GRAHAM GREENE AT HOME IN ANTIBES

IT ISN'T EASY getting to see Graham Greene. His publishers said it was extremely unlikely he would agree to be interviewed and they were right. Via his sister who lives in England, he said no with the automatic reflex of a man accustomed to tiresome approaches. A month or so later he said no again. Then the Nice Affair broke, Greene's personal J'Accuse crusade against the Riviera mafia or 'milieu', triggered by what he regarded as the cruel victimisation of the daughter of his best friends in France, Mr and Mrs Cloetta. Then a new novel, *Monsignor Quixote*, was announced by the Bodley Head. And a couple of months later he said about an interview – no. Then he said yes.

'I have a Spanish priest staying,' he elaborated on the telephone after I had been vouchsafed the private number by his sister, 'until the 13th but after that everything is clear – in principle. I have to go to Paris to see my lawyers at some point. When, I'm not sure.'

Graham Greene lives in Antibes on the Côte d'Azur. I was already driving down to stay with people, and it was agreed that a specific time to meet him should be arranged when I arrived in the South of France. From Roussillon in the Vaucluse I phoned every day for a week but there was no reply. From Saint Tropez I rang again and finally on the tenth day he picked up the phone and said – no, he'd changed his mind, I couldn't see him, he was very sorry, he was too busy. He didn't slam the receiver down exactly, just sort of dropped it by accident. 'I'm busy' from writers and artists usually means 'Please don't prod – I'm feeling too raw'.

I was annoyed. I gave him a couple of days for his moods to fluctuate – which they obviously do a great deal – into a sweeter configuration and tried again.

'Oh yes, look, I'm sorry if I was, ha, rather short on the phone the other day but I'd just got back from London and was rather tired and before that I'd been with my lawyers in Paris who'd told me not to see anyone and the *Sunday Times* were here and I do apologise and . . . well, when would you like to come over?'

Very soon was wisest.

Graham Greene is the world's most famous living novelist. He has created his own world, Greeneland, a place of dingey but crucial events. He is the chronicler of the white man's, especially the Englishman's, post-imperial fatigue. His technical gifts are for narrative suspense, sinewy prose, and the sudden simile. 'Daintry's smile resembled the painful re-opening of a wound' (*The Human Factor*) is one of the great 20th century sentences. His success with the public comes from having written from the position of an ordinary man in an extraordinary world. There is a humility here which is attractive; at the same time this has imparted something commonplace and uneven to his writing, so that when Julian Symons writes 'Greene's novels are like Kafka jazzed up,' one feels that this is precisely what they should be like but aren't.

He is at pains to avoid being a writer of the mandarin or over-literary kind. He speaks unaffectedly in a clear voice with a slight lisp and without much concern for the shape of his remarks. He is determinedly unromantic. His character is full of fear but comes across as that of a regular modern neurotic rather than that of a tormented soul.

'Nobody who lives escapes a private agony,' he once wrote. Greene has been reticent about his private life without making any secret of the pain it has caused him. So he will explain in his autobiography, for example, how as a boy he played Russian roulette with himself to stimulate his flagging adrenalin, but will not give the reader any concrete picture of the circumstances in which his desperation arose. As a result one obtains from his autobiographical books the impression of a man trying to elude direct human gaze by arranging all human events into convenient generalisations and abstract ideas.

207

Therefore I was much more interested in finding out what he was like as a human being than as a writer. Catholicism I avoided taking up – it has undermined Greene as a truly major artist and there was every reason to suppose it would have a similarly stultifying effect on the conversation. Catholicism trivialises much of his work: the novels are going wonderfully well, then this voodoo comes in at an oblique angle and the whole thing collapses emotionally, intellectually. It's the same with the later works of Evelyn Waugh. In the 20th century no writer can retreat into established religions (any more than he can into party politics) without producing an embarrassing effect.

And I didn't want to go too deeply into the Nice Affair. One admires his seriousness of purpose at an age when most men have given up but I suspected the legal situation might cause him to freeze or simply refer me to the official publications.* Besides, I discovered he was having an affair with Mrs Cloetta – strictly unofficially – and having lost the interview once, I didn't want to lose it again.

Graham Greene was born in 1905. One was prepared for a prickly old man, small, wiry, profoundly disgruntled, self-pitying. Not a bit of it. He is immensely tall, skinny and languid, with pale blue drooping eyes. He looks far younger than he is – so much so that there is something artificial in his appearance. His manner was genial and open, with the assurance of one who has travelled successfully, and he ducked just one question. He is not complacent. In all but years he is a middle-aged man with things to do. Yet he doesn't strike one as generous or a man of large culture. There is something parsimonious in his make-up. He inhabits pokey accommodation from choice and is only comfortable living in small 2-room flats, the womb that he can account for in a glance. His paranoia can't bear the idea of rooms beyond rooms. And he really doesn't like people. He likes characters. Maybe he uses his books to bridge the gap between himself and the rest of the world created by his dislike of people.

* Greene accused the Mayor of Nice of being involved with organised crime. The Town Hall sued Greene, and won, but the Mayor later fled to Latin America to escape financial scandals.

In 2 respects only was his behaviour noticeably curious and this was sufficient to give the entire encounter a Magritte-like quality, of the extremely unusual nestling within the quotidian normal (further enhanced by a small but very Greene-ish event which took place after the interview). Firstly, halfway through the conversation there was enormously loud cheering from a crowd outside on the main road that runs alongside the port. It went on for several minutes. When eventually I asked him what the noise was, he replied 'What noise?' Secondly, although I had driven a long way on a hot afternoon after a lot of bother, it never occurred to him once to offer me a drink or refreshment of any sort as we talked in his tiny, smart, modern flat, shaded by orange and brown striped awnings, with its wide plate-glass view crowded with sunshine, battlements and boats, in a building called La Résidence des Fleurs.

GG: I warn you, I have a terrible effect on those tape machines, the way my old friend Claud Cockburn did on cars.

DF: Well, let's see – when did you last live in England?

GG: I stopped living in England on January 1st, 1966.

DF: Where'd you been resident?

GG: I'd been living in Albany, Piccadilly.

DF: What made you leave?

GG: One – I got very bad pneumonia in Moscow in 1961 and the doctors advised me to keep away during English winters. So I began to rent an apartment down here. And then I found I liked Antibes and decided to leave England for good. Also at that time authors were more privileged in France than they are now.

DF: Tax reasons?

GG: Yes. We did get an automatic allowance for expenses so that one didn't have to send in every bill and so on, but that ceased a few years after I came here. It was for writers and the liberal professions – professors, doctors, lawyers, artists.

DF: What do you dislike about England?

GG: I don't dislike anything about England. I like the English countryside particularly. I liked that part of London where I lived. Before I moved to Albany I had a little flat in St James's Street. But I couldn't work in London. I used to go away to Brighton or somewhere else when I found I had difficulties with work. I found I could work better down here.

DF: What made you choose Antibes? Are you fond of boating?

GG: I'm fond of my friends' boats. It was the one place in the south which I'd liked. I used to come here 1947/48/49 because a great friend of mine, Alexander Korda, used to keep a boat in the port here and we used to go off on voyages together, and even to-day Antibes is the only place on the Côte where I would want to live. The country behind is much nicer in a way but I haven't got a car so it would be awkward to live there.

DF: Do you drive?

GG: I haven't driven since I was in West Africa in 1943.

DF: Do you have many friends down here?

GG: Yes, quite a number.

DF: And you go out a lot?

GG: Oh, yes.

DF: Do you have a favourite restaurant in Antibes?

GG: I've got 3 and I divide between them. Felix au Port where I've just come from lunch with friends. The Venise which is down a side street near here. And the Auberge Provençale which is in the Place Nationale. But alas at the moment the Venise is closed at lunchtime and the Auberge is closed completely for 2 weeks, so most of my time is at the Felix au Port which is the one I've known longest and where I feel completely at home.

DF: Do you like the French?

GG: On the whole, yes.

DF: Is there still a coherent English colony on the Côte d'Azur?

GG: There may be. But I've been rather careful to avoid it. I've got 2 English friends in Monte Carlo, 2 English friends up at Vence. But otherwise my friends are mainly French.

DF: From the sound of your address I imagined you doing a little gardening to relax.

GG: Ha, no, not a bit, nothing like that. As you can see, there isn't a garden. I have a girl who comes in twice a week to do washing up and cleaning and she does a bit of gardening on this terrace or balcony.

DF: What diet do you favour?

GG: None at all. I have a very small appetite and I like simple food.

DF: You are surprisingly thin – have you always been this thin?

GG: I've put on weight since I came to France but I remain fairly stable at just under 80 kilos.

DF: Do you take any regular exercise?

GG: I go shopping. And I have a friend with a dog and we go for walks every day.

DF: And your health is good? I must say it seems to be exceptionally so.

GG: Yes, it is. I had an operation – a fairly major one but not a serious one – about 3 or 4 years ago, cutting out part of my intestines, but it's all gone well.

DF: I always think of writing as an unhealthy profession. Unless one does something very healthy apart from writing.

GG: I've never done anything healthy.

DF: You've never suffered from backache, dizziness, grogginess?

GG: Occasionally a slight giddiness because in writing one remains in a rather fixed position.

DF: You live alone?

GG: Well, ha, that's a major question which I prefer not to answer.

DF: In the past has your preference been for living alone?

GG: Living partly alone for work purposes, but never living completely alone.

DF: When did you get married?

GG: Oh, 19 . . . I always forget whether it was 1927 or 1929.

211

DF: You have a daughter.

GG: One daughter and one son. My daughter lives in Switzerland with her two children and my son lives in Devonshire. [No socially sensitive pedantry in Greene; Evelyn Waugh would never have been caught calling Devon 'Devonshire'.]

DF: Are you fond of children?

GG: I'm not fond of babies very much. But children are reasonably . . . fun. I'm on very good relations with my two children and my two grand-children who are now practically grown-up.

DF: Was loneliness ever a problem?

GG: Not a real problem. I always took a certain holiday away from my family, perhaps up to a year. Loneliness is not a problem, except when things are not going right. Then it becomes a problem.

DF: Is your wife dead?

GG: No.

DF: But you don't live together.

GG: We've been separated since . . . 1949, I think it is.

DF: You never wanted to marry again?

GG: It doesn't mean one lives a bachelor life. But I'm a Catholic and my wife is a Catholic and it seems unnecessary to go through a divorce.

DF: What are the dangers of success?

GG: Success has two aspects. One loses anonymity. Anonymity is important for a writer, for a novelist anyway. At the same time there are certain advantages — one can call on help more easily if one is in a foreign country, and so on. But I'm not sure if overall one gains or loses.

DF: Does it alter you in any deeper way?

GG: I don't think so.

DF: Have you enjoyed your success?

GG: I don't think I contemplate it. And I don't really realise it.

DF: Then, are you aware of the opposite?

GG: One's aware of failure, yes.

DF: What is your greatest failure?

GG: Some of my early books were very bad failures, I think.

Not from the commercial point of view but from the point of view of the writing. They were failures in both, luckily. But one is far more conscious of the failures in personal relations than the ones in writing. Really I would say that one's failures were in personal relations.

DF: Does it help a writer to be rich?

GG: I don't consider myself very rich really because I've got six people dependent on me. I'm not a bachelor in the Somerset Maugham sense.

DF: He also had a number of people looking to him.

GG: He had a wife for a time, but he didn't have much else, did he?

DF: A few boyfriends, a daughter.

GG: I don't have even girlfriends dependent on me, but I have a wife, a daughter, a son, two grand-children, and – well, there's quite a lot. I'm not rich but I'm well off.

DF: It wasn't always the case, was it?

GG: No.

DF: Do you look back with any affection to the days of struggle?

GG: No. They were very anxious days. I was in debt to my publishers from the time I left *The Times* in 1930 until the eve of the war in 1939 when *Brighton Rock* sold 8,000 copies and just put me out of debt.

DF: So you came off the breadline with *Brighton Rock*? In your mid-thirties.

GG: Yes. I'd been going on with the help of reviewing in the *Spectator* every fortnight. I reviewed novels and they paid me £5 a fortnight. One would have 4 or 5 novels in one's package every 2 weeks and one could sell them to the bookshop at half price which again helped. And from 1935 I reviewed films for the *Spectator* too. One managed.

DF: How did you discover the facts of life?

GG: My elder brother, who was going to be a doctor, had medical books and we shared a room together so I was able to get the general idea, but I suppose – I don't think I had a woman before I was . . . 19.

DF: Was this first experience of a woman important to you?

213

GG: Not in the least important. And not a success either.

DF: Does it help a writer to be in love?

GG: Love can enlarge one's experience a little bit and one's sympathy a little bit – and it can of course be a great distraction.

DF: Malcolm Muggeridge once said about you 'Where Graham is, sin stops.' What do you think he meant by that?

GG: What was that again? Where Graham is . . .? I haven't the faintest idea what he meant by that. Malcolm is, er . . . I wouldn't trust Malcolm very far.

DF: Was he ever a crony of yours particularly?

GG: We knew each other quite well before the war and I got him his job in the Secret Service where he was not a success.

DF: What was your position in the Secret Service?

GG: Oh, I'd only been in for a week or so. I was recruited by my sister who'd been in it before the war. They wanted somebody with a little experience of Africa. They wanted somebody in West Africa which was to be me, and also somebody in East Africa in Lourenço Marques and so I suggested Malcolm Muggeridge who was then a sergeant or something in the Field Security Police and he had to drive a motorcycle in all sorts of weathers and I thought he would really be more comfortable in the Secret Service.

DF: You talk about it as if it were a golf club.

GG: Well, it was during the war. And, you see, it wasn't all that covert. In West Africa I had a cover, which was a rather silly one, of being CID Special Branch. This meant that all my telegrams had to come through a local police station but in a code which the police couldn't read and I had to send my cables back through the police in a code they couldn't read. Which might have made things very difficult with the Commissioner of Police who might have thought he was being cut out. But in fact we became very good friends and I had no trouble from him at all. But it wasn't very exciting work. When I got back to England I joined the counter-espionage group of MI6,

214

which was called Section 5, with Kim Philby. We were in counter-espionage in the Iberian Peninsula against the Abwehr which was the official German secret service before Himmler came along with his own.

DF: Was your life ever in danger?

GG: No, no.

DF: Has it ever been?

GG: I felt a bit of danger in Viet Nam once. And I felt a bit of danger on the Suez Canal once.

DF: Apart of course from your own exertions.

GG: The Russian roulette thing, yes.

DF: Sexual considerations aside, do you like women's company?

GG: Yes, I do.

DF: Who is your favourite actress?

GG: That's a difficult question.

DF: As a film critic you were incredibly aggressive.

GG: I'm not a regular film-goer now. I don't regard the cinema as necessarily acting, do you? I think of acting as the stage. Dorothy Tutin I liked enormously. She acted in my first play brilliantly and I've seen her since in a Pinter. But I don't feel close to the theatre or the cinema now.

DF: You don't have a video machine?

GG: No. I've got that little television over there [an extremely tiny portable is perched like a small piece of modern sculpture on a flimsy table] for news and the political programmes. I don't watch anything else.

DF: Who is the most charismatic person you've ever met?

GG: I don't think any politician. A man whom I grew very fond of and who was killed 2 years ago, Omar Torrijos, I think he had it. He was a general in Panama. And for 4 years I used to go out to Panama and visit. He was killed in a so-called aeroplane accident just as I'd packed to go back to Panama in August of . . . was it last year or the year before? He had this special quality. And a great sense of humour. In that tiny country of Panama he had an enormous influence and on the whole of Central America. He was an invaluable help to the Sandinistas in driving out Somoza. He enabled me to meet the guerillas

215

both in Salvador and Nicaragua. He was a romantic. He had the dream of making the whole of Central America social democratic non-Marxist which would be independent of the United States and at the same time no menace to the United States. His sense of humour – for example he gave me a Panamanian diplomatic passport and took me in his entourage as one of the Panamanian delegates to the signing of the Canal Treaty in Washington. It amused him. And it amused me too because I could only obtain a visa for the United States by giving notice to the American Attorney General and saying on which plane one was coming and on which plane one was leaving and limited to a stay of 3 weeks. However with Torrijos one came flying in at a military airport with the marines all lined up in the dark and a red carpet rolled out and nobody even noticed I was there. Torrijos was a mixture of this very down-to-earth human quality – he liked women, he liked drink, he liked laughter – and this romantic aim and a courage which was never in fact put to the test. He was half longing for a confrontation with the United States if the treaty hadn't gone through. He told me he could hold out in Panama City for 48 hours, and after that in the mountains and the jungle for another 2 years. And he said 'They don't quite realise it but for the first time since the American Civil War there will be a large number of American civilians directly in the firing line, 40,000 of them in the Canal Zone.'

DF: American dislike of you – is that from Haiti days?

GG: No. I think it comes from the Viet Nam days. But I don't think there is any hatred now. It dates back really to McCarthy. Because I had been while at Oxford [*Second in Modern History*] a member of the Communist Party for 4 weeks. I'd told that to a *Time* magazine man in about 1950. They were doing a cover story on me. And I showed them my party card with 4 sixpenny stamps on it. He reported it absolutely correctly as something of a joke from when I was 19 – from that moment onwards one came under the McCarthy rule and was *persona non grata* in the United States, up until Kennedy came to power.

216

DF: Who would you say was the most evil person you've encountered?

GG: I've never encountered anybody evil in the sense Hitler was.

DF: You've never felt yourself to be in the presence of evil?

GG: No, I don't think so.

DF: Is a feeling of anger important to you as a writer?

GG: I'm not aware of using that. I probably write worse when I'm angry. One tries to be cold when one's writing.

DF: Which of your critics has pleased you most?

GG: V. S. Pritchett. Because I was young and it was the first really good review I'd had and with a not popular book called *It's A Battlefield*. Pritchett's review came out in the *New Statesman* and gave me great encouragement.

DF: I read a very weird book about your work by John Atkins.

GG: Oh, a terrible book.

DF: It has a kind of quirkiness that is not disagreeable.

GG: I found it thoroughly distasteful and rather silly and not very well written. There have been an awful lot of Graham Greene commentaries – I had one from India only a few weeks ago – but I don't awfully enjoy reading them. One doesn't want to see the pattern in one's own carpet. It makes one too self-conscious and one says 'Oh, my God, it's true, I said that twice over, how terrible.'

DF: Is this similar to the dangers of Freudian analysis which can also make one too self-conscious in the bad sense?

GG: It's worse than Freudian analysis. I'm not anti-Freudian. But I am anti-reading even good criticism of one's own work. Even if it's flattering, it's bad to read it. It points out correspondences one was unaware of, points of similarity. I prefer to forget the books that are finished and not to worry whether or not I'm repeating myself.

DF: Do you have any experience of Freudian analysis?

GG: Not Freudian. But at the age of 16 I was psychoanalysed by a man called Kenneth Richmond. He was an independent – took in Jung and Freud and Adler and took what he liked from them. It was dream analysis which I think is a dangerous thing. But it gave me an enormous interest

217

in dreams. I've kept dream diaries. I write them when blocked in my work.

DF: You use dreams a lot in your books but not symbolically or in some structural way – you use them raw which I find very odd. You just slot them in.

GG: Yes? In a book called *A Burnt-out Case* I was completely blocked for some weeks. Then I had a dream which was not my own dream but the dream of a character. I could recognise it when I awoke as belonging to the character, not to myself. It fitted completely into that section of the book and made the bridge and the book went on. The character dreamt that he was a priest and something strange happened and I can't remember it now.

DF: Do you get writer's block very often? What is the nature of it?

GG: It varies. After I'd finished *A Burnt-out Case* I felt I was never going to write another book. I felt I was completely finished. That feeling went on for quite a long time. It comes at intervals.

DF: Is it connected to a general fatigue with life?

GG: That may enter into it. It's a very unpleasant state. I was in Budapest a few years back and I met Tibor Dery who's a very good Hungarian writer – he was in his mid 80s, he's dead now – and we found ourselves liking each other and we started talking about writer's block and he said, at the age of 85 or so, that he was suffering from it and I said 'How long has it lasted?' and he said '10 days', and I said 'My God, but my writer's block has been going on for nearly 3 months', and he said 'I tell you what you do. After you've had your breakfast you sit down at your table, you have a glass of whisky beside you, some paper, and you start drinking the whisky and you write *anything*'. This worked for him. But it never worked for me. I find that keeping a dream diary helps. Because it means one can still write quite a lot a day. As soon as one has a notepad beside the bed and jots down the key points of a dream as one wakes up at intervals through the night, one soon finds out that it's true what they say,

218

one dreams 5 or 6 times a night, so that even with just key points one is writing about 500 words a day.

DF: The beauty of that is that you don't have to think in terms of structure which is often the big blocking thing, knowing that somehow everything has got to fit. Do you keep any other kind of journal?

GG: Only when I'm travelling. I've got some Panama diaries.

DF: Do you see this dream diary as material for publication?

GG: Not really. But it is carefully indexed. So I can look up 'Khrushchev' and see how many times and what I've dreamt about him.

DF: I can see some big American academic computer getting at this in due course.

GG: I've got, I should think, 700 pages of manuscript.

DF: What is it like meeting other famous writers?

GG: On the whole other writers aren't one's material. One doesn't meet them very often. The French have these groups but I don't think the English writers like going into groups. Poets do occasionally in England. I was a great friend of Evelyn Waugh but we were friends who disagreed on almost everything. Norman Douglas I knew at the end of his life. I see Anthony Burgess occasionally – he lives in Monaco now. He came across and interviewed me for the *Observer*. We had to go to lunch to a very poor restaurant just across the road because his leg was so bad and he couldn't get any further. But in the interview he put words into my mouth which I had to look up in the dictionary to see what they meant.

DF: Is that slightly dishonourable of him?

GG: No, not dishonourable. It's imaginative. He amuses me. And he always accuses me of being Jansenist or Manichean or something and I say 'It is because you were born a Catholic and therefore you don't know any theology'. Whereas I am a convert and had to work it up.

DF: Do you read much?

GG: Generally, yes. But in the last month or two, because of this affair with Nice I haven't been reading much. Normally I read about 8 books a month.

DF: What was the last book you read?

GG: Actually, I can answer that. I finished it only a few days ago. A very good book indeed. *The Samurai* by Endo, a Japanese writer.

DF: Didn't he write a book called *Silence*?

GG: Yes, a wonderful book too, about the Jesuits in Japan. *The Samurai* I think is almost as good. It's a little slow in getting started but, um . . .

DF: Do you find yourself going back to writers?

GG: I re-read Henry James a lot. Conrad to some extent now – I was afraid of him for a long time because he was a terrible influence on me when I was beginning and I was going off on the wrong road as it were as a result. Trollope I re-read quite a lot.

DF: At what point did you feel you'd found your own voice?

GG: With *It's A Battlefield*.

DF: I've got a quotation here from your autobiography of your early years, *A Sort of Life*. 'Perhaps it is only desperation which keeps me writing, like someone who clings to an unhappy marriage for fear of solitude.' I can understand the idea of writing to keep chaos at bay, but do you get no positive kicks at all from writing?

GG: Only occasionally. Sometimes at the end of a morning I might feel 'Well, I think that scene came off'. But then you have to do another one.

DF: Do you find the process of writing a personal drama?

GG: It's a discipline. In the morning I give myself tea and toast and don't shave, don't bath, don't do anything until I've done my quota. There's a moment in a book I think when one feels that after a long track along the tarmac the plane has lifted and has taken over control a bit.

DF: When you land the plane and get out, what's your feeling?

GG: Great relief. Sometimes one feels one had enough of the right cards in one's hand to choose from, to feel confident about the end. Then the next day of course a feeling of 'Oh, God, what now?'

DF: Do you get post-natal blues?

GG: Yes, very much so.

DF: Do you then immediately throw yourself into another book?

GG: Well, then there's still the revision. Which is more interesting than the writing in a sense. I always imagine it is the feeling a sculptor gets a little bit. With revision one is chipping, refining.

DF: How many drafts would you normally do?

GG: 3 or 4. But they're not complete rewritings. The manuscript will go on being corrected until I have to put it onto dictaphone because nobody could read it with all the corrections. Then the proofs are yet another stage.

DF: Do you alter much at the proof stage?

GG: I try not to because it's so expensive. But a book always looks completely different at each stage. Physically one notices different things.

DF: Are those Byron's Journals up there?

GG: Yes. I enjoy them very much. When I was young Byron was down in the depths in terms of literary reputation. Nobody thought he had any merit. Then first of all Maurois did a biography which I seem to remember as quite a good one. It taught the English that Byron was somebody to be respected. And Hamish Miles, who was a man of letters in the early 30s, published an anthology in Jonathan Cape's Traveller's Library of Byron's verse, letters and journals. That sort of woke one up to the fact that he was a great writer. In the 20s he was regarded as nothing. Even *Don Juan* was forgotten.

DF: If there were a nuclear war which, say, 3 of your books would you hope survived it?

GG: I wouldn't expect any.

DF: Do you have a sentimental attachment to any?

GG: I would say *The Honorary Consul*, *The Power and the Glory*, and . . . perhaps, oh, *Travels With My Aunt*.

DF: Have you ever invented a word?

GG: I don't think so. No, I haven't. But the word 'seedy' has become attached to my name.

DF: And 'depressing' too.

GG: The English always regard me as pessimistic and the French always regard me as optimistic.

DF: What do they find optimistic?

GG: That I always give a bit of hope at the end.

DF: Mm, you're an improvement on Samuel Beckett in that sense. You haven't won the Nobel Prize. I'm led to believe that you find this rather galling. Is that so?

GG: No. It's such a big lottery. It seems perfectly natural that some people should lose in a lottery.

DF: What sort of significance can be attached to such prizes?

GG: There's a lot of financial significance in the Nobel. I think their choices for the past few years have been quite good. But there was a period – Pearl Buck for example – when it was very poor. I think even Galsworthy wasn't worth it.

DF: You've never written a novel about the USA.

GG: No. I've been a number of times, to New York, San Francisco, New Orleans, San Antonio. San Francisco I liked, San Antonio I quite liked. But I don't like New York.

DF: Have you been to Russia?

GG: 3 or 4 times. The last time was when I caught pneumonia in '61.

DF: Were you invited?

GG: No, but one's always got somebody from the bureau tagging along. I did receive an official invitation fairly recently but I refused it.

DF: Do you sell many books in Russia?

GG: When Andrey Sinyavsky, the satirical writer, went to prison I said I didn't want to be published in Russia any longer and they do follow one's wishes on these things. Now of course they've joined the international copyright thing. And now Sinyavsky is out of prison and they wanted to publish *Dr Fischer of Geneva* and also *The Honorary Consul* and I've given permission. They are doing them apparently in editions of 300,000. It is a very curious arrangement. You get a royalty according to the number of signatures – which is one of the sections in a bound book like so. A long book gets a higher royalty than a short book. I don't know how much it will be at all.

DF: Which of your books has been most successful in Russia?

GG: Undoubtedly *The Quiet American*.

DF: Why do you think they chose *Dr Fischer*?

GG: As illustrating the decadence of the Swiss?

DF: *Dr Fischer* reminds me very much of the novels of Anna Kavan.

GG: Who?

DF: Anna Kavan. She's a very Graham Greene type in a way.

GG: No, I don't know her . . . I think I've heard of her.

DF: You've been in the Secret Service, you are interested in international affairs – are you ever jealous of the man of action?

GG: I'm not aware of it.

DF: You don't feel that to write well one in some degree has to sacrifice participation?

GG: . . . I've participated a little bit. In Viet Nam during the French war for example – on both sides.

DF: In *The Heart of the Matter* you made an important distinction between pity and compassion.

GG: I did it earlier in *The Ministry of Fear*. I said there that nobody is safe when pity is roaming around. I don't like *The Heart of the Matter* as a book. I was out of practice when I wrote it.

DF: Lots of people do like it.

GG: Yes, too many people. That's another weakness. There's a sentimentality in it which appealed fairly widely. Anyway the distinction between the 2 qualities is – compassion one can have for an equal, but pity contains a sense of superiority I think.

DF: Would you have preferred to live in another age?

GG: I'm quite happy living in the 20th century. I'm glad I shan't be living in the 21st.

DF: How quickly one leaps from century to century. In that connection I'm reminded that your father met Oscar Wilde.

GG: Yes, it was in Naples after Wilde's downfall.

DF: Did your father live to see your success?

GG: If one can call it success. He lived until after *Brighton Rock* anyway. I had a good relationship with him in his

223

last years. But as a boy I was not very fond of him. He was a headmaster and I attended his school. As a young man I rather teased him. He was an old-fashioned liberal and I was inclined to go to extremes. He died when I was in West Africa.

DF: And your mother?

GG: Oh yes, I was very fond of her. She lived much longer than him.

DF: Your first memory is a dead dog at the bottom of your pram.

GG: It sounds invented but it isn't.

DF: If somebody wanted to play up certain aspects of your work . . .

GG: I know. But it is a fact. There's no horror about it. I just have a visual memory of this dead dog which my nurse had picked up and put in the pram to bring home to bury.

DF: The epilepsy you were supposed to have suffered from as a child – what happened to it?

GG: It wasn't real. It was a wrong diagnosis.

DF: Do you enjoy gossip?

GG: Yes. I read *Private Eye*.

DF: What else gets sent over?

GG: The *Spectator*. Which really is incredibly good. And *The Times* I buy here.

DF: Are you fond of music?

GG: No. Let's say – I'm completely ignorant of it. I have no musical memory. If you played something now I would like it or dislike it. And if you played it again half an hour later I wouldn't know that I'd heard it before.

DF: Really? That is unusual. Painting?

GG: Painting I do like, yes.

DF: Do you enjoy shopping?

GG: No. I just go out and get my bits. I have one meal in a day and have to go and buy the food.

DF: Do you enjoy buying presents.

GG: No. I like secondhand bookshops.

DF: Are there any good ones down here.

GG: No, there aren't. That's one thing I miss.

DF: Isn't there an English bookshop somewhere along here?

GG: I believe there may be one in Nice.

DF: Where do you buy your clothes?

GG: I haven't bought any for ages. I sometimes buy a pair of trousers in Capri. I haven't bought a suit since I left England.

DF: Do you go to Capri quite a lot?

GG: I try and go twice a year. I've got a little place in Anacapri. I work there too.

DF: What is an average day for you?

GG: If I'm working – which I'm not at present – I get up about half past 7. I finish my breakfast by 8 o'clock and then I'll be working until about 9, maybe half past 9. And then I have my bath. Shave. Shit. And go shopping. When I was young I would write 500 words a day – incidentally it is not true that I would stop mid-sentence when I'd reached that number of words. I'd stop at the end of the sentence. Now it is more like 200 or 300 a day. When I'm working, that is. And I work in longhand.

DF: Do you smoke?

GG: Not now. And I never inhaled. I stopped during the war. There was rationing. I had a girlfriend who smoked and I thought that if one was going to queue up for a couple of cigarettes she might as well have them both.

DF: Do you have any phobias?

GG: I'm frightened of bats. And birds flying about the room. I can't touch a bird.

DF: What would you say your vices were?

GG: Er, selfishness, probably. Pride probably.

DF: This flat isn't very large, is it.

GG: No. It's only the bedroom and this room and a kitchen and bathroom.

DF: I have another quotation from *A Sort of Life*. 'I live, like most of my contemporaries, an apartment life between bedroom and sitting-room.' But you are in a position to live in grander state if you chose.

GG: I don't think so. Somebody would have to go short if I did.

DF: What are your luxuries?

GG: . . . Mainly wine. I've got a cellar but not of great wine.

Of drinkable wine. It's down below in the garage. I like my drinks, aperitifs and so on. I used to buy pictures. All my favourite pictures are in Paris. Half my books are also in Paris. I rent a 2-roomed apartment in Paris.

DF: How often do you go to church?

GG: I'd say about 2 Sundays in the month, sometimes 3. There's a cathedral in the Old Town where I go.

DF: What other famous people live nearby?

GG: I don't know any. There was a popular writer called Paul Gallico who used to live somewhere around here I think.

DF: Do you know anybody who has taken a particularly good set of photos of you recently?

GG: I've got a niece who is a first class photographer and she took some 2 years ago which are excellent. My sister, who acts as my secretary in England, would have her address. My niece is called Amanda . . . I've forgotten what her surname is now.

DF: Have you been painted much?

GG: No. There's one woman whose name I've forgotten who did a small one which Tom Laughton bought. And there's a young painter called Anthony Palliser whom the National Gallery has asked to do something – he's done the drawings but he hasn't done any painting yet.

DF: How often do you go back to England?

GG: 4 or 5 times a year.

DF: Do you maintain membership of any clubs in London?

GG: No, you mustn't. In the old days anyway, it made you liable for income tax. I was told by my accountant that I must drop any clubs when I left, make a complete break. I was a member of White's at that time. But I've never been a club man and directly I became a member of White's I stopped going there. The membership which lasted longest was a shabby one called the Author's Club in Whitehall Court. I was also a member of the Reform and then I quarrelled with them during the Blitz – I was firewatching close by and used to order my breakfast very early but the Head Waiter became nasty and refused to take my breakfast order so I resigned. For a brief period of a month or so I was a member of the

Athenaeum but I resigned on the grounds that I couldn't take a friend there because the food was too bad. White's I only became a member of because I was slightly drunk one day with Evelyn Waugh who was a member and very fond of it and wanted to put me up and I thought 'It won't come through, not in my lifetime anyway' and then one suddenly heard one had been elected and I never went there again.

DF: Do you take holidays?

GG: I like a working holiday. Every summer I go to Spain because I have a great friend there, a priest who is a professor of English Literature at Madrid University. With *Monsignor Quixote* in mind, I've been going there for the last few years, driving around with him.

DF: What do you think of the Polish Pope?

GG: I admire his courage but I find him very conservative in theology.

DF: What about future books?

GG: I'm thinking of doing a non-fiction book called *The General*, my reminiscences of Torrijos, a personal memoir.

DF: No more autobiography?

GG: No, no.

DF: Did you enjoy writing *A Sort of Life*?

GG: Well, it began – in the 50s I was going through a very bad depressive period and I went to a friend of mine, Eric Strauss who was a psychiatrist, and asked for some Electric Shock Treatment. He said 'How long have you been in this state of acute depression?' and I said '2 weeks' and he said 'I won't consider the electric shocks until you've been in that condition for 4 weeks. Meanwhile, start writing early memories.' And so I started, the depression left, and I put the writing in a drawer. Then a long time passed and I pulled them out and looked at them and thought 'This isn't a bad beginning' so I went on with it.

DF: Have you got the knack now of outwitting depression?

GG: Yes. It doesn't come seriously now. I'm on a kind of plateau.

DF: What were the specific symptoms?

GG: Complete boredom, complete disenchantment.

DF: I think your affair with Nice is a latter day version of the Russian roulette, something to pep up the atmosphere a bit, get the blood moving.

GG: But I never expected the explosion of publicity which followed my letter to *The Times*.

DF: What made you make your move when you did?

GG: The violence thing was becoming too much – when that girl's nose got broken ... I'd already written to the Minister of Justice some time before which resulted in an inspection and some shuffling round. Then things got worse and suddenly after dinner one night I thought 'Let's try and get things going again.' So I wrote to *The Times*.

DF: Do you think British society on the whole is pretty OK from this point of view?

GG: You get police scandals in England every now and then, don't you. But it's not built-in corruption like here.

DF: Which parts of the world haven't you been in?

GG: Ha, quite a lot really. New Zealand I don't know.

DF: Australia?

GG: I've only spent a few hours there on my way to Tahiti – I think it interesting that unlike Canada, Australia seems to have produced quite a number of people in the arts.

DF: China?

GG: I've been there, yes.

DF: The poles.

GG: No, I haven't been to the poles. And I haven't been in Peru, Venezuela, Colombia.

DF: India?

GG: A little bit. I rather liked Goa. I went with a Goanese friend. We went up to a little village where his aunt had a house. We'd come from Panjim to spend Christmas. On the way we stopped at some other relations of his. I said I wanted to pee and my host led me up some stairs. He said 'You won't be afraid of the pigs, will you?' And directly I started peeing I heard them come honking round underneath. The pee was going down and it was like a signal –

they were expecting something more substantial to follow. Then we reached the aunt's house and the first thing one was given was pork. Ghosts used to wander round outside the aunt's house apparently. She said we must sleep indoors but we insisted on sleeping outside on the veranda, so she locked us out there. The church bell rang at I think it was half past 5 in the morning. Nobody stirred out at all then. It rang again at 6 o'clock and people would set about their work – you could see the torches moving round. You could get up at the first bell but were not supposed to venture out until the second bell. But the aunt's sister had a mango tree in her garden and one night there had been a high wind and the mangoes had been blown off. She was afraid that they would be stolen and went out before the second bell to gather them up. She was taken by the ghosts and put up in a tree on the seashore and had to be rescued by the fishermen when they turned up for work. Also, if you see a pig after dark in Goa it is supposed to be a spirit – unwise to use the loo after sundown. I was there for about 2 weeks. We used to go down to the seashore every morning at about half past 8 and take some Indian gin and squeeze limes into it and between 8.30 and about half past 9 in the morning we'd drink gin and lime and get a bit drunk and then it became too hot to stay on the beach. This was the rhythm of one's day. My Goanese friend lived in Bombay and had lost his wife – she was in the kitchen, her sari caught fire from the stove, and she was burnt to death.

It was about 5 o'clock in the afternoon when I left and I decided to go for a walk before driving back to Saint Tropez. My route took me round Fort Carré, a large rocky promontory with fortifications on the edge of town. It was deserted and I was alone with the rocks, the ruins, the surfy sea. Then I saw against the horizon a couple slowly approaching. A small highly-groomed dog was dancing about their feet. As they came closer I saw that one was a petite French woman of about 50 or so, very pretty and chic and up-to-date. The man was much taller and bending low to catch what she was saying – it was Graham Greene. This produced a curious sensation, that the one person one encountered on the deserted path should be him, and that he should have been with his mystery woman. It seemed right not to intrude. I know he'd seen me and thought the same. So not the slightest flicker from either side acknowledged the mutual realisation that we were passing each other – a very English gentlemanly form of understanding I thought at the time (in his letters he always wrote 'Dear Fallowell'). In retrospect it seems rather pathetic and childish. As they went by she was saying something to him in English. He was on her left, bending that ear very low with his hands clasped behind his back, and in this rapt way they moved gradually round the wide curve of the rampart and eventually disappeared.

(1982)

GOING ROUND THE RODD

Sir Sidney and Lady Nolan in Herefordshire

'I HAD A BAD fall some time ago – fell into the orchestra pit at the Sydney Opera House – I went to the doctor recently to make sure everything is fully mended. He said "Go out, don't be lazy" – so I want to take some time off from money-making and do lots of posthumous pictures which tell it like it really is because it's a bit . . . difficult to come out with it when you're alive,' says Sir Sidney in his soft amiable voice and crumpled grey suit and brown slip-on shoes, lolling with ease in a plump armchair of bluish brocade in front of the library fire. This library with its little clocktower on the roof and minstrel's gallery, is a modern (1953) 'Agatha Christie Tudor' extension to the verable beamed mass of the Rodd, Nolan's early 17th century house on the border of England and Wales – it's in Herefordshire by just a few yards. The house, which has 20 acres of land, is set close to the Presteigne–Kington road, along with a range of fine old farm buildings including an ancient tithe barn in superb condition. Though clearly in residence here, there is something light and unemphatic about Sir Sidney's tenure (he's lived at the Rodd for 4 years but has met the neighbouring farmer only once) just as there is something weightless in his paintings and in the movements of his body. Born in 1917, he moves around without giving the slightest sense that physical activity can be a chore.

'Like the Patrick White thing for instance,' he continues. 'He should never have published that last chapter of his auto-biography while he was alive – his statements were libellous because they were written down – so far in law there hasn't been a libellous painting, but I want to paint a number of libellous paintings . . . for posthumous exhibition.'

'You haven't made it up with him?'

'No, it went too far – he blamed me for my wife's suicide – which is quite disgraceful because one always blames oneself anyway. Patrick and I were extremely close so it's quite a loss. His novel *Voss* is the great interior drama of Australia, played out in the central desert – but Patrick never set foot there, oh no, he wouldn't go into the bloody dead heart – you see, he hates Australia, hates it good and hard – he was educated in England and has a contempt for Australians – until he got the Nobel Prize and thousands of letters from people saying how much his books meant to them – this touched him and he softened up a bit towards Australia – at which point he started accusing me of living abroad – but he's got emphysema so the English climate would be bad for him. You know, all Patrick's desert experience came from when he was in the Air Force in North Africa during the war – and also from my desert paintings. He evoked the Australian desert marvellously – without having been there.'

'Is writing important to you?'

'Very much – I keep a journal – I write . . . well, not poems, it's doggerel. Robert Lowell was a great friend of mine – he cracked up every year for 16 years on the trot – it was genetic – and he drank too much . . . Do you want to look round a bit?'

The Rodd used to belong to Lord Rennell. In one of the narrow hallways is a portrait of Sidney Nolan's present wife, Mary, by Lady Rennell. 'My wife was a great friend of Lady Rennell. When Lord and Lady Rennell died, the place was inherited by their 4 daughters none of whom could afford to live here, so it came onto the market. I have no personal connections with this district otherwise – Nolan's an Irish name.' (For many years Lord Rennell's heir was his brother, Peter Rodd, the husband of Nancy Mitford and a model for Evelyn Waugh's character 'Basil Seal'.)

Sir Sidney leads the way upstairs to what he describes as his 'morning room'. It is the most elaborate room of the house and has a richly carved fireplace bearing the figures of Adam, Eve, and the snake – many windows and a bright view of hills. Tables are piled with correspondence in neat stacks.

232

'There's always a lot of business to attend to,' he says. 'The art game is a very tough game. A successful artist would have no trouble being a successful member of the mafia.'

Up more stairs between black-beamed walls to the attic floor, a private region to which Nolan can always withdraw when too much is foaming below. Up here there's very little furniture – several tables for sketching. On them are a series of beautiful crayon drawings suggestive of alchemical practices, plenty of blank paper, boxes of compact discs to feed to a sleek laser sound system.

'I designed my first ballet in 1941. Now I'm designing a new *Ring* over the next 5 years for Covent Garden. I like doing stage designs because it's working with people – in the studio you're on your own. Love of music is one of the reasons I have to spend part of every year in London – I'm very pro-London and want to do a series of London pictures but can't find the form. Let's try this thing out . . .'

The moving parts of the laser sound system glide silently into action. A silver disc flashing rainbows is placed on a little tray and this is absorbed into the stomach of the machine. One of Richard Strauss's *4 Last Songs*, apparently disconnected from any earthbound source, pours into the air and rotates voluptuously in space . . . Kenneth Clark once compared Nolan's paintings to the music of Benjamin Britten, especially in the sense of menace, of something very strange just over the horizon, 'but I think your work is more sinister than Britten's.'

'Oh dear – really?'

'It's a compliment.'

'Yes . . . I suppose it is. Britten could be fairly – he was very polite and boyish, but steely underneath – a lot of people who thought they were pretty close friends of his, suddenly found themselves not friends. He came to Australia with me in 1970 and we saw a lot of aboriginal boys near Alice Springs – he became very interested and wanted us to do a ballet based on their circumcision rites and link it with another story about a friend of his, some very well-known chap whose name I've forgotten, who hanged himself on the morning of his wedding day. We never did it – I still want to – Peter Maxwell Davies has now agreed to do the music but we don't have a choreographer – Kenneth Macmillan said it sounded too much like *The Rite of Spring . . .*'

'I don't see any aboriginal content in your pictures.'

'That's right. But I know a lot more about them than I let on. They are the only race on earth who've had a continuous way of life for 40,000 years in one place.' [NB. The official estimate of this period is 18,000 years.]

'You mean they've done the same thing for 40,000 years? Failed to evolve?'

'No, no, it's highly evolved – but their society reached perfection – for its circumstances – they couldn't grow anything – they had only fire.'

But people have found places in Australia where crops can be raised – Sir Sidney's point remains abstruse. He leads the way downstairs to the ground floor and a small temporary studio with dozens of canisters of spray paint gathered on tables.

'I might buy a house near Dublin and set up a museum of my paintings there in conjunction with the Irish Government – but I'd still live basically here at the Rodd – which will also house my paintings after I've gone. And I'm doing the same with our place in Australia – that one's pretty far advanced already.'

'You seem quite rich.'

'Nah, not really. I've always spent on houses and travel. All Australians want to travel. I spent 20 years going to Angkor Wat, the Grand Canyon, Chartres, just to prove to myself they existed. This is one of the advantages of living somewhere that's a long way from everywhere else.'

'What's it like growing up in a place with no history?'

'Wonderful. I was just thinking that this morning. This is maybe why I developed an ironic attitude to history. The Ned Kelly pictures were ironic – but the irony backfired, so now I'm stuck with Ned Kelly round my neck.'

'Why did you give Kelly a square head?'

'It isn't square – it's a cylindrical helmet which appears square in silhouette.'

But irony and curvature are secondary. In the first instance, Kelly's head is a black box with 2 desperate eyes staring out of it: trapped, frightened, alienated: very 20th century.

In the large old kitchen, a cooker with 4 pans steaming on top is marooned pitifully in the middle of one of the long walls. The pans are being tended by Sir Sidney's daughter, recently arrived from Australia, who, with a number of children and cats about her feet, is preparing dinner. As yet the Rodd has no dogs. In passing, Sir Sidney points out a wooden beam which Lady Rennell always said was the longest domestic beam in England – it travels through 2 rooms and is over 50 feet long. We go out of the kitchen door and into the garden. The front of the house faces England but its paddocks run back from it into the romantic prospect of a Welsh valley.

'What do you think of the English?'

'They're just as odd as the aborigines. The English have this wonderful consensus way of life – like the Chinese. I've been a lot to China. No one has the reputation for facetiousness that the English have.'

'Do you feel especially Australian?'

'I actually feel quite Irish in temperament. Australians are supposed to have difficulty with their identity – I've never had any problems seeing myself as an Australian, despite spending half my life away from it.'

'I think one's national identity goes into sharper focus when one lives abroad.'

'Perhaps. Lots of them hate it – Xavier Herbert, a great writer who died recently, cursed the Australians as he was dying – he called them rogues, liars, bastards. Patrick will curse them on his deathbed too. I had a big row with Xavier over my knighthood – he was a republican – we made it up when I visited him in hospital. Of course I betrayed my working-class origins. I really accepted it, I told him, for my mother – he said "You bastard, your mother's been dead 12 years", and I said "That makes no difference". My wife Mary didn't like the knighthood much. My father would've thought I got it by foul means.'

'You mean he thought painting a bit of a con?'

'He did. He thought everything should be earned through the sweat of one's brow. He was a tram driver. He always thought I wasn't tough enough, even though I was an athlete.'

'What's the worst thing about being Australian?'

'To feel colonial. I never felt colonial, probably because my background was Irish, not English. I came from a tight-knit working-class family in Melbourne and in my early days was too busy surviving in a factory to wonder if I was colonial or not. It's the middle-class ones who suffer that way . . . There's the valley . . . See that woodland over there? We let that go –I did the deal on the phone from Australia – I'm trying to get the woodland back.'

It is a cool fresh evening. The orientation of the property in the landscape is effortlessly correct. The sun is setting on a central axis at the far end of the valley in this pylonless Arcadia.

'What do they think of you in Australia?'

'I got quite a shock. I started coming over here from 1950 on – I thought I was pushing ahead as an Australian painter – but when I met the younger generation of artists from Australia, I discovered that they thought me contemptible – they thought I'd sold out. It took me 12 months to get over it. And when I went back the reporters at the airport said "Why are you coming back? Can't you make it over there any more? Why don't you stay away?" It still goes on. This business with the Cultural Centre in Melbourne – they commissioned a series of paintings from me. I delivered them and they rejected them. It's almost as if I was set up for a slap – I'm still trying to find out what really happened.'

'What is ugliness?'

' . . . . It's in people – a kind of psychotic selfishness like Iago's. There's no such thing as a dishonest work of art. But there are dishonest human beings.'

Return to library: tea and chocolate biscuits. Lady Nolan enters in a very chic mackintosh. She is petite and slightly spaced-out, with soft ivory-coloured hair parted school-girlishly in the middle. She has laryngitis to-day but this does not prevent her expressing forthright opinions on any subject going – both Sir Sidney and Lady Nolan have the unusual gift of being simultaneously soft and decisive in their natures.

'I wish you wouldn't tell jokes . . .' she appeals vaguely to her husband who is embarking on a New Zealand joke which is to Australians what the Irish joke is to the English and the Polish joke to the Americans.

'I'm Australian, I like telling jokes,' he says somewhat abashed.

236

'Anyway, an Australian booked a cut-price boat trip back to Australia from England. When he arrived at Southampton – '

'I still say you shouldn't tell jokes,' she asserts, looking up at the minstrel's gallery.

'Let me finish,' says Sir Sidney, lifting a soft decisive finger. 'When the Australian arrived at Southampton they strapped him to a plank and floated him off and away he went, much to his astonishment. A New Zealander comes along and gets the same treatment. So there they are, flat on their backs, floating across the equator, and the Australian looks across and sees the New Zealander and says "This is really terrible – and they don't even give you any food". And the New Zealander says "Yes, it is terrible – we got food last year" . . .'

'Is that it, Sid?' asks Lady Nolan. 'Is that all?'

Sir Sidney seems put out – his smile, normally so unalloyed, looks alloyed, and his eyes scan the room for support because it's not a bad joke.

'Are you Australian too, Lady Nolan?'

'Yes, I am.'

'But she doesn't sound Australian, does she?' interpolates Sir Sidney. 'I do but she doesn't.'

'Oh I do, of course I do.'

'No, you don't,' he insists (and she doesn't). 'Mary's the sister of Arthur Boyd.'

'Arthur Boyd?'

'A famous Australian painter. And her uncle was Martin Boyd, a famous novelist.'

'Oh it doesn't mean anything, really it doesn't,' she protests with a coy turn of the head and driving her finger into one of the plump sofa cushions.

'What are you working on at the moment, Sir Sidney?'

'I'm not. My method is – I don't work for 2 or 3 months, then I work for 2 or 3 months. I want to do a lot of these private libellous paintings and there's an Antarctic series and – I reckon I can work at full, um er, until about the age of 80. I want to go to Russia soon!'

(1985)

237

STRANGE COCKTAILS
MARY LUTYENS

IN A CUL de sac off an avenue off the Regent's Canal, in that part of London where Little Venice starts to become Maida Vale, is a small modern brick house with a yellow front door. This is opened by a robust figure in a cravat. His name is Joe Links and behind him in the hall, petite and silvery, bobs his wife Mary. Inside the house, a full tea is laid at one end of the sitting-room in which valuable and valueless articles are harmoniously arranged.

What could be more conventionally British? But outside a thunderstorm is starting up and one is reminded that things aren't always what they seem. For few people have found themselves in so many peculiar worlds as Mary Lutyens. And yet, apart from a volume of autobiography which ended at the age of 17, she has never put on record the details of a life which represents a sort of alternative history of the British Empire in its final, fantastical phase.

Of course it all began idyllically in a beautiful 18th century house – 29 Bloomsbury Square, where Mary was born in 1908, youngest of the 5 children of the architect Sir Edwin Lutyens. Sir James Barrie was a family friend and Lutyens had designed sets for the first stage production of *Peter Pan* in 1904. It was through the windows of Mary's night nursery that the Darling children had flown off to Never Land.

The first crack in the idyll occurred in 1910 when Mary's mother converted to occult religion. Lady Emily Lutyens was an Edwardian eccentric, the daughter of Lord Lytton, Viceroy of India. In her youth she played the guitar and was loved by

Wilfred Scawen Blunt. Now her conversion to Theosophy led her to vegetarianism and socialism, but most of all it led her to Krishnamurti. When in 1911 Annie Besant brought Krishnamurti and his brother to be groomed in England, Lady Emily fell in love with the boy-god. Later on Mary Lutyens fell in love with his brother Nitya.

This bizarre new element in their lives caused a rift between the cool, high-minded Lady Emily and the ribald, prankish Sir Edwin (who for example was mad about dancing – he once performed a ballet, taking all the parts, during a dinner party). When in 1914 the family moved to 31 Bedford Square, transporting the fireplaces with them, Lady Emily used the opportunity to break off all sexual relations with her husband.

'This deeply affected our childhood,' says Mary, 'because it made Father so miserable that he never came up to the nursery again. He simply couldn't bear to go past his old bedroom and had a bed made up on a lower floor.'

Lady Emily later wrote to him 'I know I am a rotten wife', and went on to say that if he wanted to take a mistress, she wouldn't mind.

'There was no certainty but it seems that Lady Sackville, the mother of Vita Sackville-West, became his mistress. We all very much hoped so.'

Mary loved the Bedford Square house but everyone else hated it. Periodically Lady Emily would retire to the shrine room which she'd fitted up off one of the landings.

'With a Buddha on one side and a Crucifix on the other,' says her daughter, 'she'd sit in there burning incense and meditating in her yellow shawl. She was a member of the Yellow Group. There was also a Purple Group. She belonged to many things. Co-Masonry was another.'

But eventually the atmosphere became so disagreeable that Lady Emily decided to have the house exorcised – not of course by any familiar body but by another of her beribboned cults, the Liberal Catholic Church. It was typical of Lady Emily's rarefied social conscience that she felt it wasn't necessary to have the servants' quarters done. A Roman Catholic housemaid was bitterly offended by it all and left.

'Have you ever seen a ghost?'

'No. I'm not at all psychic. But I've had 2 weird experiences. The first was in a supposedly haunted house in Dorset. I'd been nursing a lover called Tid Ralli who died from cardiac oedema while I was with him – this was in 1943. His will and important papers were in a dispatch case with a combination lock and he'd forgotten to tell anyone the combination. But my hands were absolutely guided – I got it open immediately.

'The second experience was more recent, when I was with Krishnamurti at Brockwood Park. He said "Can't you feel the power in the room?" I couldn't feel a thing and he said "But it's getting so strong". We were in the drawing-room in the west wing. Then he had to go upstairs and lie down because his head began to hurt – this was the morning. In the afternoon before leaving, I went to collect my coat from that same drawing-room. I was about to enter it when through the door quite suddenly came a terrifying force which almost knocked me over. It was liked being caught in the wind of an aeroplane propeller and very frightening – I felt that it was hostile.'

'Did you ask him about it?'

'Yes. He wasn't surprised – he was used to it but couldn't define it. He associated it with what we called "the process".'

This 'process', Krishnamurti's tendency to painfully incapacitating fits, is one of the most contentious aspects of his life. Mary says 'I'm sure it wasn't anything simply physical like migraine. I believe something psychic or mental was expanding in his brain cells and this was the cause of the pain.'

In 1918 the Lutyens family moved again, to 13 Mansfield Street, near Portland Place, 'by far the biggest of our houses – instead of 7 servants, Mother needed 10 to run it'. And the best cook they ever had had to be dismissed when it was discovered she washed her face each morning in her own urine.

It was in the front drawing-room at Mansfield Street that Queen Mary's Dolls' House, now at Windsor Castle, took shape in the early 1920s, designed and supervised by Sir Edwin. But he was often away. From 1912 he spent the winters in India building the new capital at Delhi.

Both sides of the family now had a strong Indian connection. Mary's maternal grandfather, the Earl of Lytton, had been Viceroy from 1876 to 1880. He shocked Simla society by smoking cigarettes between courses at dinner but it was during his administration that Queen Victoria was declared Empress of India. Mary didn't know him – he died in 1891 – but she very well remembers her grandmother, the Vicereine.

'She was accustomed to send her hair-combings to Paris to be made up into curls which the maid then pinned to the front of her head. She lost her memory but kept her manners. I would say "Granny, don't you remember me? I used to be Mary", and she'd say "I'm afraid I don't remember you but I like you *very* much". She liked us to play piquet with her and she used to cheat a good deal. Her daughter – our Aunt Con – lived with her and was a suffragette and went to prison 3 times. Once in prison Aunt Con was forcibly fed without them testing her heart first and she had an attack and was paralysed all down her right side – but she continued to do beautiful Japanese flower arrangements with her left hand.'

The Lutyens children went to London day schools, 'except Elizabeth who was difficult and boarded away', and when Mary came home at tea-time she always hoped to see Krishnamurti's and Nitya's pale grey Homburg hats and gold-topped canes on the hall table – Krishnamurti was a great fan of P. G. Wodehouse (and later on, like Gurdjieff, was mad about cars).

'One of the sources of these 2 boys' charisma for us was their smartness and terrific cleanness. It was such a contrast to the grubbiness of our British upper class regimen – insufficient baths, no bidets, changing underclothes only once a week and so forth. Father always had black fingernails. He didn't believe in cleaning them on principle.'

While Father was raising his imperial masterpiece of New Delhi, Mother was in alliance with Annie Besant, passionate advocate of Home Rule for India. In December 1923 Lady Emily took Mary to the Subcontinent, first to the Theosophical headquarters at Adyar, then on to stay with Uncle Vic, Emily's brother, who was Governor of Bengal.

'We'd been terribly happy at Adyar and made lifelong Indian friends and span cotton for Gandhi with our little wheels. Then having to go into this heavy formal atmosphere of Government House in Calcutta – Uncle Vic was very natural and nice but his wife Aunt Pamela, well, it was so shocking, she expected us all to curtsey to her!'

Pamela Lytton, née Plowden, was a beautiful woman with many suitors in her day. 'She was very social. Winston Churchill wanted to marry her but she turned him down and chose my uncle who wasn't social at all. And in Calcutta the Lyttons had not a single Indian friend!'

A year later Krishnamurti and Nitya suggested that Lady Emily should take Mary and Elizabeth to Australia to be trained in advanced Theosophy by Charles Leadbeater. After an unjust homosexual scandal, Leadbeater had felt unable to live in England and so developed a community far away in Sydney where he could be a bishop in the Liberal Catholic Church and wear gorgeous floor-length robes.

Despite Sir Edwin's disapproval, Lady Emily arrived in Sydney with 2 of her daughters, plus Krishna and Nitya, in April 1925. Bishop Leadbeater came prancing along the wharf to meet them 'like a great lion in a long purple cloak, a large amethyst cross bouncing on his breast, and holding on to the arm of a very good-looking blond boy of about 15.' (This was the jaunty Theodore St John, his chief acolyte, who was killed at an early age in a motorbike accident.) Leadbeater was 78 at the time, full of fun and sparkling with health.

The party travelled to Leadbeater's headquarters in the suburb of Mosman, a large house called the Manor containing a community of about 50 devotees.

'They all had centre partings. All good Theosophists had centre partings. The house had been taken because its millionaire builder had for some reason lined many of the rooms with beaten copper and Leadbeater said that copper conserved magnetism and good influences.' Up the road at Balmoral, a temple and a 2,500-seat amphitheatre had been built for Krishnamurti to speak in as head of the Order of the Star in the East, the organisation which had been set up to assist his earthly passage. 'The place is now a car park I believe,' says Mary wistfully.

Leadbeater spoke of the Masters who lived in Tibet, especially of the protector of the Theosophical Society, Koot Hoomi, a reincarnation of Pythagoras. He produced Koot

242

Hoomi's portrait, painted by Theodore's mother from her memory of a visit to the Master on the astral plane. But most of the time Mary was fretfully in love with Nitya who had gone off with Krishnamurti to California.

On the girls' journey back to England the ship put in at Melbourne and it was here that Theodore St John casually informed Mary that Nitya had just died in California from tuberculosis. This fact would eventually shake her awake and lead to an utterly different sort of life, but for the moment she was devastated and struggled on as best she could.

'Leadbeater very much wanted Mother to present us at Court so that we could spread Koot Hoomi's word in Society but we arrived back too late to put our names down. Elizabeth didn't go in at all and went off to the Royal College of Music. But I tried to go in and went to one debutante dance in Queen Anne Street. The trouble was I didn't know anybody and the English won't speak to you until you've been introduced, so I was a wallflower and soon fled.'

Briefly she transferred to Krishnamurti all the love she'd felt for his brother and there was a rumour they were to be married but Sir Edwin put a stop to it.

Since Krishnamurti's death in 1986, it has come to light that he had a mistress, Rosalind Rajagopal, the wife of his best friend. A book has been written on this strange triangular relationship. Mary won't read it but for me the book clarifies a number of uneasy questions and makes Krishnamurti more human and appealing. Rosalind had 3 abortions by Krishnamurti who had no children nor wanted any. Since he maintained such a chaste public demeanour, I asked Krishnamurti if he'd known sexual love and he replied 'Little bit'. In fact it was a very passionate and long lasting affair. I ask Mary why she didn't include this aspect in her biography of him – which is in 3 volumes and otherwise exhaustive and impeccable.

'Well, he was still alive until I wrote the last part. But his pronouncements on sex were very intelligent and revealed that he knew what he was talking about. He said that holy men who deny sex end up tearing out their eyes and tongues and performing penances and deny all the beauty of life. He also said go to bed with whom you like but don't make a problem out of it because sex is only a fragment of life.'

'Was he ever a lover of yours?'

'No!' she laughs. 'But sometimes when we were young we very innocently climbed into bed together and lay completely still.'

After Nitya's death, Mary decided to break completely with Theosophy – and this meant breaking with Krishnamurti too. 'I'm not in fact a very religious person and had only gone along with it to please Nitya.'

Already she had abandoned at the age of 18 the vegetarianism in which she'd lived since the age of 2. 'When I started to go out in London, vegetarianism was such a nuisance. It cut you off from people so much. At parties while everyone else ate something delicious, I'd be offered an underdone egg. So I made myself eat meat and heaved at every mouthful but persevered. I still can't eat a steak or an oyster.'

Through her father's introduction she was taken up in 1927 by Sir Roderick Jones, chairman of Reuters, and his wife Enid Bagnold. 'You see, when I left Theosophy I lost all my friends. Roderick and Enid helped fill the gap. He was a very dapper little man and an extraordinary thing happened – he fell in love with me. He gave me an allowance of £5 a week to boost the modest one I had from my family. At one period I spent almost every weekend at their house in Rottingdean, which had belonged to Burne-Jones, and met everybody.'

'Apart from Krishnamurti and Leadbeater, who is the most charismatic person you've met in your life?'

'Mrs Besant.' (She pronounces the name with emphasis on the first syllable. After her divorce Annie Besant always pronounced it thus, to dissociate herself from her husband's family.)

'Apart from all those ones.'

'I should think . . . Bernard Shaw. Uncle Vic had this big house called Knebworth and once at a lunch party Pamela sat me next to Winston Churchill and opposite Bernard Shaw. I tackled Churchill – he was frightfully surprised – and said he ought to support Home Rule for India. At 18 I thought I'm sitting next to him, I must try something. Then Winston and

Shaw began to converse and the whole table fell silent to listen. I can't recall what they discussed but I do remember that Shaw absolutely *wiped the floor* with Churchill – Shaw was so full of life! Oh dear, I'm talking too much. I haven't offered you anything to eat. This cake is very good. Do have some.'

'Did you make it?'

'It comes from Marks & Spencer.'

Another important new feature of her life – she began to write a novel, encouraged by Rosamund Lehmann 'who was a great friend of my sister Ursula because they both lived in Northumberland. Rosamund was married to Leslie Runciman at the time and very unhappy with him.'

'Why was Ursula in Northumberland?'

'Because she'd married a man called Lord Ridley who lived there. Nicholas Ridley was their son. I didn't agree with Nicholas's politics but I loved him as a person. Nick wanted to go in for designing furniture and did have an exhibition at Heal's as a young man. His elder brother Matthew inherited everything. Matthew is right wing but old-fashioned Tory, part of the Royal circle, Lord Lieutenant of the county. I think Nick had a chip on his shoulder because he said all his father left him was a bankrupt engineering firm.'

But the main force for change was that Mary met a young man and married him, Anthony Sewell, brought up in Paris, tall, good-looking, Eton, Cambridge. They were engaged in April 1929. In August of that year another important event took place – Krishnamurti dissolved the Order of the Star, breaking his connection with all organised cults including Theosophy, and declaring that 'Truth is a pathless land'. From now on his importance as a spiritual philosopher grew – but Mary didn't have any contact with him for a further 40 years.

She and Anthony were married in February 1930: a grand wedding at St Margaret's Westminster with a blue carpet to match her pale blue velvet wedding-dress.

'I married him because he couldn't't've been more different from the life I'd known. He never read a book. He always wanted to be out on the town, and if we did stay in he made me play 6-pack bezique for money. He had a very inferior job, selling advertising for the *Daily Express*. But he soon got the sack and became a stock jobber.'

The rot set in early. Anthony grew bored on the honeymoon at Cap d'Ail because the nearest racecourse was at Cannes and had bad meetings. So he went up to Paris. A mysterious figure, with whom Mary had begun to fall in love even before her marriage, was in Monte Carlo. 'This man, who was a friend of Anthony's, had assured me my marriage would not take place. He came to the wedding and at the altar I was expecting him to stand up and forbid it!' She spent the rest of her honeymoon with him in Provence. It was her first passionate, sexual relationship. He was 20 years older and lived in Paris where she often visited him – no one, including Anthony, ever knew. But it didn't last.

'I was shattered when in December 1931 he committed suicide with Veronal. On one occasion previously I'd taken the Veronal away from him but he'd laughed, saying that in Paris it could be bought over the counter.'

Meanwhile, back at the marriage, she and Anthony weren't well-off but found a picturesque flat in the Temple once occupied by Charles Lamb. 'I wasn't in love with Anthony and I don't think he was with me but we were fond of each other. We both went our own ways and had terrific love affairs.'

This period lasted for 14 years and the affairs included Peter Rodd, husband of Nancy Mitford, and Robert Boothby. Mary had no difficulty appealing to men – she was smart, pretty, warm, and lively, a liberated spirit hungry for experience.

'I was very advanced in having a contraceptive device called the Graffenberg Ring, like a coil but made from silver. It was invented by a German and only 2 doctors in England could fit it.'

It was taken out when she and Anthony, who was becoming rather successful as a stockbroker, decided to have a child. 'I didn't want to get pregnant until I could afford a nanny. I prefer the old-fashioned system. I don't believe in mothers bringing up their own children.'

A daughter was born in 1935 – she is now a medical herbalist in Broadway, Worcestershire. Afterwards Mary employed an alternative method of birth control called 'galvanism'.

'If you were 2 days late you made an appointment for "tummy treatment" with a very old doctor. He would put the Faraday machine on your stomach, which brought you on. It had to be done within 2 or 3 days – so you never knew if you were really pregnant or not. But it was infallible. Several of my friends used nothing else.'

When the old doctor sold his lucrative practice, the young doctor who bought it was horrified to discover what most of the patients came for. He got rid of them by saying that they had to ring for an appointment after 7pm – when most of the husbands were at home. 'If I had not been married I could not have behaved as I did. Marriage protects you in 2 ways. The man you're having an affair with is not afraid that you'll want him to marry you. And or if he does want to marry, you can say you don't want to break up your own marriage. Incidentally, by having no more children I thought I was being kind to my daughter – I'd've loved to have been an only child. But she regrets it terribly.'

So she was a pioneer of much that didn't become widespread until the 1960s – vegetarianism, oriental philosophy, free love. Was she aware of this?

'I was aware that I was living what was then considered a very immoral life!'

'Were there problems as a result?'

'A lot of hurts. But my motto became: do exactly what you like but don't squeal if you get hurt. Also I had the rather awful idea that you couldn't take a man away from his wife unless he wanted to be taken. But none of my lovers was casual. They were all very intense while they lasted.'

This was also a time of gambling, dancing and nightclubs. She attended a tap-dancing school for chorus girls near Piccadilly Circus and went out dancing night after night 'to our wonderful 1930s tunes'. During the more virtuous hours of morning, the writing was going well and a novel was published by John Murray.

During the Second World War Mary worked, among other things, as a barmaid. In 1943 she met Joe Links who was at the Air Ministry with her brother Robert Lutyens. Joe's father, a Hungarian Jew, had died when Joe was 21 and left him the

247

family fur business. Mary lived with him for a year and they were married in 1945.

'At last I'd found the person I'd always been looking for, the one who meant I didn't need anyone else. And he wasn't interested in having children which was good. Luckily Anthony met a girl he wanted to marry at exactly the same time but she didn't want to be cited in the divorce, so I was very happy to be the guilty party.'

After the War, Mary embarked on her series of biographies, leading to the success of *Millais and the Ruskins* in 1967.

'Tremendous things happened from that one book. It got me into *Who's Who*. It got me to 2 Royal Academy banquets. It got me invited to 2 royal garden parties – but I wasn't interested in those and didn't go. I'd been presented when young, so didn't need to look at Buckingham Palace.'

'Oh, I thought you said you'd missed out on that.'

'Yes, but I did it later. Anthony wanted me to be done, so in 1930, the year of my marriage, I was presented to George and Mary. I wore pale pink satin and feathers, long gloves, an emerald brooch and green satin shoes to match it. When I got to the Palace, first of all I was dreadfully shocked – they didn't even have commodes in the cloakroom, just chamber pots put out on the floor. Then as we were going upstairs one of the equerries saw my shoes and said "You can't go in wearing green shoes" and I said "What shall I do, go home?" He had a brainwave and asked "Can you stoop so that the hem of the dress covers your shoes?" So I had to shuffle along bent at the knees and try to curtsey without exposing my green feet which was terrifying. And all the while, Mother was waiting for me in the Mall, reading a book on Communism.'

Outside in the small Little Venice garden, the rain has stopped and a certain brightness suggests the sun might break through. So – finally everything worked out all right for Mary. But what of her brother and sisters? Did they too eventually find happiness? Alas, not. Their fates were very different.

Robert married at 19 a Polish Jewish woman who became a successful dressmaker in London while he became an interior designer of renown. 'But unfortunately they had an odd son who became odder and odder. It was partly their fault – they starved him and he developed rickets. But while his body wasted away his head grew and grew.' He died a few years ago in a home. Robert had already become an alcoholic and had died from drink.

Elizabeth became a disciple of Schoenberg.

'I hated her music but she hated my books, so that was all right. She was an alcoholic too but cured for 20 years. Her second husband was hopeless and wouldn't get a job but she struggled and managed to keep her family by doing brilliant scores to horror films. I introduced her to an acupuncturist who'd cured me of frozen shoulder. She went to him for depression which she very much suffered from and he said "Have a whisky", and she became an alcoholic again and died from a combination of alcohol and anti-depressants.'

Ursula?

'Father's favourite. She had a very happy life at first and was the only one of us children never to be involved with Theosophy. She and her husband Lord Ridley were very much in love but she hated being shut away in Northumberland. Ursula had been mad on horses and used to hunt with our other sister Barbara every winter but the moment she had a baby she lost her nerve. Ursula had no occupations – she even refused to learn bridge – and her husband was always under a motor car – he broke the record at Brooklands – so she got desperately bored. After his death, she became manic depressive and eventually committed suicide after several botched attempts.'

Barbara's fate was perhaps the most tragic of all. A beauty, adored by everyone, she had a magical life until she was 40, with 3 sons and 2 stepsons, having married a rich Scotsman called Euan Wallace.

'Then the war came. Euan died of cancer in 1942 while he was Minister of Transport. Both stepsons and her own middle son were killed in the war. She married again in 1945, to an American writer called Herbert Agar. He had a hip operation which resulted in a bone infection and he lived in agony until his death in 1955. Her eldest son had an operation for a polypus in his nose and died under the anaesthetic. That left only her youngest son, Billy Wallace, who was supposed to marry Princess Margaret and didn't. He died a horrible death – cancer of the tongue. She survived them all but having no grandchildren, Barbara decided to kill herself too.

'She was quite cold-blooded about it and said that directly the couple who looked after her were settled in their own house, she'd do it. She also said "I'll haunt you if you have any kind of funeral. I want the undertaker to do everything and scatter the ashes". And she said she had the sleeping-pills. I wouldn't have dreamt of stopping her – I'm a member of Exit but don't want to die unless I'm gaga. Joe and I went down on a Thursday to Beechwood, her wonderful house in Sussex, and Barbie took me round saying "Look, is there anything you want?" which was awfully awkward because there were lots of things I wanted but I couldn't really say so. Then she said "It's going to be this weekend but I shan't tell you when". It was very nasty saying goodbye. She made me take one or two things – for example that oval urn clock over there which Father designed with expanding hands. I rang her Friday evening and she said "I feel happier than I've felt for years" and talked about a book she'd just read, so I thought it won't be to-night and went to bed quite happily. At 9 the next morning her butler, dear Mr Claydon, rang and told me she was dead.'

'Have you ever wanted to commit suicide?'

'Yes, I tried. Once.'

'When?'

'May 10th, 1933.'

'Why?'

'I was terribly in love with a man and knew he was being unfaithful to me. Curiously enough – I suppose it shows that one's writing didn't mean a tremendous amount to one – it was the very day I received a letter from my agent saying that John Murray had accepted that novel for publication. I rang this man to tell him and he didn't answer for a long time and when he did he was out of breath and I knew what was going on.'

'What was your chosen method of suicide?'

'That other lover of mine, the one I'd taken the Veronal away from, well, I'd kept the pills. Unfortunately, as I then felt, I was rescued after being unconscious for 36 hours – Anthony came back home. The worst thing is the waking up. It's *hell*.

Because the reason for trying it is still there. The means of escape has gone – they even removed my dressing-gown cord from the room. You feel physically very ill. They watch you constantly. And there's the guilt over all the people you've hurt – in my case especially my mother. You wake up very gradually. I didn't go to hospital. Anthony fetched the first doctor he could find and was furious because the man wouldn't do anything until he'd been paid! Then he brought out his stomach pump. I was quite cross afterwards because he chipped my front tooth. The Veronal worked frightfully quickly – I don't remember an instant after taking the stuff. There's no courage needed in putting oneself to sleep.'

One last feature of her life must be mentioned. In the late 1960s she renewed contact with Krishnamurti, though in a less personal way.

'His ideas were now very different from those of the young man I'd grown up with and struck me as profoundly wise. Apart from doing the biography, I edited several volumes of his talks which is the most intellectually exciting work I've ever done.'

'What was Joe's reaction?'

'Joe liked Krishna personally very much but is too happy to need him – and disagrees with many of his ideas.'

'Do you mind living in a small house without servants?'

'Oh, I love it! A Spanish girl comes in 2 mornings a week. Servants were an awful bore. You couldn't do what you wanted because it put them out and they were cross if you were late for a meal or home late at night and they were always squabbling among themselves.'

'And finally is there anything you've retained from the old Theosophical days?'

'Yes. A respect for everybody else's beliefs but not wanting to belong to any religion myself. And a horror of those afternoon meetings with Marmite sandwiches!'

(1991)

251

POP STAR

MICHAEL JACKSON

MICHAEL JACKSON ACHIEVES heroic status by accomplishing a number of impossibilities. For example, he has tricked time. He has always been around – but remains young, outside the loop of nostalgia. We have watched him grow up and fail to grow up, seen him loom larger and closer yet become less real, more elusive. As Nijinsky in his famous leap managed to swell that hiatus between his rising and falling, so Jackson too has managed to spin the illusion of operating outside the normal laws of perception. Presumably, eventually, he will topple and fall into time's abyss, but not yet, not at the moment.

His professional fall has been many times predicted – when the Jackson Five break up, when his voice breaks, when Prince takes over, when Madonna takes over, when he suffers a nervous collapse. Once on the beach at Saint Tropez in 1985 I overheard 2 very modish boys talking. 'Ah, Michael Jackson, il est mort!' said one. The other agreed with a sage nod of his ringlets. One would believe it impossible to survive such Gallic scorn – but he has done so. How? Not simply by being one step ahead so much as being one step to the side which has added mystery to his appeal, conferring that tantalising ambivalence which all great stars have, of being both intimate and beyond reach.

Another trick – outside time but dynamic: he has evolved. This is Puck, Ariel, Pierrot, Mercury, Harlequin, Pan in his demonic vitality – but not Peter Pan frozen at 5. On paper he is 33 years old – and what relevance is that? Well, it is astonishing – he is not giving off thirty-something vibrations at all. And here is the tragic aspect. The dream of timelessness is doomed on this earth. The clock is ticking in the wings even as we are hypnotised by Jackson's fandango on the high wire, and this injects an anxiety into the performance, a concentrate of that 'in the midst of life we are in death' poignancy which is always around us.

To be outside time is to be outside sex. He exerts the fascination of the divine hermaphrodite, a Farinelli for our more boisterous age. The speaking voice is almost pre-pubescent, the social manner is that of the adolescent writhing with self-consciousness. His hypersensitivity is not effeminate (because he is in no respect a cliché) but it is poetical, a form of androgyny which disorientates then charms. He is more comfortable with children. A whole dimension – or encrustation – of adult awareness appears to be missing. So of course there is nightmare too – for him. And for us – that sinister edge towards an abnormality which is not ashamed of itself but wholly innocent and fully operational. This is his threat which can be thrilling or make you cringe, according to taste.

Recently he was crowned King of an African tribe and giggled nervously during the ceremony. This is serious/not serious: carnival, circus, commedia dell'arte. It is also macabre. I think of the television series *The Avengers*: the clang of the doorbell as Steed enters an old toyshop in a London sidestreet; there is nobody within; but the toys are disturbingly alive. One of them is Michael Jackson, the boy who dances like an empassioned robot. His thinness allied to his energy is of a creature honed onto his very nerve-endings, a prodigious doll, a show business machine. He could easily be grotesque but is not because a sweetness of character comes through. He could easily be whimsical and sometimes is, especially in his films, but never merely that, because he is too intense, and too talented. Never before has a performer operated at such a pitch of tension in his performance, as though Jackson has taken into himself all the stresses of the world and twisted them up into fine flexible wires, spraying them back at us in an ecstatic desperation. His raw material is the panic of the age and his style is urgent – it's there in every taut vocal phrase, in the hectic geometry of every explosive dance step. And at the end of the show he says 'I love you' and vanishes. Never an encore. So the audience leaves bewildered, with a feeling of having been rejected by their idol. There is something creepy and alien about the whole thing. The euphoria occurs the following day.

The triumph of weirdness is not the least of the impossibilities. To become the world's greatest star and at the same time be thoroughly peculiar, thoroughly yourself, this is rare. Of course our cultural heroes and heroines must in every field contribute an element that is quite new, quite exceptional. This is always difficult and one of the reasons why public recognition of them is sometimes delayed. But it is especially difficult in popular art which operates through simple, direct common denominators; even more difficult in the USA whose corporate mentality is unnerved by the odd; and more difficult still at the end of the 20th century when the pressures towards technological standardisation are so immense.

It is thought-provoking that the most popular entertainer on earth should constantly challenge our notion of what is acceptable in appearance and conduct. But again if our age must have a star that is highly wrought in tension, perhaps it must also have one that is outlandish. In the millennial mood, cosiness can only take you so far. And how could he ever have become a regular bloke? Michael Jackson, finest flower of the USA's first family of entertainment, has grown up in the synthetic heart of the American Dream, in the innermost chamber of its Potala Palace. But no dalai lama or queen termite was more curiously nurtured, more strangely sustained. More than Judy Garland who started earlier than he, Jackson has from babyhood occupied the absolute eminence of razzamatazz. Both Temple and Garland were whirled about in an era of relative media modesty. He is the child of the media explosion. Countless computers and factories and organisations are at work every second upon promoting the idea that he should prevail. Is there life without fame? He has never known it, never known a world which doesn't reflect himself back to himself a millionfold.

And what is star quality? It is, for example, an essence in a context. He has the courage to live out his foibles, as well as his talents, in public. The plastic surgery, the shopping sprees with young friends to Hamley's toyshop, the attempt to acquire the relics of the Elephant Man, the visit to comedian Benny Hill in hospital – there is a grand eccentricity at work here. Probably Jackson doesn't see it; probably irony is not among his gifts. He is simply acting out his wishes and has the wealth to do so, providing additional spectacle for us all. In the European tradition heroes are not supposed to be involved with money – it would limit their freedom of action – but in the American tradition millionaires are worshipped. For me Jackson's extravaganzas resemble the ink which an octopus will squirt to hide itself from the cold gaze of the world.

Star quality is also the universal in the particular. MJ lives a certain torture which has usually gone with a large destiny (and often with no destiny at all!). This is the discomfort created by the violent trafficking between one's inner and outer life, a violence which all but shreds the safety curtain between the two. Jackson is a black man, a fact which is supposed to carry enormous charge. But to universalise, he partakes of whiteness, just as Elvis Presley, the Beatles, the Rolling Stones partook of blackness. This is the chemistry of our imploding cultures. And Jackson goes a step further in universality – the element of androgyny latent in those earlier pop idols in him becomes explicit. Skin bleaching, hair straightening, lip thinning: he now comes from everywhere. And nowhere. Which means he has loneliness to endure as well. All heroes have ultimately to be alone with themselves. I'm afraid it comes with the job.

Jackson's world tour is pledged to a good cause. It will last for 18 months and is expected to raise about £100 million for children's charities. The dream, the hype, the ambition, the energy, the problems, the scale, the noise and oddness of it all are extreme. But in a manic world vibrating between greed and despair as it rolls towards its various catastrophes, Michael Jackson – terribly vulnerable but terribly strong too – strikes a shimmeringly optimistic note: the herald of sweet mutant freedom. So before you ridicule or scorn this unusual song and dance man, just ask yourself what you have done lately to brighten up the place.

(1992)

THE POET IN CHELSEA

SIR JOHN BETJEMAN

SIR JOHN BETJEMAN, the Poet Laureate, was invited to lunch by myself but on the day in question Sir John had already made his arrangements and so reversed the invitation – 'Please join us. It will be me and 2 extremely nice old friends, the Reverend Gerry Irvine and his sister Rosemary.'

The following conversation took place at Sir John's house in Chelsea in the middle of a sunny day: blue sky, daffodils, and daisies. There are 2 background activities: (1) The rapid progress through bottles of champagne. These were by Dagonet and the speed is faster than usual because they were half bottles. (2) The attempts to take some snaps with an over-sophisticated polaroid camera.

'You've done your hair up in a new colour!' was the first thing he said with his toothy, crooked grin which is so open and fresh and artless and hasn't changed since he charmed his mother's tea guests with it as a little boy carrying a teddy-bear by one arm.

'No. I went to the tropics.'

'That's very brave of you. In the summer I like to go north, to the Faroe Islands, mist-laden Atlantic wonders. It stays cool up there. They roof their churches with sods. Would you like to have a little bubbly? Mr Glover, where are you? Oh, there you are, let's have another glass. And let's have another bottle.'

DUNCAN: I'm a bit late actually. The King's Road is blocked off.

SIR JOHN: It's not the punks is it?

DUNCAN: No, steamrollers. They're making a new road.

SIR JOHN: Mechanical punks . . . Can't offer you a cigarette. Haven't got any.

DUNCAN: I've got some Camels.

SIR JOHN: I love the smell of it.

DUNCAN: Have you an ashtray?

SIR JOHN: Use that Chelsea Arts bowl. They kindly presented it to me, the Chelsea Potters, a lovely firm.

DUNCAN: Why did you move here from the City? I loved Cloth Fair.

SIR JOHN: Driven out by the noise. I really liked the City better. But you know that great Barbican thing glaring down at one. Horrible great thing. It's only in the morning that you need this champagne to drink, you know.

DUNCAN: What do you have in the afternoon?

SIR JOHN: Sometimes I have a rest.

DUNCAN: I've brought some gadgets. This one is American. It's supposed to take polaroid pictures. Somebody told me how to use it but I've forgotten.

SIR JOHN: Do you want to take a picture?

DUNCAN: I thought I might. The picture shoots out of the bottom here and you watch it developing under your eyes.

SIR JOHN: Oh, let's have a go! Am I against the light do you think?

DUNCAN: Er, possibly . . .

SIR JOHN: Is this the first you've taken?

DUNCAN: I took some in a pub. You are supposed to hold it very still. They were a complete mess.

SIR JOHN: A man asked himself to luncheon here and he comes out of your past. Oh, look, it's shot out the front! Let's have a look.

DUNCAN: It should come up like a proper photograph!

SIR JOHN: I believe it's doing so. Something's happening.

DUNCAN: It's very clever . . . I think this one's going to be a bit dark.

SIR JOHN: I liked your things in the *Spectator*.

DUNCAN: Did you ever know any of those *Spectator* people?

SIR JOHN: I knew Peter Fleming. He said that each number of the *Spectator* was *semper idem sed numquam verbatim*.

257

Which do you think is the dullest periodical? *Punch*, I
suppose. I dare say the *Investor's Chronicle* is quite dull.

DUNCAN: The *Farmer and Stockbreeder*.

SIR JOHN: Is that dull?

DUNCAN: There used to be a livelier farming journal called the
Muckspreader.

SIR JOHN: Who publishes that? Odham's?

DUNCAN: I think it's gone now.

SIR JOHN: There are some publishers with absolutely no
character at all – Harrap's for example. No kind of house
style whatsoever. Methuen. It all comes through on
rollers like the London Brick Company. Not like my dear
old publisher Murray. Murray's've got somebody's
Forest Trees, I think, which keeps them going – it's the
standard book on the subject.

DUNCAN: Did you get any of my postcards from India?

SIR JOHN: Yes, I did! Lovely. Those wonderful Raj churches
which should have been in Surrey or Edinburgh.

DUNCAN: I sent one of St Paul's Cathedral in Calcutta.

SIR JOHN: That's obviously wonderful.

DUNCAN: It's the Regency version of Canterbury Cathedral.

SIR JOHN: Is it well-attended, St Paul's Calcutta?

DUNCAN: Mm, well, the out-patients department is. They
have a crack saviour service in jeeps.

SIR JOHN: High?

DUNCAN: No, they can't really afford the candles. But they're
eccentric. I heard a sermon there about Thackeray. He
was born in Calcutta.

SIR JOHN: I've never been there but my wife has.

DUNCAN: I saw her in Hay-on-Wye, incidentally.

SIR JOHN: I used to go and stay there but she has no water or
electricity or heating and all the windows are open with
the wind whistling through the place – well, I'm rather
frightened to go now in case it kills me. But I like Hay very
much. My wife knows India well. Did you come across
Rose Aylmer's tomb? It's in the cemetery at Calcutta.

DUNCAN: That cemetery is quite extraordinary. Full of
obelisks and pyramids but they are all at an angle of 45
degrees with urns falling off. And goats eating the grass.

258

SIR JOHN: That's right. There should be goats. I'm very much in favour of goats doing the grass rather than ATCOs. Or sheep too in graveyards – that's how it should be. Mr Glover, what about another bottle of this? ... he's disappeared. We've got a terrible smell of cats in the house, did you notice it? Can't make out where it comes from.

DUNCAN: Let's try another picture, one with the knob turned to light. And if that's wrong we can try it turned to dark.

SIR JOHN: And let's have the drink. I tell you who came to lunch. Dr Sutton from Magdalen College.

DUNCAN: Was he the man from my past you referred to?

SIR JOHN: Well, he must have been a don when you were there. American. Or maybe Canadian. I couldn't make out quite which.

DUNCAN: I can't place him.

SIR JOHN: With a wife. A chemistry don. Oh, that machine again! I don't think these photographs are going to work. Look what I had in to-day, from Southend-on-Sea, a lovely place. This letter, read it, it seems they've saved the Royal Hotel there from demolition. It cost £350,000. Southend got its name from being at the south end of the parish of – some other name, I forget ... Cricklewell! In Essex. The little picture at the top shows you what Southend's like – a lovely Georgian terrace.

DUNCAN: Ah, for a moment I was thinking of another hotel. Like a château on a bluff, one of the first purpose-built Victorian hotels – near Skegness, was it?

SIR JOHN: Scarborough! Now that's strange, I also had a letter in about that one to-day. I wish they would hold on to these things. These buildings are worth anything to the country. Anything with a gable or a tower is worth saving.

DUNCAN: I like the new aerial roadways in Birmingham.

SIR JOHN: Newcastle was lovely until Poulson was let in. Now there are just a few streets left in order to show you what it was once like. Newcastle Central Railway Station is still there. I think in Peter Parker we've got a good man for British Railways. He thinks like we do so perhaps they will stop trying to demolish St Pancras Station. Forgive my brushing my hair but I suddenly found this hairbrush and it's the most delightful sensation, what little hair I've got left, like a scalp massage. It's an ivoryback brush.

DUNCAN: I've one similar to that but I can't use it, it slides over the surface of my hair.

SIR JOHN: The bristles are so delicate. Whenever you go bald, should that ever happen to you, and I don't think it will –

DUNCAN: I think it might.

SIR JOHN: No, it seems to be bursting out quite boldly.

DUNCAN: That's because I've been living a hectic life for the past 3 weeks.

SIR JOHN: Where? In Lancaster Gate?

DUNCAN: Sometimes in Lancaster Gate. Everywhere . . .

SIR JOHN: What is your magazine?

DUNCAN: Very modern.

SIR JOHN: Bled-off pictures, things like that?

DUNCAN: Oh at least. £1 a copy – which is revolutionary. It has been maximum 95p until now.

SIR JOHN: A pound is a shilling. And a shilling a copy is very cheap. Is it an exciting job?

DUNCAN: It's fun. But it's not a job. I'm doing it freelance. It takes all one's time of course. Mary Whitehouse* wrote something for us.

SIR JOHN: I wonder what she's like. And I wonder what Mr Whitehouse is like – that's the mystery.

DUNCAN: I expect he's like Mr Thatcher.

SIR JOHN: Mr Whitehouse. I like to think about him. Are there kiddies?

DUNCAN: I think there's a son who's a disc jockey. Are you working hard for the Queen?

SIR JOHN: I tell you one nice thing I discovered – the Poet Laureateship is not what the newspapers presume it to be, it isn't a command to work when something important happens. It is meant to be a kind of reward for having worked for a long time – much better. Still, official people do sometimes phone up – one must avoid promising too many things on the telephone.

---

* A campaigner for puritanism.

DUNCAN: Are you invited very often to Buckingham Palace?

SIR JOHN: Not often, but I have had invitations. The Queen is very, very bright in the head, very well-informed. She's an awfully good conversationalist.

DUNCAN: Do you see the children much?

SIR JOHN: There's one who's awfully good on architecture. Richard of Gloucester. Prince Charles is a very humorous man, witty like his mother, great powers of mimicry. The family has an ear for music which is not something I have particularly. They really are better company than almost anyone you could meet, certainly better than the local council would be. Is it right to put all this down, do you think? On the whole I think it's better that people should say what they like. Whether it should all be printed and read – I'm not so sure.

DUNCAN: What do you think of this media explosion of the past 20 years then? You've participated in it.

SIR JOHN: I'm very pro it as far as poetry is concerned. I think it is now the only way you can get people to like poetry. And I'm very fond of filming. And I like the combination of verse – oh dear, do I sound too serious? – of verse and vision which makes a documentary.

DUNCAN: I saw your programme about Metroland.

SIR JOHN: That was all really the clever producer, Eddie Mirzoeff. My daughter worked on a book of photographs with Christopher Sykes of people's front gardens. It was a lovely idea but really it's a film I think. You see, when you get down to deckchair level every garden suddenly becomes Richmond Park, so you could have a helicopter filming on the ground then lifting up and you see the front of the house. That would be full of surprises. Nobody has ever thought of doing front gardens before. She and Christopher Sykes spent about a year going round looking at front gardens – and they found an interesting thing: that commuters don't build particularly interesting gardens. The best ones are built by people who stay at their houses all the time, and much better in the North Country, in Cheshire, than in Metroland.

DUNCAN: Perhaps commuters are Sunday gardeners like Sunday painters.

SIR JOHN: Yes, Peace Roses and things. Have some more champagne. Gerard Irvine is coming to lunch. He's vicar of St Matthew's, Great Peter Street, Westminster. *Extremely* high. And his sister too. She is headmistress of a girls' boarding school.

DUNCAN: The only vicar I've come across in London, apart from the Bishop of London, was the one from, I think, St James's Piccadilly who was known simply as 'the Vicar' and was rather grand, liked grand parties.

SIR JOHN: Oh, that was Bill Baddeley, Hermione Baddeley's brother. No, these people are from a good old slum parish in Westminster near all the MPs. Gerard Irvine's church was burned down last week, I'm very fond of that man who did the *Eagle* comic thing – Marcus Morris.

DUNCAN: He edited *The Best of Eagle*.

SIR JOHN: Yes, Marcus Morris, the son of a vicar in Southport. He's now head of Condé Nast.

DUNCAN: Our magazine is more punk.

SIR JOHN: Oh, punk rock! That's frightfully funny! Oh gosh, it's a frightfully good idea, very clever of you – have some more of that stuff. Mr Glover, can we have another bottle? Where's he got to, do you think?

DUNCAN: It's a fine name for a butler.

SIR JOHN: No, he's not a butler or anything. He does odd jobs around. At the moment he's doing some electrical rewiring. Do you have problems with printing strikes? It would be very nice to print it yourself . . . with arty-crafty people . . . rather slowly. Then you could charge £5 a copy. That would be lovely. Done on vellum. £5 a copy would be nice.

DUNCAN: With a candystripe cover.

SIR JOHN: Yes, and everything hand-painted by gentlefolk.

DUNCAN: The printers have advanced computers however . . .

SIR JOHN: Commanded about by their machinery. Like people who buy deep freezes and find themselves obliged to eat things they normally wouldn't want just because it goes into the freezer.

262

DUNCAN: But I love all this toy-like technology!

SIR JOHN: I like what that camera thing did just now. Did any of it come out?

DUNCAN: Let's see, well, no . . . only in a kind of arty sense.

SIR JOHN: Oh dear me, it's quite out of focus. And very funny colours. It's what is known as a 'camera study'. My red tie's come up rather marvellously, hasn't it? I like this one because I look almost invisible. It's like a spirit photograph. Very pale colours. It looks as if it's a picture by Marie Laurencin. She was a French painter. Lesbian. This is a beautiful photograph — my tie looks much better here than it does on me.

DUNCAN: This camera is perfect for artwork.

SIR JOHN: You mean it gets everything out of focus, that's why.

DUNCAN: Yes, it messes it up automatically.

SIR JOHN: That Marie Laurencin one is absolutely lovely.

DUNCAN: I received a poisonous letter from a writer called Michael Moorcock.

SIR JOHN: Who is he?

DUNCAN: He writes fantasies for children and hippies, churns it out. Pretty feeble stuff, and I said so. He said if I said so again he'd break both my legs with an iron bar.

SIR JOHN: Where did you run him down?

DUNCAN: In print.

SIR JOHN: Oh, they never forgive print. They think it's going to be there forever. I always believe anything that's said against me. And if anything is said in my favour I think they're only trying to be nice. To this day I think that. And I can only remember things said against me.

DUNCAN: One very occasionally meets these pop singers who've been subjected to massive adulation very suddenly.

SIR JOHN: Do any of them remain sane?

DUNCAN: I should think Mick Jagger is about the sanest.

SIR JOHN: He must be rather a nice man. Is he any relation to the sculptor, Sergeant Jagger? A wonderful sculptor who did the machine gun memorial opposite St George's Hospital. And the thing of the soldier reading a letter on Paddington Station, do you remember?

DUNCAN: Paddington Station?

SIR JOHN: Platform One. The War Memorial. I think he's a wonderful sculptor. If you look at that machine gun memorial you'll see that the machine guns are in stone and the people are in bronze. It's a sort of 1924 Modern. What's the latest President of Magdalen like? Griffiths, is it?

DUNCAN: He's said to know a lot about drink.

SIR JOHN: And a very sensible thing too. I hear he's very keen on the reproduction of music by mechanical means. He's got very elaborate gramophone and amplification arrangements. He's probably very musical. Let's see if Mr Glover's around and we can have another nip of that stuff.

The Reverend Gerard Irvine arrives with Rosemary Irvine. He is in a soutane, is very jolly and flushed and eighteenth-century looking. His sister is more contained, wears intelligent shoes, and has a dry sense of humour.

SIR JOHN: Shall we all have a spot of bubbly before we set out?

GERRY: Do you know whose birthday it is today apart from the Queen Mum's?

SIR JOHN: Osbert's [Osbert Lancaster]. I rang him up. Here you are, Rosemary, drink this.

ROSEMARY: Mmm . . . mmmmmmm . . .

GERRY: I'm going to stay at Rosemary's school next week before we go to Siberia – I thought I might drive out to see him if they're going to be there as they probably are.

SIR JOHN: Give him a tinkle. I've got the number. It's what they call Compton and I call Cumpton.

DUNCAN: Siberia?

GERRY: Yes, Rosemary and I are off on our holidays.

DUNCAN: Shall I have another go with this strange machine?

SIR JOHN: Try getting Gerry.

GERRY: Ah, no! No, I'm fearfully unphotogenic. Really I am! No, please, oh Lord!

ROSEMARY: Look, what are you going to do with that machine? Tell me.

264

DUNCAN: It's a very modern machine which I can't use alas.

GERRY: But you must realise how awfully ugly I am. It makes me terribly self-conscious. Please, oh, no . . .

ROSEMARY: Oh look, it's shot out! Did you see that? It shot out the front.

GERRY: But that's marvellous. How very clever.

DUNCAN: You have to wait a bit for the picture to show up.

GERRY: Can I see?

DUNCAN: There are some examples of my craft on the table – they're rather abstract.

SIR JOHN: They're camera studies.

DUNCAN: Do you smoke?

GERRY: No thank-you.

ROSEMARY: We're all too scared of lung cancer.

SIR JOHN: I wasn't scared about it, I, er – oh, er, yes, I think I was scared of that one, of course, who wouldn't be? . . . I found I became so nervous trying to give it up by cutting down that I had to give it up entirely because I got into such a state. Have you got everything in your glass, Rosemary? Have some more – isn't it lovely stuff in the morning?

ROSEMARY: Mmm, it is good stuff.

GERRY: Gorgeous stuff.

SIR JOHN: What we'll have – we're going to Au Fin Bec in Draycott Avenue. We'll start with oeufs Benedict which I think are better there than anywhere else I know. Oh, I was with somebody holy – I went to Mass at the Traveller's Club.

GERRY: Upstairs with old Father Gilbey?

SIR JOHN: That's it. There were some extremely right-wing people there.

GERRY: I'm sure there were. Everybody. I'm not a member any more. I've gone off it. It is now £150 a year – it used to be £45.

SIR JOHN: The food's better there than at the RAC. I joined the RAC because it was so empty and nobody spoke to one. And because it had a country club at Epsom which I've never been to but I always like to think that it's there if ever I want to. Perhaps we should have gone there for lunch since we've got a motor car.

GERRY: Has anything come out on that picture?

SIR JOHN: I look like Edward Heath in an off moment. His ghost. Wouldn't it be awful if we went out and found he was dead?

ROSEMARY: Would it be awful?

DUNCAN: I had a very odd experience the other day. I read an obituary of Bapsy Pavry. Do you know her? I discovered her in *The Indian Year Book* for 1941–2. Well, in this obituary I discovered a lot more about her – that she had since become the Marchioness of Winchester, then the Dowager. I checked it out from another source and found that she had indeed become the Marchioness and done these other things.

GERRY: She had a battle for the Marquess with Mrs Fleming.

SIR JOHN: Peter's mother.

ROSEMARY: And Ian's.

DUNCAN: Apparently Mrs Fleming sued her for alienation of her husband's affections. But the funny thing was that when I telephoned *The Times* for a copy of the obituary, they said they hadn't published one. I thought then that maybe I'd read it in some other paper and telephoned the rest – none had published an obituary. In fact hardly anyone had heard of her. So I phoned Nigel Dempster, who's a gossip columnist, and he said he'd last seen her alive and well at Ascot a few years ago. So where did that obituary come from which revealed to me new and accurate information about her?

GERRY: You should put it down now while you remember. We might be able to use it as an example of precognition. Her husband was the oldest Marquess ever. He died at the age of a hundred or something.

SIR JOHN: Shall we go and eat?

Rosemary drove and there was a moment of frisson while crossing the King's Road, followed by some disorientation in a cul de sac. There were several ribald remarks about a certain block of flats used for prostitution, by which time the car had been brought back to dirigibility. We eventually found ourselves at the destination and hit the dry martinis. Oeufs Benedict broke and dribbled to perfection. The veal was moist and wittily served. The spinach a tour de force of deliquescent greens and buttery yellows. The red wine a swooning fermentation of superior fruits from a hillside chosen by wizards. Cutlery and tableware were creditably amenable to the machinations of one's hands which were no longer needle-perfect in their coordination. The electric lighting, as befits a sunny day, was golden yet languorously subdued. The chairs were comfortable but not so excessively as to induce somnolence. The clientèle, insofar as they impinged, seemed to be delightfully enthusiastic about life without being overzealous on the matter. Our talk grew bawdy.

(1977)

HIM AND A GLIMPSE OF HER
THE KOESTLERS, MONTPELIER SQUARE

8 MONTPELIER SQUARE; the evening of November 6th.

Arthur Koestler is a tiny dapper figure with greenish blue eyes and yellow, fleshless skin. His elfinlike air reminds one he is Hungarian, not German. And the head is not the massive piece of masonry suggested by those official photographs of the European Thinker (one hand always propping up the side of his face, clear eyes focused on the Immensities) but round and detailed like a finely carved billiard ball. His smile is sly, even coy, and redeems the somewhat unhealthy impression given off by his overindulgence in ratiocination.

He wears the costume of the Old Left. This is the same as that of the Old Right except that all the materials are rough instead of smooth, tending to light rather than dark (in Koestler's case, tending to green), and nothing matches anything else: check shirt, woollen cardigan, tartan tie, tweed jacket, and so on. This costume exhales the authentic ether of Guernica and the Left Book Club, of long nights in London trying to solve the world with Bertrand Russell and George Orwell, of getting drunk in Paris with Sartre, Camus, Malraux, and Simone de Beauvoir (who described his personality as 'tumultuous'). Koestler resigned from the Communist Party in 1938 as a result of Stalin's purges and his novel *Darkness At Noon* (1940) conveyed the inner nature of that regime. During the Spanish Civil War he was imprisoned in a death cell by Franco. At the outbreak of World War II he spent 4 months in a French concentration camp. In the 1950s he turned away from politics and now he is more famous for his interest in the area where science appears to touch the paranormal.

Sitting very uneasily in a pool of lamplight, Mr Koestler seems low. His wife Cynthia, a gentle woman who wears no make-up and has the look of one who has only recently stopped crying, explained downstairs that he is not at his best – he is recovering from a viral infection which is how the Koestlers describe a cold. Cynthia is much younger than Arthur and will presumably tend with love and pride his posthumous reputation. She began to work for him in 1949 and had to watch him divorce 2 previous wives – Dorothy in 1950, Mamaine in 1953 – before taking her place officially at his side in 1965. She has the semi-numb Buddhist detachment of one who has spent a lifetime in surrender of her will to another.

While I'm trying to regress him to his days in Vienna as a student of science and psychology, back to the 20s of Freud, Koestler suddenly shakes himself into the present: 'I used to be a journalist – what is the peg for this interview?'

Koestler is drowsy to-day and tires easily – or rather, bores easily – but when he does come alive it is abruptly, like a compact and efficient reptile sensing danger. Pegs? Well, the Danube Edition of his Collected Works continues to grow, volume by volume, the most recent being a volume of essays and reviews on favourite themes of his: paranoia, ESP, nuclear catastrophe, canoeing. Also Iain Hamilton's much-delayed official biography of Koestler, 10 years in the writing, has been published – and disowned by its subject. But the most important peg is quite simply that Mr Koestler avoids personal publicity with some determination and is therefore an object of curiosity. He avoids it not out of modesty (he is sufficiently vain to have written 4 volumes of autobiography) but through a fear of anything he can't control.

He dislikes being interviewed and nearly always refuses. 'And I'm recovering from a viral infection,' he moans. He dislikes tape-recorders because he says he rambles when he talks. He doesn't ramble. It is just that he is so terrified of being misunderstood or worse – misused – that he is disinclined to make any remark that has not been rendered watertight by years of cogitation. Perversely, this can oppress and diminish his ability to deal with the truth – spontaneity and lightness have their value too. He dislikes appearing on television and radio 'because my accent is too thick and it embarrasses me.' When I ask if a photographer might call, he cocks his head to one side, frowns and says 'I'd prefer to avoid it. I know where you can get good photographs of me.' One feels that the list of his dislikes could be extended quite a way. What does he dislike most of all?

'Stupidity.'

'What about your own?'

'Including my own.'

He was born in Budapest in 1905. 'I'm from typical Central European Jewish family. Middle-middle. Before the ceiling fell in.'

'The ceiling?'

'1939. 1942 mostly. Auschwitz. My mother was Viennese but my father Hungarian. He was an industrialist who had too much imagination and financed disastrous new inventions. He said too much time is wasted opening envelopes and big business needs an envelope opening machine, so one day a huge machine came into the house – it would have covered half that wall. The inventor came with it. He looked like one of Snow White's 7 dwarfs the way he hopped around his machine. It was plugged into the electricity, turned on, there was an enormous clattering and shuddering, then flames started to lick here and there about it and we all got terribly scorched. Another invention was radioactive soap. You must remember the time, 1918-ish, when curative properties were ascribed to radioactivity. This soap was supposed to make you glow with health and vitality but it didn't catch on.'

He falls silent, as if he'd prefer to nod off in his chair. I imagine sleepless nights on the racks of impossible logic, the torture of preposterous dilemmas. Does he suffer from insomnia?

'No. I used to sleep 7 hours a day. Now it's closer to 9 which is one of the disappointments of old age. They always promised one would sleep less. I sleep very well and always have done, even in prison.'

'You were in a concentration camp for 4 months. Was that a useful experience?'

'I was in a Spanish prison before, in a death cell. I didn't know when my turn to be shot was coming. Afterwards the French camp was easy to bear. It taught me among other things the relativity of freedom. Solitary confinement is rock bottom. I was in solitary most of the time.'

'Was that frightening?'

'In fact I preferred solitary to sharing. It depends on the individual. But it's generally considered rock bottom.'

'You opposed Fascism, then you ditched Communism – '

'No, I didn't. Communism ditched me by turning into Stalinism.'

'Do you have faith in any political philosophy?'

'Nothing very original or specific now. Please don't let's talk about politics.'

'Oh, all right then. Am I being too formal? I get the feeling that I'm too wooden.'

'You're doing all right, coping with a strange alien and feeling your way.'

'Have you ever felt you were going mad?'

'No.'

'What would be madness for you?'

'At the University of Michigan there was an awfully nice English psychiatrist who persuaded me to be a guinea pig taking the psilocybin mushroom. When I was under the influence of it I had what is called a very bad trip. I noticed the psychiatrist had a scar on his neck – from a mastoid operation perhaps. His face went green and the scar started gaping as a wound. For some reason I thought "Now at last the Gestapo have got me!" Or was it the KGB? Then the psychiatrist had a table lamp and suddenly the base of it developed bird's claws. I flipped for a moment into normality and told myself "You are hallucinating, that's all. If you touch the claws they'll go away." But they didn't go away. Not only a visual but also a tactile hallucination. It was extremely frightening. So when you ask me what madness is – it is when your perceptions are dramatically deviating from reality. This is not a scientific definition however. When I came back from this experience of induced schizophrenia, the after-effects lasted for several months. Timothy Leary went round the bend of course.'

271

Koestler came to live in England in 1940 – 'because France collapsed in the most shameful way, Europe was kaput' – and became a British subject after the war. 'I lived in North Wales for 3 years, just about enough. Snowdonia. And on and off in France and America. But I couldn't put down roots in the USA. When I was in America it became very obvious to me that I am a European. For this purpose I would include England in Europe – but not for all purposes. When I first came to England I enlisted. I had to join the Glorious Pioneers, *digging for victory* as the slogan went.'

The intelligentsia of the Left, especially George Orwell who wrote an essay on him, were impressed by Koestler's credentials, i.e. his sufferings, although these were hardly outstanding by the standards of continental Jews. However his status as a free-thinker who had been beaten up by monsters in uniform was important to his future and all the biographical data issued by publishers on his behalf continue to give great prominence to his periods of detention as a political prisoner.

As for England, 'what appealed to me about it originally was what Orwell described – the sticks-in-the-mud, the old maids bicycling to Holy Communion through the fog and mist, a nation of darts players and pigeon fanciers, knobbly faces with gentle manners and bad teeth, and so on. Then history made a perverse somersault and it turned out that England was the only country which lost the war.'

This cliché of materialism is unexpectedly crude for Koestler.

'But there didn't used to be skinheads and muggings in England,' he says, his voice fading, his whole system seeming to deflate. Then he makes one of his abrupt rallies. His method is to shift the ground sharply, in both the physical and mental senses. He stands up to look for a newspaper clipping and the years drop away. When he walks it is with a dancing gait, the toes pointing outwards in their tiny buff suede shoes, and the knees are lifted to an unusual extent. If standing still his shortness means he holds himself very erect, determined not to lose a fraction of those precious inches, the backs of his legs very straight in their little pipes of navy blue corduroy. About the whole there is something androgynous and

272

attractive, a combination of chocolate soldier and ballet master.

'Did you see a magazine,' he asks, 'called *The New Musical Express*? It turns out there is a pop group called the Police and they made a record of *The Ghost in the Machine*. I didn't know about it until the clipping agency sent me this review a while back. A rather difficult book has become the inspiration for a pop group. It came as a great surprise. I've had no contact with them. I'm slightly tickled by it,' and his cheeks pucker with pleasure. Koestler resists elevation to gurudom, but worldly success is important to him as evidence of effective communication. 'I'm ambivalent about the mail in the morning. It's an awful bind. The fanmail is hell. But no fanmail would be worse hell.' And he is sufficiently proud to have included in his *Who's Who* entry not only the customary list of his own books but also a list of those written *about* him – a remarkable piece of self-aggrandisement.

The Koestlers divide their time between this house in Montpelier Square almost opposite Harrods (where Koestler has lived since 1952) and Suffolk where they have a farmhouse (as opposed to a farm). 'We had a house in the Austrian Tyrol for 12 years.' Koestler becomes dreamy – he knew the Tyrol as a child. 'I loved it. Then the tourists caught up with us and the village was ruined. So 10 years ago we bought the house in Suffolk. I love the climate of East Anglia which as you know is the flat part of England. You feel very braced by the weather and vigorous in the daytime, and at night-time you sleep like a doormouse. Dry continental climate blowing over from Siberia.'

This was the only occasion when he used the word 'love'. His big book *The Act of Creation*, a psychological investigation of 751 pages, doesn't deal with love at all, not even in the disguises of marriage or sex. He is in no sense a family man, 3 marriages – but childless, at his insistence. Apparently his reason was that babies would be a distraction from work. 'My family,' he says, 'is just my wife and one dog. It used to be 2 dogs.'

David, a Lhasa Apso, lifts his cloudy white head off the carpet in acknowledgement.

('David is mine,' explained Cynthia earlier when Arthur was out of the room. 'Arthur dislikes small dogs. His dog was Goliath, a Newfoundland. It died.')

'Cynthia used to be my secretary,' he continues. 'So she's part of the work too. A most stabilising factor in marriage – shared work.' In the same slightly chilling way, the dedications of his books are not so much to friends as to literary agents and the directors of institutions.

He is not interested in character, only in ideas; not interested in Tom, Dick or Harry, only in mankind. He scorns gossip. He expresses the mental collectivism of an ex-Communist and the indifference to personal feeling of the wholly dedicated European intellectual (a breed which gave you all the 'isms' including totalitarianism).

But Koestler's distrust of the heart is also the fear of violence and chaos, qualities of which he is understandably suspicious. This was evidenced in his wish to see a transcription of our conversation before anything was written up. 'Just to make sure I didn't say anything vulgar or silly.' The horror of vulgarity or mischief – this is coming close to a distaste for life itself. It has something of Beckett's wormlike bleakness, Sartre's nausea, and could well be the black hole of the Koestler universe through which all his works will be sucked away into oblivion.

'Sir Thomas Gold, the British astronomer, tells a story of when he was going round America on a lecture tour explaining the Big Bang theory. There's a very old lady at one of the lectures who says "Mister, I've got a much better theory about the universe. There's a huge tortoise with a thin covering of earth on its back – that's the universe." And Tommy Gold said "But what is the tortoise standing on?" And she said "On a much bigger tortoise of course. It's no use arguing, mister. It's tortoises all the way down." That just about sums it up. The Cosmological Quest – an infinite series of recessions.'

At the terminus of the intellect you find either a concentration camp in the outer world or a pagoda of tortoises in the inner world. So the next step forward for Mr Koestler is the leap into mysticism, although he cannot quite reconcile himself to the incipient giggliness of a state which ridicules unhappiness. Does mysticism include the paranormal?

'I do believe that the evidence for telepathy for example is overwhelming and that it is a part of reality that is above science. Science allows us only to glimpse fragments of reality. There are concepts such as infinity in space and time which science cannot fathom.'

'What about occultism?'

'You mean wise men in Tibet and all that? No, no, no.'

The room is predominantly green with green walls. Its furniture has an Empire flavour and there are interesting pieces of Egyptian sculpture in it. On the coffee table is Barbara Pym's *Quartet in Autumn*. And also *The Dancing Wu Li Masters: an Overview of the New Physics* by Gary Zukav. On the front of this book the man at the *New York Times* says 'The most exciting intellectual adventure I've been on since reading *Zen and the Art of Motorcycle Maintenance*.' This is Koestler's Hungarian shamanism and his Jewish Kabbalism coming through.

Otherwise he remains a model of self-control. A slow and deliberate reader and writer for example. (When in due course the transcription was delivered, Koestler swayed over it like a praying mantis, taking 1¾ hours to examine 9 pages and making only 3 or 4 very minor adjustments.) He prides himself on being the only writer who twice changed the language in which he writes, from Hungarian to German at 17 and from German to English at 35.

'But in any language it is a struggle to make a sentence say exactly what you mean. English has a muscularity with the fat massaged away. German is a very woolly language. French has a so-called Cartesian lucidity but – no, cross out that remark, it's getting too complicated.'

So let's move away from ideas and get into character. 'What are your vices?'

A long pause. ' . . . . . Is smoking a vice? I drink the normal amount . . .' A longer pause. The doors to long-forgotten chambers are cranked open by a process that is almost audible. But found to be empty. ' . . . Funny, I can't think of any. I'm trying but I can't.'

'You try to be good.'

'Look at that viking ship over there made out of balsa. For

20 years now there has been something called the Arthur Koestler Award for Prisoners, competing with paintings, model-making, writing etc. It isn't much publicised because there's no point in doing so. That's my do-gooding side.'

'What are your failures?'

'Let's come back to what makes a good man. I don't know what makes a good man. I was active in the campaign for the abolition of capital punishment. I'm Vice President of the Euthanasia Society.'

'Who's the President?'

'There isn't one. But we've had a terrible setback recently . . .'

'I think people are nervous about giving others the right to kill them.'

'Oh, quite.'

'I think that's understandable.'

'Oh yes.'

'One must be very careful.'

'Indeed.'

'Don't you agree?'

'Mmm . . .'

'What is your idea of paradise?'

'That's a silly question.'

'It doesn't have to be a silly answer.'

' . . . ugh . . .'

Koestler descends into one of his grunting phases and can manage no complexity of response. Then out of the blue, quite without warning, he begins to make a very peculiar noise, a wailing half-yodel. 'Hoo-ooo-oo.' I look about me but detect no obvious reason for it. Is some energy from the long-denied earth principle forcing itself out through an unguarded fissure in his otherwise ever-vigilant mind? Has some Tyrolean atavism finally by-passed decorum and flung itself forth? Here it goes again. 'Hoo-ooo-ooooo!' Eventually . . . Cynthia staggers up from her private lair downstairs and stands a touch tautly in the doorway of the drawing-room. Evidently this curious wail is her summons.

'Can we have some more drinks, angel?' asks Koestler, 'because I want to get on with this.' The gentleman from

Budapest is accustomed to servants, it seems, because the drinks tray is *very* close to his elbow.

'When a writer loses his doubt, his uncertainties,' he goes on, with a refill of much-watered malt whisky, 'he loses his humility – then he's finished, then he'll go on writing the same book again and again like an idiot.'

'Are doubt and depression connected for you?'

'Always.'

'This means you must always be unhappy.'

'I'm happy when work goes well. You know, I would like to die in harness. Vices – I've just thought of one. I'm a workaholic. If I stop working and just try to enjoy myself, I get very neurotic and guilt-ridden and so when sometimes I displace myself to a sunnier climate I always take the office with me. But I love playing games like Scrabble and chess. That's not wasting time because it is an effort. Anything which is an effort is virtuous, is work, and worth doing.'

But because the mind, like the body, cannot maintain constant exertion, Mr Koestler's concentration collapses without his permission. In other words he suffers from depression. It results from a subconcious refusal to accept that life cannot be all glamorous intensity, that one is obliged to accommodate the passive as well as the active mode. And this is presumably exacerbated by the problems of growing old.

'Whenever I get depressed.' He dances up to a floor-to-ceiling bookcase. 'Which I often do.' He places a hand on his hip. 'I come over here and look at these.' He extends the other hand towards the shelves in a gesture of demonstration. 'If ever I wonder what on earth it was all for, here is the evidence. The 30 books I've written plus all the translations – 42 different languages including English.'

Croatian, Ukrainian, Norwegian, Telugu, Russian – 'in samizdat of course.' (Barbara Cartland, the world's most prolific writer, has only been translated into 21 languages.)

'My comforter,' he muses, surveying the wall of print.

'You must have said something.'

'I must have had something to say,' he corrects, with an extremely sneaky, boyish smile.

(1981)

277

Postscript. 15 months later Arthur and Cynthia Koestler formed a suicide pact and killed themselves with an overdose of pills. The maid arriving in the morning found a note saying 'Don't go upstairs' and telling her to call the local police. The couple were found slumped in armchairs in the room where this interview took place, with the curtains drawn. For him a very logical death. For her a very emotional one. He was said to be suffering from Parkinson's disease. She could not envisage a life without him. The dog David had previously been given to friends.

TIMOTHY LEARY, WONDERLAND PARK, LOS ANGELES

DR TIMOTHY LEARY, experimental psychologist, youth freak, and advocate of mind-expanding drugs, indeed of mind-expanding anything, is currently living in a bungalow in Wonderland Park, Laurel Canyon, north of Sunset Boulevard in Hollywood. This isn't Bel Air grandeur, just comfortable middle-class college-professor (Leary taught at Harvard until expelled in 1963 for LSD experiments) West Coast finelife among irrigated hanging gardens. 'It's rather like the French Riviera, don't you think?' he enquires.

The house is very Californian, big cream floor cushions instead of a sofa in the sitting-room and neurotechnology books in the study – plus a bar in one corner and a Filipino maid to clean up. 'It used to be a bohemian area, then it became quite rock 'n' roll. Ex-governor Jerry Brown lives a couple of doors away.' The sun is blazing outside; the air inside is rinsed and rendered somehow hard and unreal, faintly metallic and perfumed and irritating to the sinuses, by air-conditioning. Leary has a young wife (his fifth) and a young son. One can't imagine him having anything else. California, the youth-obsessed. Everywhere the tight rubbery flesh of youth, lightly muscled, deeply golden. And home of the ageing immortalists, of the cryonic engineering which freezes you into coffins for resurrection at a later date, of physioplasty and psychoplasty.

The look of Southern California is rather 1950s. The nicest thing about it is that it is horizontal and adjustable like a box kit. 'Understanding' is one of its commodities. Jung liked to distinguish between understanding and knowledge. Understanding, he said, had in it the diabolical element which kills. California's loose brain can absorb and neutralise in its benign

279

mush even the greatest ideas. Californians, like all Americans but much more so, are under tremendous pressure never to be caught without a smile. They talk a language called 'mellow' to avoid frightening each other with direct statements. Mind-expansion becomes lack of concentration or worse: anaesthesia. They understand neurosis, but not tragedy –

TL: Hang on, hang on a minute. Wolves eat rabbits, I know that. Our animal brain is wired to be paranoid, jumpy, panicked, to go into jungle action, I know that. But I would say that the East Coast and European mentality is to centre obsessively on terror and suffering. I'm always amused when people attack my optimism as if I'm avoiding the hard issues. I've been in prison, in solitary, in eyeball-to-eyeball, life or death confrontations with the Sicilian Mafia, the Corsican Mafia, the Afghani Generals, the Black Panthers and Weathermen, the CIA. I've had tremendous personal tragedies. My life right now is pain every day because of my children and God knows what else – my God, I face these things, I sweat through disasters – maybe 99% of life is that. But the 1% I'm interested in is a precise optimism and skilful growth technology that I've been studying all my life and can pass on to other people. That 1% of intelligent scientific virtue is what interests me.

Dr Leary was hoping to visit London for the opening of the film debate *Return Engagement* but the Home Office said no. In the film Leary defends the rights of the individual against Gordon Liddy defending the power of the state. Liddy masterminded the Watergate break-in, although 'mastermind' is not exactly the right word since it was Liddy's incompetence which collapsed Nixon.

TL: This is the positive side of Liddy's work. It's mildly flattering that the Home Office considers me so much more dangerous than him. There was no problem about *him* going to England and his crimes were much more glamorous than mine. My crime was merely possessing less than half an ounce of marijuana.

But Leary also then escaped from his Californian prison, for which he subsequently got another 5 years. He fled in a roundabout way to Algeria and entrusted himself to Eldridge Cleaver and the Black Panthers. This was a mistake. So he engineered another escape – from Cleaver's grim 'protection' – and fled in a roundabout way to Afghanistan where he was kidnapped by federal agents and forcibly returned to American gaol. After the fall of Nixon, Leary's case was reviewed and he was released.

DF: Altogether how much time have you spent in prison?
TL: 42 months.
DF: How many different gaols?
TL: 40.
DF: What! . . . What did you feel in prison?
TL: I felt no guilt. I chastised myself for stupidity only, for falling into traps.
DF: What did you learn from it?
TL: I learned a great deal about how the law and order industry works, this factory procedure of taking bodies and putting them through the justice system. The prison system in the States is extraordinarily decent compared to, say, the South American.
DF: You're very gregarious – was loneliness ever a problem?
TL: No. I was in solitary confinement 29 months. When I was at West Point Military Academy as a young man I was 'silenced' which is like being in solitary. It is a luxury. No phones, no demands, no events. In solitary I found myself locked up with one of the most amusing minds of our time.
DF: How many LSD trips have you taken?
TL: Oh, I don't know, several hundred.
DF: What was the worst one?
TL: I've had quite a few moments of ontological terror and philosophical angst in many, many sessions. The worst

281

one was during the break-up of my marriage to the woman I call Jeannette in the book. I felt truly isolated.

This refers to his autobiography *Flashbacks*. One of the problems with this book is its lack of rigour. It says things like Madame Blavatsky studied with wise men in Tibet, Wordsworth was a pioneer hashish explorer etc.

DF: Do you know Ireland well?

TL: Not well enough. The older I become the more I see my life as conditioned by an unconscious Celtic character. Ireland is wonderful because it's as far west as you can get in Europe. My theory of neurogeography is that freedom and intelligence have been moving east to west. Even the centre of Hollywood is still moving west. When you go east you travel back through a time tunnel until you get to a mediaeval police state in Siberia.

DF: What about Japan?

TL: From our map in California the extreme west is Japan and Australia. There is a great alliance between California and Japan in the new computer world of artificial intelligence. The Japanese are converting their island into a knowledge factory.

DF: What makes you angry?

TL: I consider anger a destructive, unintelligent response if indulged in for more than 5 minutes at a time.

DF: Anger can be a very quick and efficient discharge of negative energy.

TL: Yes, as long as you keep it quick and focused. It's also a very useful way to shock, to awaken.

DF: Why does the American Government support cruel dictatorships in South America?

TL: We have heavy commercial interests in these countries. Fruit companies and oil companies prefer dictators: they are quicker and easier to deal with. The men who run America are East Coast WASPs. The good side of the American experiment is the frontier, freedom, innovation, individuality. The flip side is a dark puritanism, gloomy, anti-human, the world's a bad place. As Gordon

Liddy says in the film 'The world's a bad neighbour-hood'. They're cruel therefore, anti-freedom, anti-fun, anti-ecology. In the Reagan Administration the big term of scorn is to call someone a snail-data type, i.e. someone who is interested in the impact of industry and pollution on the lowly snail. These men who run America have a ruthless hard-boiled contempt for human happiness, which almost mirrors the Russian view.

DF: What are you bad at? In the sense of – clumsy at?

TL: I'm clumsy at getting my signals out. There's a sense of mischief or self-indulgent bravado in the way I present what I believe to be tremendously important issues. A desire to shock a bit.

DF: I think this jokey side is part of your Americanness.

TL: It's Celtic too. James Joyce had it. And Mark Twain, who is my American hero. The title of my book for example – *Flashbacks*. I should have called it, if I didn't have this flaw, something like *Remembrances and Regrets*.

DF: Oh God.

DF: I tried to have the title changed for the paperback but it's too late. In all I wrote 3000 pages which were cut to 600. In movie parlance I shot 5 to 1. I could have written 3 books at least on prison.

DF: You did that book *Jailnotes*.

TL: No, I didn't. I tried to stop that thing. They were just notes I was sending out and concealed in them were escape plots and so forth. It was published without my permission. But there was nothing I could do because by that time I was in exile in Algeria being protected by Cleaver – what a disaster *that* was!

DF: Have you been barred from Britain before?

TL: The previous time was January 1973. Just a few months previously a Chinese diplomat had defected in Rome. He'd been captured by the Chinese, drugged, and flown forcibly to Paris for a connection to Peking. He was being brought through Orly Airport and the French police saw this, stopped it, and freed the Chinese defector. The French came out as heroes in the defence of freedom. Well, although I wasn't drugged, I was in exactly the

283

same situation, being forcibly returned to the United States after being kidnapped in Afghanistan. As I was being forcibly escorted through Heathrow Airport I appealed to the cause of freedom but they didn't want to know. It's a shame. England had this tradition of being the home of exiles, eccentrics and fugitives. The psychedelic impulse came from England. It was the great transmitting station east to west. Shall we have some lunch? Let's wait 2 minutes and then we'll eat.

DF: Why 2 minutes?

TL: So that I can finish my cigarette. Still – England is less puritan than the USA. I can't believe what you say, that it's possible to publish 'fuck' in *The Times*. They've only just allowed 'damn' into the *New York Times*.

DF: Why were you released? People said you were informing on drug rings and revolutionary groups.

TL: I served 4 times the official sentence for my original crime. Besides, possession of that amount of marijuana had since been reduced to the status of a traffic offence. The government put out statements that I was informing, (a) in order to discredit me, and (b) to sow the seeds of paranoia among the various groups, and in this they succeeded. But no one ever went to prison because of anything I said. Until about a month before I got out on appeal I was still involved in escape plots. Have you read that bit in the book about Joanna and the guns and all that? My attitude towards life is basically an Alice in Wonderland, somewhat bumbling openness. I don't claim to have it off pat at all. I've made hundreds of mistakes. Eldridge Cleaver was more than a mistake – I must have been nuts. At the same time it was a funny, interesting episode. When I found myself in Algeria in the power of Cleaver, well, you simply couldn't trust anyone. Everybody was a triple agent. It was a period of tremendous confusion and lowered self-esteem. I was totally helpless.

DF: Do you believe in evil?

TL: No. It's in the nature of a rattlesnake or scorpion to poison you.

Leary has been accused of having gone round the bend, but that's clearly nonsense. A bit shell-shocked perhaps, but his inner and outer worlds correlate very well – he can make a living out of his convictions.

DF: Have you ever felt you were going mad?

TL: .... No.

DF: What is madness for you?

TL: Madness is basically not receiving information, not attending to what's coming in. And imposing the same programme on the world even though it's not working.

DF: Then most people would be mad.

TL: Yes, I think so. What is madness for you?

DF: Um – being unable to buy a pint of milk because of interference from outer space ... What's the closest you've been to death?

TL: I almost drowned in this cove in Mexico. I've taken ketamine many times which is a drug which produces what we call an experimental death experience, a classic replica of an out-of-the-body experience. It's wonderful, it's the safest anaesthetic, they give it to babies.

DF: I hear the birth rate dropped.

TL: Modern kids in California are the most consciously conceived kids in history. The birth rate plummeted after 1964. They are very clued-up kids, very into the computer world of artificial intelligence. I think the concept of the 'programme' is extremely useful. I was playing chess with a computer once. I'm not very good at chess and said I wanted to end it. The computer answered 'illegal move'. So I said 'Fuck you' and the computer answered 'illegal move'. This went on for a bit until a kid told me that to get out of the game you had to press the button marked 'exit'. This is what mental suffering is – not knowing which button to press to get out of the game, to get a new programme. The Industrial Age is over, the Information Age has arrived.

DF: What's it like getting older?

TL: Less breath.

DF: More reflective?

TL: I've been reflective all along. I'm a philosopher by blood and bone. You are as old as the last time you changed your mind, as old as the people you hang out with. I'm always playing around at computers with young kids. Reagan never goofs around with anyone young – he'll just about shake hands with the girl scout troupe from Mississippi. Have you seen photographs of those geriatric dinner parties? I'm into paedomorphosis. A generation of humans is a continent in time. You can jump continents.

DF: But as the voice of experience, what is your message for the youth of to-day?

TL: Intelligent distrust of all authority: spiritual, intellectual, political. And precise scientific optimism about continual change.

DF: I was thinking particularly of an unemployed youth with no future, suffering from alienation and depression. What would you suggest he did?

TL: Move. For Christ's sake, move! Sometimes migration is the only answer. People are so afraid to move. You don't have to move alone. Get 2 or 3 friends and move together. Allies are very important in life ... Most people are involved in conspiracies to hold each other down. Most families and friends don't *want* you to change – it threatens them.

Continual change, very Californian. In fact there is some history hereabouts. John Barrymore lived in that house over there. The Spanish heritage still lingers – a block down the road is something called 'El Snack Bar'. But if California has a function it is the escape from history. This is its freedom, its exhilaration for the visitor. And Hollywood is still a film town – the big headline is: *Bette Davis loses breast to cancer and courageously battles stroke*. They get up early here, not only because they have to telephone New York, but because the film community does. Overheard in café: 'You'll never guess who I've just seen on the other side of the road. Yul Brynner. With Carol Channing. Yeah, just across the road.' American psychology, like almost every other American industry, aspires to the condition of show business. There is much originality in the USA – but it is not in ideas. It is in the marketing of ideas. The local home-grown guru is Carlos Castaneda whose great success was in rejecting understanding and having a go at knowledge. His stories make the long overdue connection between the modern California of products and an older Indian past rooted in the landscape. Behind all the plasticity of modern America is always overwhelmingly the landscape. Dr Leary is chewing heartily on a variety of chicken limbs.

TL: I've met Castaneda, but he's only an acquaintance. He's one of these mystery people. I found him very guarded. It's his warrior idea, that if you give away any truth about yourself, you give away some of your power. So he just mirrored everything back that he thought would impress or satisfy me. It was rather transparent, kind of . . . dull. He's no fun at all to be with. But he's supposed to be giggling inside. Castaneda was married for I think 8 years and the wife, an American woman, says he's as much a mystery to her as to anyone else. She said that when they were divorcing she was living back in the East and Castaneda was in New York and they got together for a week-end, a little fling. She was perhaps hopeful that they'd get back together again but he disappeared afterwards. She saw him a couple of years later and said 'That was such a wonderful week-end we had in New York – how come you never called me back?' And he said 'What are you talking about? We never had a week-end in New York. The Hotel Plaza? I've never been there.'

DF: This is like those power games that governments play which you were referring to before.

TL: Yes, it's very irritating once you've seen through it.

DF: I see you're not a vegetarian.

TL: No, I'm not. I hate all forms of righteousness and prudishness. I tried it once at Millbrook which was our experimental place in New York State. We tried everything there. The only violence we ever had was irate vegetarians attacking convinced carnivores in the kitchen.

DF: Do you eat much?

TL: No. And I've always been very slim – I blame it on my genes.

DF: You were the chief apologist for LSD in the 60s. What about the problem of drug abuse?

TL: Psychedelic drugs like LSD, mescalin, marijuana are probably among the safest of all drugs, obviously much more safe than alcohol, nicotine, heroin, speed. People say that drug use has declined. It hasn't, but self-indulgence has. These things are incorporated rather more intelligently into the daily pattern. There are 30 million regular cocaine users in the USA – a few lines for a party. But the flamboyant cases get all the publicity. I'm glad the drug culture is over. Blind faith in drugs is ludicrous. Drug abuse in the 1970s made people more thoughtful about drugs which is good. Just as herpes made people more thoughtful about sex. The average herpes victim is young, attractive, college-educated, affluent – I don't mind being put into that group.

DF: The same might be said for the average hepatitis or AIDS victim. Have you seen this advertisement in the newspaper? *Robert Aay Products After-Sex Genital Body Wash for the Disease Conscious Male.* Do you have many blind spots?

TL: Aesthetically, I'm rather vulgar. A little bit loud. I've solved this problem by having my wife Barbara who's extraordinarily aesthetic. My worst fault, and I blame my genes again, is a tendency to exaggerate the positive, to make promises that are probable but not necessarily certain – sometimes I disappoint people. An Irishman's fact is a Celt's hope. One of my biggest mistakes was ever getting involved with lawyers, being drawn into that labyrinth. However I suppose I have to go back to them because I intend to fight this English ban – look, this is the appeal form they sent me to fill in. This is the third time I've been barred from England. It was a disappointment to me because I was hoping for a big reception in London which would then play back to America because, as you know, a prophet is not honoured in his own country.

(1983)

ANDREW (THE DUKE OF DEVONSHIRE: MAYFAIR, CHATSWORTH, LISMORE)

Chesterfield Street, Mayfair

Dukes are a varied group but they are somewhat like kings in that they find their characters subtly modified in a way that's appropriate to the mantle. Dukes don't want to write novels, for example. Or indeed write anything at all. The Duke of Devonshire is an exception.

'Yes, I did write something. It was about my horse Park Top, the greatest English-bred filly since the war.'

'What was the book called?'

'*Park Top*. I'm writing another book now. It's got a good name cribbed from Disraeli. Called *In My Anecdotage*. It's not really an autobiography. It's about things that have interested me. It says things like how you can't look at Suez without referring to Munich, the sense of shame in the Conservative Party, and how they over-reacted to Nasser and all the rest of it. It's great fun but my eyes are bad which is tiresome.' He is also colour-blind.

Dukes are cosmopoliton in outlook, international, not county. So usually are marquesses. Widespread 'blimpishness' begins to appear only with the rank of earl. Viscounts tend to be 'odd', sometimes with a touch of petulance. Barons are usually 'blimpish', unless they are life peers in which case they can be anything. Baronets tend to 'odd' or 'blimpish' or both and, because they occupy the lowest inheritable rank, can be staggeringly snobbish. If you can't go the whole hog and be a duke, being a baronet is probably most fun.

Of all the ranks, dukes are the nicest because it is impossible for a duke to be pretentious. But not all of them are grand. The old Duke of Leinster, Ireland's premier peer, gambled his life away and committed suicide at an advanced age in a bedsitter in Pimlico. His son, the present duke, is rather straight and runs a flying school in Oxfordshire. The Duke of Newcastle, the greatest name in Whig patronage in the eighteenth century, now lives in a terraced house in Lymington.

Some *are* grand. The Duke of Atholl, the only duke who is a bachelor, is also the only man in Britain permitted to maintain a private army. The most ducal duke is probably the Duke of Devonshire. He owns 80,000 acres in Derbyshire, Ireland, Yorkshire, and Sussex; Chatsworth, Bolton Abbey, Lismore Castle, the resort of Eastbourne, a house in Mayfair; and various other bits.

'But Devonshire doesn't exist, does it.'

'Now look here, that is, with respect, *highly* intelligent of you, because you are quite right, it's the County of Devon, and to talk about Devonshire is like talking about Cornwallshire.'

'Rather wonderful to be duke of a place that doesn't exist.'

'Well, when we were created earls, whenever that was, the Earl of Derby was a very powerful figure and said so long as I'm Earl of Derby there's not going to be an Earl of Derbyshire, so perhaps my forbear said right I'll call myself Devonshire, it's got the same number of letters and I can still have D on the coronet.'

The house in Chesterfield Street, off Curzon Street, is the Duke's London home and carries a blue plaque to say that Beau Brummel lived here. It is small and his own, belonging to him as Andrew, not as the Duke of Devonshire. In the ground floor sitting-room where he receives guests, all the newspapers are laid out overlapping, with *The Sporting Life* on top. There is a large green baize easel with the day's appointments clearly displayed. Lady Jane Rayne arrives at 2. The drinks tray contains everything, including quarter bottles of champagne, a couple of little rows of them with their wire-twist release mechanisms already pulled out through the foil like hand grenades.

The Duke wafts into the room, tall and slim and jittery and

smelling lightly of fine soaps and talcs. 'What will you have? I've got this theory that *really* people like to pour their own drinks so that they can have as much as they need. So you go ahead. Then I'll do mine.'

Andrew is in town dress. A grey double-breasted suit hanging just so on the elegant figure; a thick cream silk soft-collared shirt closed at the wrists by cufflinks and at the neck by a pale blue tie; soft black slip-on shoes, low cut showing white silk stockings. The effect is *soigné*, slightly 18th century, very much *not* the city gent. He drapes one long grey leg over the other while his hands twitch about on the chair arms, including the hand holding the drink. In fact Andrew twitches quite a lot, so does his voice, soft, scrambled, breathless, coming out of an upper body that twists and stretches toward the listener, while he expresses himself in fits and starts. This anxiety mixed with eagerness is very appealing.

'I do like the town but I'm spending more time in Derbyshire now, but after a week or so I begin to feel restless and come to town where there's opera, concerts, theatre, none of which you can find in Derbyshire. I've recently become very keen on opera for the first time. I don't quite know why. Then after a few days of it I start thinking of the country.'

'I expect you belong to lots of clubs.'

'Yes. Lots. I love clubs. I used to like White's very much but it's gone down hill. The Turf I like – but that's more my son's generation. The Athenaeum is nice and quiet.'

'I've always liked the idea of Pratt's – do you belong to that?'

'In fact, it belongs to me. My father bought it.'

In the early 19th century, the Duke of Beaufort came up to London one evening and found White's closed and was furious. He said he'd have to knock up his valet who occupied a place across the road. The valet's name was Pratt and that is how the club started.

'I think that of all the things I enjoy however, it's my books and pictures more than anything.' Colour-blindness notwithstanding, the room is stacked with modern paintings. The mantelpiece is covered with photographs and a variety of model greyhounds. 'Oh yes, and I like gambling very much. I found a lot of old chips the other day from all over – Deauville,

Crockford's, Monte Carlo. I had them mounted on green baize. They're hanging in the hall. Come and look . . . They look rather good, don't they. I used to gamble more than I do now.'

'I suppose dukes have to be rather economical these days. Did you know that the Nizam of Hyderabad, who was the richest man in the world, used to collect up the dog-ends after his guests had departed and re-roll the tobacco into cigarettes? What is your most ingenious economy?'

'I wouldn't have thought I'd got one. Being economical is not my strong suit! Oh – well – I have got one or two racehorses, very few. I *love* horse-racing and I'd like to have a lot more. But I have to cut right back on them.'

'Have you indulged in a piece of sheer extravagance lately?'

'Well . . . I have a weakness for buying jewellery. Not modern. Diamonds and things like that.'

'What do you find hateful in life?'

'Saying no to a function that I know I ought to go to but am, uh, just too lazy.'

'You're not lazy, are you?'

'Yes, really I am. My family always has been.'

'How does this laziness manifest itself?'

'Oh totally totally. Total laziness.'

The family motto is: Safety with Caution. Which should be altered to: Softly with Cushion.

'What's it like being a duke?'

'It has advantages. It's easier to get a table in a restaurant.'

'Or a seat at the Coronation.'

'But it has one great disadvantage which is that dukes are an anachronism and people do tend to think that one is different from other people. And one isn't. I care just as passionately about how Derby County does as, uh, football is a source of great pleasure. And, uh, people do think that if one's a duke one's an absolute bloody fool. But if they give themselves time to discover one's only a bloody fool as opposed to an absolute bloody fool, then there's sometimes a certain favourable backlash. But it's . . . being thought to be . . . *not* a proper person. That's the disadvantage. I care passionately about the football team.'

The Cavendishes are not an ancient family, as families go, and their fortune is based on 2 aggressively self-made people. First, Bess of Hardwick, the greatest self-made woman in 16th century England who through clever marriages came from nowhere to be the Countess of Shrewsbury and own most of Derbyshire. She didn't get on with Shrewsbury and it was to the establishment of the Cavendish dynasty – through the offspring of her second marriage, to Sir William Cavendish – that she devoted most of her energies. The second figure was the greatest self-made man in 17th century Ireland, Richard Boyle, 1st Earl of Cork. His descendants entered the Cavendish family through marriage bringing, among other things, Lismore Castle in County Waterford.

'Oh, it's the most wonderful place,' says the Duke, 'built up on a rock overlooking the Blackwater River. You can fish out of the drawing-room window. I inherited it from my uncle, Charles Cavendish.'

Andrew inherited Lismore, as the younger son, from a younger son. He was not in line for the dukedom until his elder brother William Marquess of Hartington was killed in the Second World War. William Hartington was married to Kathleen Kennedy, President Kennedy's sister, herself later killed in an accident. In this way Harold Macmillan and President Kennedy were related through Cavendish marriages – Macmillan married Andrew's aunt. This is typical of the Cavendish family – perhaps they are a bit lazy, they never do anything terribly striking, but they are always splendidly there.

'But Lismore is, you see, to use an awful phrase – please, you must forgive me – is *a holiday home*. It's a bit like Ireland itself and this is a fairly quotable – oh no perhaps unquotable, perhaps we'd better not – oh no, yes, yes, this is quotable I think – that Ireland is like a mistress. You go to it but you don't live with it.'

'You've never had a home abroad – the Mediterranean or something.'

'No, I can't really aff . . . oh no, it's not strictly true to say I can't afford it. But if you've got a house abroad, you've got to go to it. Whereas if you haven't got one, you can go anywhere.

I'm going to Israel quite soon. I'm closely involved with the Jewish community in England.'

'Did you marry into it? Are you partly Jewish?'

'No. But my father longed to be Jewish. He could be seen leafing through the Peerage saying "My family's not very old, but we've married lots of different people, there must be some Jewish blood somewhere," but he never found any, to his great regret.'

'Lismore sounds fabulous.'

'It is. You should go and look at it. Officially it belongs to my son.'

'Are you planning to go there soon? Could we continue our conversation there?'

'I may be going. It's uncertain at the moment. If you mean is there any chance of my coming over with you for a day or so, well, that wouldn't, I'm sure, be too difficult. There's a couple there who look after it, and I think someone to cook for us. Yes, I think we could go there without too much trouble. The view from the drawing-room is absolutely, absolutely . . .'

'Is the castle a foil to Chatsworth? Gothic versus classical.'

'Yes, and I like that too, in that, well, to say Lismore is shabby is perhaps . . . *over*stating the case but – it's not posh. Because I've got in Chatsworth a re-la-tive-ly posh house. And so deliberately I've, and my wife entirely agrees with me, kept Lismore – different. Un-grand. You'll see.'

'It's wonderful to have both the gothic and the classical, isn't it? I'm terribly glad we were colonised by Rome.'

'Oh, so am I! I'm terribly in favour of Rome. I daren't think what we'd have been if they hadn't come.'

Chatsworth

There is something absurd about one's first sight of Chatsworth. Built on the edge of the Peak District, it looks as if an enormous town hall has landed in a remote place. The park, though immaculately upholstered, does not quite have the lush Arcadian prettiness associated with English settings. And immediately beyond the perimeter an austerity in the region reasserts itself.

As the ducal empire contracts, Chatsworth becomes the redoubt. Other houses are sold off or let and Chatsworth grows more magnificent as choice pieces find their way here. Andrew became Duke at the age of 30. His father died in 1950, 14 weeks before the crucial tax deadline – as a result the Duke was taxed at 80% of all resources.

A man opens a tall wrought iron gate and says 'Drive up to the front door and His Grace will let you in' (heavy crunch of gravel past a string of venerable urns and statues). That is the Devonshire way. If you've got a front door, use it, like everybody else, even if your front door is gigantic and set into a massive façade by Talman. And so the Duke prances out through it waving his arms, wearing country dress, tweeds, twills, fawn suede shoes, a red and white neck-square tied at a jaunty angle. His face has again that air of surprise bordering on alarm, so that when he breaks into a smile, which he regularly does, there's relief all round.

'Good morning, Duke.'

'Good morning. Do come in.'

His study is immediately to the left of the hall. Its walls and ceiling are painted with classical figures in colours faded to pastel and the shelves carry new as well as old books. There is another appointments easel here – at 7 pm, a meeting of the Peak Mineral Society.

'Now, what'll you have?'

There they are again, all the drinks on a large tray, with the mini-champagne bottles lined up, firing pins at the ready.

'I wonder why the aristocracy stopped being patrons of art in the 19th century.'

'Very *very* good question. And I've often asked it myself. And I don't know the answer. Perhaps they thought they'd got enough. Later on, Edward VII's set were fearful philistines. One of the few things I take pride in is that I've, uh, *collected*. Mostly modern paintings.'

At the end of the 19th century it was the task of the 8th Duke's librarian to walk round Chatsworth with him before a house party and tell the Duke something about his possessions.

The Bachelor Duke's work with Paxton in the first half of the 19th century, here and at Lismore, was among the last great aristocratic enterprises.

'Why did your grandfather blow up Paxton's Great Conservatory?'

'He didn't do it. My grandmother did. She was a very dominant character. Purely economic.'

'But they can't have needed the money so badly. It was such an amazing building.'

'Although my grandfather was immensely rich, it was a time – 1921 – when the rich began to think that if they couldn't live on the income of their income they were poor.'

'Does this explain why the aristocracy sold off their London palaces? Which led to their subsequent demolition by developers and which I consider a tragic loss to the capital.'

'Yes, it was. But here we've tried to make, uh, amends. We've built a modern greenhouse where we grow pineapples and paw paw and the Cavendish Banana.'

Nowadays money is a constant juggle and the Duke has had to sell off a small part of Chatsworth's famous collection of old master drawings in order to refurbish the private apartments and top up the Trust. They made £21 million at auction, 4 times what was expected.

'If it wasn't for Eastbourne . . .' he muses dolefully. 'Eastbourne is what keeps us going really. I love Eastbourne. My second home is the Grand Hotel.'

He means fourth or fifth home.

'Bolton Abbey isn't big. It was the gatehouse to the abbey and rebuilt by Paxton as a shooting lodge. But wives can't come. The rooms are so small there's only room for the guns. And Lismore is not as big as it looks. Oh and, uh, I'm awfully sorry but I shan't be able to come over with you after all. It *is* a shame and I am awfully sorry but it would be an enormous bore for the Irish Government – I had a quick word with their embassy here – who would have to put 20 or so policemen all round the house because of the IRA. I might possibly be a target as a sort of, uh, representative Englishman – and I feel really that I couldn't put them to all that trouble. But um, er, my goodness, *your* visiting it poses no problem at all. That is, if you want to go ahead without me. I'll see that you're looked after.'

Chatsworth is now established as a charitable trust. 'I decided that because – well, I'm not quite sure what my motives were but, uh, anyway I decided that steps must be taken to preserve Chatsworth whether or not my family lived here. These days, for tax reasons, nobody can afford to own anything.'

'I read in the paper that Lord Pembroke's been approached by the Getty Museum to sell off bits of Wilton. Have you?'

'No, I haven't. But the public part of the house, and all it contains, is no longer at my disposal. The Poussin was the first piece to be sold from here other than to meet death duties.'

'What is the greatest treasure here now?'

'We've got a very good Rembrandt, and there's the Poussin – '

'But I thought – '

'Ah well, one of the reasons we sold the Poussin was because we, uh, had 2.'

When death duties struck 'I decided to sell off relatively few tip-top things.' One of the family casualties was Hardwick Hall, the Elizabethan masterpiece built by Bess and mono-grammed by her – the letters 'ES' 6 feet high in stone, 18 of them on the roofline, 3 on each turret. She spent her last years there needlepointing. The place is now run by the National Trust and is full of softly decaying tapestries and gently warping woodwork. Hardwick's most charming detail is the group of 18th century graffiti in the little banqueting pavilion up on the roof which includes a springy 18th century cock straight out of *Joseph Andrews*. But Bess herself was not a greatly cultured woman. At her death the library at Hardwick numbered 6 books.

'You have a very nice private library here, Duke. I mean, it's a proper reading library.'

'I like to think that when I'm finished with it, an educated man could spend many happy hours in this room. English fiction this side. Foreign fiction that side. Biographies. The top shelf at that end is my favourite – the disaster shelf. It's got most of them – the R101, the Titanic, the Lusitania, the Great

Earthquake of San Francisco. The disaster shelf gives me enormous pleasure.'

'Were you brought up at Chatsworth?'

'Nope. We lived in a relatively – I use the word advisedly – modest house 5 miles away called Churchdale. My father was the local MP. The house had 10 rooms.' Was the Duke himself ever in politics? 'Mrs Thatcher and I were junior ministers together so I knew her at one time. She was very masterful. We don't get on.'

'You're not a Tory now?'

'No.'

'SDP?'*

'Yes.'

'Among other dukes, is any particularly a friend?'

'A number of them. Charles Rutland's a very old friend of mine.'

'What about the Duke of Portland? That Dukedom is a sort of offspring of the Cavendishes, I believe.'

'He's a most charming man, very old, and when he dies it's a great tragedy because the Dukedom comes to an end. He had 2 daughters, one of whom died tragically. The other married a strange count from Capri and they've a son who'll inherit the estates but he won't be a duke. The Portland property is enormous. And when I say this I'm not exaggerating – if you go to Welbeck Abbey it's got 21 different lodges. Although the actual big house has been let to a school.'

'Who is your most unpleasant ancestor?'

' . . . Oh dear. The 5th Duke perhaps? Or is that unfair? . . . I know so little about my family.'

'Do you ever feel overwhelmed by the past?'

'I don't think I get overwhelmed by the past. But I get overwhelmed by the present. We've got a big estate here. There are 2 estate villages – Edensor and Pilsey. Edensor was built by Paxton. No 2 houses are the same. And until recently no 2 chimneys were the same, but it got too expensive to keep that idea up. The community, if you count those who work on the estate, their families, and pensioners, is 750. They've got to be

* The Social Democrat Party which has since gone in with the Liberals.

298

housed, looked after, and so on. I regard that as my first obligation. God knows, I'm a lucky man – but there are certain pressures. To maintain the estate as it's been maintained for so long . . .'

'I must say, the moment you enter the Devonshire part of the landscape, I don't mean just the park but the agricultural land, it's very obvious, very spruce.'

'Well, it's, uh, very very very very nice of you to say so,' says the Duke, straightening up like a plant hit by the sun.

The Duchess bursts in, throwing off her cape. 'God I need a drink – the committee went *on and on*.'

Lismore Castle

Brief history. There has long been a castle on this site. Richard Boyle arrived in Ireland with nothing in 1588 at the age of 22. In 1602 he purchased all Sir Walter Raleigh's estates in Ireland, including Lismore. At his death in 1644 Boyle had become the Earl of Cork and one of Ireland's greatest landowners. One of his sons was Robert Boyle, the father of modern chemistry, who was born at Lismore in 1626.

The 2nd Earl of Cork became the 1st Earl of Burlington. In 1748 the 4th Duke of Devonshire-to-be made, against the wishes of his mother, extraordinary to say, the most illustrious of all Cavendish marriages. This was to Lady Charlotte Boyle, daughter of Lord Burlington the architect earl, connoisseur and arbiter of taste (the architect Juvarra dedicated a book of drawings to him, the architect and designer William Kent was his lover). Charlotte brought remarkable augmentation to the Devonshire holdings: Bolton Abbey and Londesborough in Yorkshire, Chiswick House and Burlington House in London, Lord Burlington's great collection of architectural books and drawings, and Lismore.

The castle was then in a somewhat puny condition. And stayed that way until the Bachelor Duke – who seems to have been the most creative of all the dukes – began to restore the castle in 1811. However the 19th century romance in stone which eventually emerged is largely the Bachelor Duke's work with Paxton in the 1850s. The stone was quarried in Derbyshire and transported ready-cut to Ireland. Much of the furniture and the rich interior of the Banqueting Hall is by Pugin.

Lismore was the seat of Lord Charles Cavendish, the brother of the 10th Duke, from 1932 to 1944. He married Adele Astaire, Fred's sister.

The drive from Cork Airport to Lismore is just over an hour with the sun going down. There is something odd about the towns and villages en route. What is it? The countryside is soft and wet and yielding and green and hilly. County Cork and County Waterford is prosperous farming land – it is dotted with subsidised EEC Spanish hacienda bungalows, brand new. What was that village called? Watergrasshill, Rathcormack, Ballyduff? It had an oddness, like all the others. What is it? . . . Ah yes! The houses which line the streets have no doorsteps. There is no distinction between outside and inside floor levels. This gives to the towns and villages of Ireland a quirky stunted look, as if they've been chopped off at the ankles.

Dusk is deepening into night. At Lismore there is a sharp left turn and a rough drive flanked by ancient encrusted walls – the precinct of the castle comes right into the town. But as you begin up the drive the town shoots away behind, everything becomes fantastical and dreamy. A gateless gatehouse of elfin charm approaches and is passed through, and ahead rises up a magnificent fairyland tableau: complicated black silhouettes of towers, turrets and battlements among black trees are set against a rich purple sky glowing with stars and a half moon. So this is what 'un-grand' is.

At the rampart a light goes on. Heavy wooden doors creak open, spaniels jump out yapping through the widening crack. The car moves forward into a large gravelled parade ground (around which the castle is arranged in 4 asymmetrical wings), crosses it to what appears to be the main entrance to the interior, and stops. No one emerges from this impressive porch, but from an oblique angle a dark figure approaches through the turretted gloom.

'Hullo.'

'Hullo.'

'You're staying in *their* bit,' he says. It's Paul Burton, the agent, about 50 years old, skinny and droll, with an extravagantly upper-class voice. He used to work for the Londonderries. The father of the playwright Congreve lived at Lismore as agent of the Burlington estates in Ireland, he says.

'There's a couple there who look after it, and I think someone to cook . . .' the Duke had said. Such modesty. The whole place is in full-swing at the drop of a telephone call.

Going through the front door into the hall the first impression is . . . smell. A powerful wave of perfume from pots of hyacinths quickly placed throughout the main rooms breaks across one's brain, blotting out for a moment all other information. In this lovely smell, delight and extravagance and repose are mingled. This is underlined by the reassuring smell of wax polish and on proceeding across the hall to the sitting-room, by the more vigorous aroma of a log fire.

The principal living wing was always on the north side, the rooms looking out across the sumptuous Blackwater valley with its many varieties of trees. The interiors, many designed by Atkinson in 1811, have a levity belied by Paxton's dramatic exterior. When approached from the north the pile, because it is built up on a rock, appears by an optical illusion to be much more massive than it is. In fact this is a lighthearted castle.

Nonetheless the large gothic drawing-room is used only on unusual occasions. The family generally uses the cosier sitting-room. It also is gothic and done up in a cheerful chintzy style by the present Duchess, a Mitford girl. The log fire burns, lamps give out a soft light, a clock ticks. There is an atmosphere of sherry-imminent.

Logs have been split and stacked in piles, fires have been lit in the main rooms, hot water systems set gurgling, corridors of radiators set creaking with heat, chandeliers switched on. Everywhere these pots of hyacinths have been introduced and bowls of pink camellias cut freshly from the garden. The kitchen, way over in that direction somewhere, is whirring into action. An electric blanket meanwhile is roasting a bed by Pugin in a distant bedroom. Even the billiard room, which is not part of the main suite, a billiard room circa 1925 in feel, though everything in it looks older than that, even this has been warmed up just in case.

'All for me?'

'Yes, all for you. We had this phone call.'

One is in good company. King James II stayed at Lismore, and so did Lord Clarendon when Viceroy of Ireland – both in the absence of the owner.

'Would you like a drink? You'll be dining in the dining-room later. Would you like my wife and I to eat with you for the first night? We thought you might like that.'

'Yes, I'd love a drink. And I love this sitting-room.' The tapestries in it come from Compton Place at Eastbourne (now let to a girls' school) and are scenes from Don Quixote. 'And I'd love you to join me for dinner. I shan't be changing.'

'Oh good.'

The dining-room is large, overlooking the bluff where the wind blows. 3 huge windows along one side are black with squally Irish night. A black marble fireplace blazes at one end. A chandelier of crystal prisms hanging from a high simple ceiling throws rainbows onto the white damask tablecloth. A large bowl of pink camellias sits in the centre of the setting.

'You *must* wander about the garden to-morrow. Mustn't he, Paul?'

Paul grunts.

'It's one thing the Duke absolutely insists on,' continues Arabella Burton who was brought up in Australia and Shanghai and whose voice is rather more explosive and chaotic than her husband's. She bats big girlish eyes at frequent intervals and adds '*He's* interested in the garden, not the farm. *She's* interested in the farm.'

'What a tremendous sideboard.' A terrific, dark thing, richly carved with pineapples and bunches of grapes, has suddenly asserted itself at one end of the room.

'It's by Pugin. There's lots of Pugin here. Paul, you must take him to Careysville! That's the Duke's fishery where he spends *all* his time when he's here. He's interested in fishing, not hunting or shooting. *She*'s interested in shooting. In fact she's one of the best shots around.'

'This soup's delicious – what is it?'

'I don't know what it is. But the cook here's terribly good,' says Paul. 'They want her to go and cook at Chatsworth but she doesn't want to live in England.'

'She's called Kate. And her brother is the head maintenance man here and he's terribly good too,' says Arabella.

'These rolls are wonderful. I'm sure she baked them herself.'

'Wonderful beef!'

'Wonderful creamy horse-radish sauce!'

'Wonderful purple sprouting!'

'Actually,' says Paul drily, 'it's white sprouting.'

'Oh my goodness, what a joy, white sprouting! I'll miss vegetables like this when I go to France . . .'

'I loathe the French,' says Paul wryly. 'I think they're *poisonous*. I've got a French sister-in-law.'

'She and Paul don't really get on,' says Arabella in an explanatory aside.

'Why do I think they're poisonous? Oh, Agincourt and all that.' Paul emits a slow giggle.

'Wonderful chocolate mousse!'

'Rather disappointing wine,' he says. 'It's Beaune. I think it's too old. It hasn't got a date on it.'

'Oh yes, it's too old,' says Arabella, pouring herself another glass.

'That's the problem with the cellar here,' says Paul. 'All the wines are too old!'

'What's that big church outside the castle?'

'The Cathedral of St Carthage. Church of Ireland, not Roman Catholic. He died at Lismore in 637AD. Sometimes at evensong we and the Dean's wife are the only congregation. 3 of us in that huge place.'

To bed.

'You're not afraid of spooks are you? You'll be all alone in this big main bit of the castle.' Arabella is very comforting. 'You don't want a cat or a dog or something for the end of your bed? But really this is the cosiest, unspookiest castle you could ever have.'

'I'll take another whisky with me.'

'Right then, we'll be off to the piggery.'

'The what?'

'The piggery! That's what we call our bit. It's on the other side of the quadrangle. Just open a window and scream if anything happens.'

'You better lock the door behind us,' says Paul. 'You never know.'

As they leave through the battlemented porch, the big green door heaves shut with a thundery noise and I slide the fat bolt through its polished brass casing with a sense of amazement.

Alone in a castle. 1a.m.

Things flicker briefly in corners, then settle.

Where is the switch to turn off the great hall lights? Damn. The servants will think they've been left on because of nervousness. It is not so. However the switch is not to be found and perhaps something deep in the unconscious is rather pleased that lights will have to burn all night.

The bedroom is of medium size at the end of a long corridor. There is a sudden chill at the door and one pops quickly inside. It is cosy and welcoming and faces towards the north, crucial for the morning view. The corridors have had their woodwork left brown for visual warmth but in the bedrooms the Duchess has had it mostly painted white. It produces a pretty effect with the bowls of camellias and the ivory curtains painted with swags of red and pink roses (these curtains are over 100 years old someone said and like all the best curtains in Ireland their linings are in shreds). There is a wallpaper of ducal strawberry leaves. Pugin's high bed is also painted white and stacked with plush bedclothes a yard deep all sizzling hot from the electric blanket.

Books in the bedroom: *The Secret of the Coup d'Etat*, edited and with an introduction by the Earl of Kerry; *Lord Lansdowne* by Lord Newton; *The Diary of a Nobody* by Grossmith; *A Sleeping Life* by Ruth Rendell; *The Beast in Me* by James Thurber. There are dozens of other little book selections in dozens of other bedrooms – whenever are they

304

opened? The Duke comes at most for 2 weeks a year and didn't come last year . . . and each bedroom is furnished with little desks carrying Lismore writing paper curled by damp – when will these letters be written? . . . The print series on the bedroom wall is *The Marquis At Home* including the Tipperary Boys. A background excitement of the nerves, horribly alert to every novel noise, prevents me from falling asleep.

Morning bath.

'It's a bit of a trek,' Paul had said and it is. In the corridor on a windowsill a tortoiseshell butterfly flexes its wings, roused by unfamiliar heat at the wrong time of year. The bathroom is painted yellow with crimson felt on the floor. In one corner is a proper weighing machine and a contraption for measuring your height in case it has changed in the night. On the walls are photographs of Fred Astaire and Ginger Rogers scudding about some highly polished surface in the Art Deco world.

The bathwater is blue. Bright blue. It comes out of the mountain like that. Just past the bathroom at the end of the corridor under the window a glass panel covers a piece of wall peppered with shrapnel. Underneath, it says 'Caused by Machine Gun Fire 1922'.

Breakfast divinely in the dining-room. The windows, so black last night, are now filled with a charming drizzle. Eggs, bacon, sausage, fried bread keep warm on heated trays behind the screen. Walking slowly backwards and forwards across the dining-room at the dictates of one's appetite, with the occasional pause to throw another log on the rampant fire, is a very good way to get into a.m. gear. By the end of breakfast one has walked a considerable distance in a casual sort of way, is both loosened up and nourished, and made semi-alert by excellent coffee.

'How many acres here, Paul?'

'8,000. It stretches over to the Knockmealdowns.'

'So the estate's quite profitable?'

'No. 5,000 acres of it is mountain and you can't do anything with mountain except look at it. Well, actually, I discovered another 600 acres the other day. They'd been let in 1928 and forgotten about.'

A walk in the garden. The Duchess has planted flowering cherry blossoms in the Lower Garden. They look ragged and dejected all year except for the fortnight in the spring when the Devonshires are there to see them. It is for Easter and fishing that they come, if they come at all.

The Yew Tree Walk is 300 years old, looks very venerable, and is noisy with *red* squirrels. There are masses of pink camellia bushes at the end of it. Blue bathwater, butterflies in the corridors at the wrong time of year, red squirrels, pink camellias – this is Lismore. And stone serpents set into greeny grey stone walls. The serpent is a Cavendish device.

The elfin gatehouse is called the Riding House and dates from 1631. It is the route to the Upper Garden where vegetables and box hedges, fruit trees and greenhouses struggle valiantly to justify themselves against the cheap commodities available in local shops.

When walking up the Upper Garden, turn round, and numberless turrets and towers swim among trees at about waist level. One is level with the top of the castle.

'What is that beautiful tree against the wall?'

'Merthel.'

'Er, what?'

'Merthel.'

'Could you spell that for me please?'

'M-y-r-t-l-e.'

The gardener is very Irish indeed. He not only pronounces his 'th' as 't' but, with indigenous logic, pronounces his 't' as 'th'.

The stables have been turned into a timber yard. No horses are kept at Lismore. Altogether, including the household, the estate employs 60 people.

A typical Anglo-Irish conversation.

'It was the Dorrien-Smiths, I think. Or was it the Smith-Dorriens? Darling, do help. You see, there are two families. They are related but they're not the same.'

'Oh, that's like the Dalrymple-Hamiltons and the Hamilton-Dalrymples in Scotland.'

'Oh yes, or, uh, the Montagu-Douglas-Scotts and oh the Douglas-Scott-Montagus.'

'Oh, ah, oh, yes! Ah, uh, or like the Hovell-Thurlow-Cumming-Bruces and the er, the er, uh Cumming-Bruces!'

'Oh gosh yes! The poor plain old-fashioned one-measly-hypen Cumming-Bruces!'

'Well, I think there's something a bit bogus about multiple surnames. If you're really grand, one will do.'

'Like Windsor, you mean.'

'Yes, or Plantagenet.'

'Or Romanov.'

'Or . . . or Orsini.'

'Or Cavendish, I suppose.'

'Yes, or Cavendish.'

'Have you noticed all the bits around?' asks Arabella. 'Adele was fond of bits . . . Darling, is there just a teensy bit more gin?'

Paul belts across the Waterford countryside to Careysville, a pretty Regency house overlooking the Blackwater. The fireplaces in the dining-room and drawing-room are fitted with enormous manual wheel and strap apparatuses for blowing air into desultory peat fires. They are made by the Wexford Engineering Company and must have looked hideous when first fitted. Now they have the dinosaur appeal of relics from the age of mechanical (as opposed to electronic) ingenuity. Down on the river a Frenchman squeals with pleasure as, with the help of the ghilly, he lands a salmon – the first catch this week. Paul undulates with uncertainty, then makes polite congratulations in pigeon French. In the drawing-room at Careysville there is *another* butterfly flexing its wings at the wrong time of year.

Miss Clodagh Anson for drinks: Miss Anson is old and bright and extremely gregarious. She wears purple tweeds and knows everything about the locality. 'When the rebels occupied the house in 1922 they used to shoot seagulls without opening the window. The place was full of glass and torn-up floorboards . . . Yes, old Charlie Cavendish used to drink a bit. He woke up one morning and someone said "So you're going to marry Adele Astaire, are you?" And he said "Am I? Did I propose to her?" So they were married. I remember once at a party somebody coming up to me and saying "Oh, do come and get Charlie, he's looking for poachers under the stairs." He was the loveliest man . . .'

Morning in the sitting-room. At the writing-desk in front of the window, writing a couple of letters. Fog is pressed up like marshmallow against the window, thick and very white and impenetrable.

There are gothic bookcases on either side of this window. Among the ordinary reading books, something special sometimes lurks – a red, re-bound edition for example of *Papworth's Rural Residences . . . consisting of a Series of Designs for Cottages, Decorated Cottages, Small Villas, and other Ornamental Buildings . . . by John B. Papworth, Architect, author of Essay on the Dry Rot, &c.&c . . .*

The volume is inscribed 'James Dugdale, Sezincot'.

The log fire has passed roaring and settled into a deep fluttering purr. Every 15 seconds or so there is a spit like a firecracker and a slight shift as various pieces of wood settle deeper into the orange, quietly singing embers. Once in a while there is a large collapse, accompanied by violent spitting and throwing out of sparks.

The fog is still solid against the window. Then something curious happens. It suddenly grows a more brilliant white and then sunlight filters through. With uncanny speed the landscape becomes apparent like a coloured photograph developing quickly in a pan. It is most ghostly and magnificent, the speed with which it happens, the last threads of fog vanishing in rich sunshine on a landscape of vivid greens, oranges, purples under a clean blue sky. It is magical that the entire transformation, from complete white blank to sharp and highly coloured view, should take less than 15 seconds.

The great drawing-room is absolutely silent. Sun shines into it. Games covered with sunshine are laid out on a long seat in front of the window. Scrabble, roulette, jigsaw, backgammon, playing cards from Asprey, used but now untouched. Probably untouched for years. The entry prior to mine in the Visitors' Book was 2 years before. A car winds away up the far side of the valley. There is a distant yap of dogs.

(1984)

ANDY LIVES

WARHOL IN NYC

IT'S RAINING HEAVILY in New York. I ring Warhol's studio.

'Andy's in Milan.'

'Oh, that's a shame.'

'But he'll be back to-morrow.'

'What time?'

'About 2 in the afternoon.'

'He'll be tired.'

'Yeah, very tired, he'll wanna rest. Why don't you come round about 2.30?'

Next day it's still raining heavily. And in the afternoon I walk to this remarkable man whose studio is in the phone-book, who seems so accessible, who needs only ½ an hour to recover from a transatlantic flight. Contrary to expectation, Warhol does not spend his time discussing money with homeless noblemen, Manhattan zanies and millionairesses. At least not during the day. He is a working artist. 'We run an office here. It's strictly 9 to 5,' he declares. It is known as the Factory.

Much has been made of his adoption of the principles of industrial manufacture but in fact his studio just as easily resembles the workshop of a Renaissance artist, a natural focus of production, with pupils, assistants, parasites, intrigue and scandal.

The Factory is about to move. But for the moment it is still on Broadway at 17th Street, the first floor of a corner building, with huge windows overlooking Union Square and secret rooms leading off the main space. One is panelled and has electric candles on the walls in the English pub style. This presumably is for signing big deals. Another suggests a small cocktail lounge on a pre-war Cunard liner. And everywhere are Art Deco-ish mirrors, chairs, cupboards, plinths, etc, all placed about very à la nothing. A stuffed dog barks in one corner.

Several supercilious and not very good-looking young men sit non-committally at desks, hoping to attract the attention of people they then intend to ignore. An unyoung female secretary – a stenographer! – sits behind a large black old-fashioned iron typewriter with brass attachments. She is knitting something long and the remains of a bun lie on a paper bag beside her machine. The wooden floor is a beautiful honey-colour, unspattered by paint.

This main space is dominated by stacks of large, approximately 8' x 6' canvases of Dollar signs, painted in various combinations of brilliant and pastel colours, leaning against the walls. The dollar sign has become Warhol's logo. On the floor are many small canvases in lurid blue, orange, green, red, yellow, of some peculiar lizardlike image. A round bald man moves among them, picks up a few, puts them under his arm, picks up a couple more, puts one from under his arm back again, picks up another, switches some round on the floor, picks up different ones, moves across, puts one down, puts another down, puts another under his arm, a process of selection and reselection that goes on and on and on with no end: he is paddling happily, feverishly (happiness in New York is to be feverishly involved) among pictures. Heavy rain pours noisily down the big studio windows. Meanwhile Fred Hughes, Warhol's 'manager', comes in and out of the main space with statements of a vaguely businesslike nature. He has a jacket & tie & rolled umbrella image, rather overdone, almost satirical. The points on the collar of his shirt are extremely long. The stenographer stops knitting and looks at the remains of her bun.

Warhol is of medium height and his voice is a soft American voice and its chief characteristic is unaffectedness. His demeanour is not at all theatrical but simple, his intentions wholly straightforward. One of the keys to Warhol's great

311

social success in a very dirty town is that he has a very clean mind. As for art, you do not become a great artist by being affected but by doing what comes naturally to an extreme degree. This innocence and curious self-effacement of his is one of the ways he managed to draw out the so-called Warhol superstars. He is a great one for getting others to go over the top. He himself went over the top with the Campbell's Soup Tin and never looked back.

Warhol walks about with his funny white wig sticking up like a crested grebe. His eyebrows are blackish; the hair in the nape of his neck is blackish and scrubby. He is wearing a white nylon polo neck sweater, old blue jeans, and blackcurrant running shoes. His complexion is agelessly bad but his expression is very open and attractive, very boyish. Like many of East European blood, he has a yellowish tinge. The collar of his polo neck cuts exactly across the centre of his Adam's apple which is covered with a fine membrane of parchment-coloured skin emphasising all movements of gristle beneath it. Warhol's skin is soft, creamy, fatless and lightly pleated, like something you'd make very expensive gloves from.

AW: I thought you were going to phone.
DF: No.
AW: I thought we were going to do it on the phone.
DF: They told me to come at 2.30.
AW: I really thought we were going to do it on the phone.
DF: It's a bit impersonal.
AW: People do everything on the phone in New York.
DF: But then you only get verbal information.
AW: It's quite popular to use the phone.
DF: There's this whole sex-on-the-phone thing in New York.
AW: Yeah, they charge it to your credit card and phone you back.
DF: I didn't know you weren't expecting me.
AW: I thought we were going to do it over the phone.
DF: Somebody told me to come.
AW: Did they?
DF: He didn't say who he was.

312

AW: Gee, I'm sorry.

DF: I don't want to talk much.

AW: I don't talk much.

DF: Just half an hour or so.

AW: But I've got nothing to say that lasts half an hour.

DF: That's a shame.

AW: Gee. I'm sorry.

DF: I'm soaked. I walked here.

AW: I know, it's really . . . raining, isn't it.

DF: I'm staying only a couple of streets away, so I walked.

AW: I walk sometimes.

DF: Which was stupid because I'm soaked.

AW: Gee, I'm sorry.

DF: Where do you live?

AW: I live uptown.

DF: Were you born there?

AW: No. I was born in Pennsylvania.

DF: Pennsylvania?

AW: Yeah. McKeesport. The Czech getto.

DF: Who was your hero as a child?

AW: Walt Disney.

DF: Do you go out much?

AW: I go to parties.

DF: What's the smart nightclub in New York now?

AW: One opens every day. The one that's opening to-night.

DF: That's the Kit Kat Club but I don't think it's going to be very —

AW: I don't know that one.

DF: There's one just opened on Hudson Street, the Area.

AW: I heard about that one.

DF: It's where the William Burroughs party is on Friday.

AW: Will that be a good party?

DF: I don't know.

AW: I mean, will there be food?

DF: I don't know. Do you eat?

AW: Sure I eat.

DF: What do you eat for breakfast?

AW: A bunch of vitamin pills.

DF: Who's the richest American artist?

313

AW: Any of them who turns out really good work.

DF: Who's the exciting new artist in Manhattan?

AW: The street artists. There's lots of those.

DF: I like the roof artists as well.

AW: Roof artists?

DF: From my room I can see people painting bits of roof.

AW: Oh really?

DF: Yes. You can only see it properly from planes.

AW: Really? I must look next time. I was in Milan yesterday.

DF: What do you like about money?

AW: Everybody asks me that. I don't know why they do.

DF: Look at those big dollar signs over there.

AW: They're just for a beer commercial.

DF: What do you dislike about money?

AW: I don't dislike anything about it.

DF: Have you bought a skyscraper? Someone said you had.

AW: No. It's just a building we're moving into soon.

DF: Why?

AW: Because they raised our rent here a lot.

DF: Where's the new Factory?

AW: Up on 30th and Madison Avenue.

DF: What's happened to Jo Dallesandro?

AW: He's working out in Hollywood.

DF: What's happened to Viva?

AW: She's at the Chelsea Hotel.

DF: What makes you afraid?

AW: Oh, er – just being alive.

DF: Do you know anyone who's died of AIDS?

AW: Er . . . no, not really.

DF: Do you have a problem in New York with contaminated people?

AW: Er, I don't think so.

DF: What do you like about Europe?

AW: The cream of the kids of Europe come to see us here in New York.

DF: Are you making any more films?

AW: We're always on the verge of it. It never happens.

DF: What's your biggest problem at the moment?

AW: I guess, just getting up in the morning.

DF: Do you prefer hotels or people's houses when you're away?

AW: I don't like to travel, so . . .

DF: You don't like to travel?

AW: No, but I do it all the time. I was in Milan yesterday.

DF: Who is the richest person you know?

AW: Gee, er, well, I don't know any of the people on the Forbes 400.

DF: Have you ever been arrested by the police?

AW: No.

DF: Do you like California?

AW: It's my favourite place.

DF: You prefer it to New York?

AW: Oh yeah.

DF: Why?

AW: The weather is much better.

DF: What's the nastiest thing you ever saw in New York?

AW: . . . I can't think about that.

DF: Have you suffered any terrible diseases?

AW: Er, no.

DF: Do you drive?

AW: No.

DF: Do you have any friends from your childhood?

AW: No.

DF: Are you into computers?

AW: No, but I really wish I was.

DF: Why not get into them?

AW: I'm not smart enough.

DF: Are you happy?

AW: I'm happy.

DF: You don't want to live with anybody?

AW: No.

DF: What's your current ambition?

AW: To get up to-morrow morning.

DF: Do you have a house in the country?

AW: Yeah, I do but I rent it out to other people.

DF: Are you interested in science?

AW: Oh yeah, I like science a lot.

DF: Which aspects of it?

AW: Oh, just any of it I like!

DF: What's your biggest mistake?

AW: Everything's a mistake.

DF: Is it?

AW: Yeah.

DF: But your mistakes seem to have worked out all right.

AW: Yeah – but it was a mistake.

DF: Do you believe in God?

AW: Yeah, I do.

DF: In any of the official ones?

AW: Yeah, I'm a Catholic.

DF: Do you go to Mass?

AW: Yeah, I do.

DF: And confession?

AW: Not for a while. I'm overdue.

DF: Do you believe in life after death?

AW: In an abstract way.

DF: What's your favourite programme on television?

AW: The News.

DF: What's your newest project?

AW: The cable TV show we're working on.

DF: Your own show?

AW: Yes.

DF: Have you ever been to Canada?

AW: I have. It's fun.

DF: Have you ever been mugged?

AW: We've been mugged in our studio here.

DF: Have you got any brothers or sisters?

AW: Yes.

DF: How many?

AW: A couple.

DF: A couple of each?

AW: No, only two.

DF: One brother and one sister?

AW: No, two brothers. I get along with them. They don't live in New York.

DF: Those are very beautiful over there.

AW: That's Ryuichi Sakamoto who was in *Merry Christmas Mr Lawrence*.

316

DF: But he had much shorter hair in it.

AW: I know. I wish I'd known before I did the picture. I'd have preferred him with very short hair.

DF: Why does that man keep picking up and putting down those pictures?

AW: He's organising an exhibition of children's art in the Midwest.

DF: He's in an obsessional state.

AW: He wants me to be in it.

DF: As a child artist or as an artist appropriate to children?

AW: I don't know. You must ask him that.

DF: Do you like interviews?

AW: I like to be on the other side where you are. I usually do some interviews for *Interview* but they always send someone else along with me because usually I only ask one question or something.

DF: I'm going to give you a copy of my book.

AW: Gee, that's wonderful! I'd really like that. Let me see.

DF: It's sort of embarrassing.

AW: No, I really do read all these things, you know. Some people don't, but I do. You must sign it for me . . . and I'll give you a copy of my book.

DF: It's silly to get embarrassed by this.

AW: Fred, have we got a copy of the book? Hold on . . . Here's the book I did. *The Philosophy of Andy Warhol from A to B and Back again*. I'll sign it for you and I'll do some drawings in it. That'll make it more valuable. And perhaps it will make up a bit for not being able to do the interview with you. Perhaps we could do it over the phone some time, if you're going back to London. I'll draw in some dollar signs . . . Is it true that some books are worth more at auction if you don't sign them? Somebody told me it was true.

DF: It depends I expect on who does the signing.

AW: He said it was true.

DF: Are you looking forward to your new place?

AW: Oh . . . yeah.

And that's Andy Warhol, the first autonomously American artist (just as the Beats are the first autonomously American literary movement), the first not to look to Europe for a rating. Quite simply – he opened everything up, hugely enlarged the territory. Duchamp took pieces of the street into the art gallery – Warhol did it the other way round. He took art into the world. He is the first artist of consumerism, the media and technology. And talking to him I'd say he is the only *natural* person I've met in New York.

Over on the floor, the man from the Midwest is still picking pictures up, putting pictures down. Another man comes in, props a dripping umbrella in the corner, and says 'It's really raining out there'. The stenographer finishes her bun. I descend in the damp lift and walk out into the grey slanting deluge.

(1983)

3 WOMEN SMOKING IN 3 HOTELS
CARDINALE, MINNELLI, MOREAU

Claudia Cardinale at the Athenaeum

Claudia Cardinale, who lives near Rome, was filming in London, enjoying her second wave of success. The first wave was in the 1960s. Fellini's *8½*. Visconti's *The Leopard*.

'I saw *The Leopard* on television.'

'Oh, it's no good on television,' she says in a smoky voice. 'You lose the background. I hate television.'

Blake Edwards's *The Pink Panther*. Sergio Leone's *Once Upon A Time In The West* (a film described by Leslie Halliwell as 'beautiful, empty and very violent').

'Did you enjoy the 60s?'

'I always enjoy. I'm not unhappy.'

'Did you enjoy *la dolce vita?*'

'No, I never did that.'

'Drugs?

'No – a little smoking marijuana.'

'You lot of smoking nicotine.'

'Yes, it's nerves. It's theatrical. To do with the hands,' and out go her arms like 2 swans' necks.

Her first starring role was in *Big Deal On Madonna Street* (1958) with Marcello Mastroianni. 'Claudia is the only normal actress I know,' he said. Her style is not the Cinecittá screech typified by Magnani, but low, contained, chic, yet warm too, with a sense of comedy that saves even the weakest scripts.

'But I prefer dramatic parts!'

'Do you cry easily?'

'*Very* easily.'

About 70 films and quite a few dramas later, her second wave of success began with Herzog's *Fitzcarraldo*.

'Jason Robards got jungle fever and had to leave, the river we were using dried up, we were attacked by Indians, Mick Jagger had to leave to do a tour with the Rolling Stones, and it all had to be made again with Klaus Kinski. Very interesting. Everybody said how will you survive in the jungle with 2 crazy men, Herzog and Kinski? They are a bit eccentric, but I like eccentric people, they are more fun, more exciting. Suddenly the critics discover I'm an actress after 20 years.'

In it Claudia Cardinale played the madam of the local bordello.

'The Americans and English think I am the foreign woman, the sex symbol.'

Has she ever taken her clothes off in a film?

'I don't never take my clothes off. Sex appeal is not this – it comes from inside, the eyes, the whole. They often ask me and I always refuse, and now it's too late.'

'Oh, I disagree.'

'No, at 44 ...' And in an extraordinarily crude but unconscious gesture of modesty, she closes up the scalloped edges of her open-necked tomato blouse which, in gaping slightly, had been revealing nothing whatsoever. To-day the outfit is white baggy trouser suit with tomato blouse, tomato espadrilles, tomato accessories. Dark glasses on, 2 television screens in thin tomato-coloured frames through which the soft eyes can be discerned just enough to prevent alienation. A tall glass of iced fresh orange juice is raised clinkily from time to time to the unlipsticked lips.

'I like to live naturally,' she says, lighting the umpteenth cigarette.

Weight?

'Always the same, between 55 and 57 kilos.'

Vital statistics?

'What?'

'You know – here, here, here.'

320

'Oh, I see, yes. 94–60–94. That's in centimetres. And 170 centimetres high. I used to be a bit rounder.'

Her bosom was often described as 'generous' (not true; that's just lascivious journalism), her beauty as 'urchinlike', her type as 'gamine'. She still has a light girlish nature, a catchy boyish smile, is pliable but not malleable, streetwise but delicate.

'I'm not delicate. I'm Aries. I believe in this a little bit, because I'm very strong, I like to fight with life. The more it's difficult, the more I'm excited,' she says in this disarmingly soft, moist, brown, furry voice with its gently swaying Italian undulation.

But her appearance cannot have been a drawback for getting into films.

'Films was an accident. I was supposed to teach children in the Sahara.' She was born in Tunis in 1939. Her mother was French/Italian, her father a Sicilian railwayman whose family had lived in Tunisia for 3 generations. 'I won a contest for the Most Beautiful Italian Girl in Tunis and the prize was a trip to the Venice Film Festival. In Venice they make offers but I wasn't interested. I wanted to stay in Africa. Then everything changed.'

'Changed?'

'I had a bebby.'

This was what first brought her to London in 1958, ostensibly to study English.

'I was only 18. It was very difficult, so I came to Kensington, to Phillimore Gardens, to do it quietly.'

'You weren't married?'

'No. I have never been married. I never want to get married. I always want to be independent. I was one of the pioneers.'

'You wanted to be an unmarried mother?'

'No, it was an accident – but after the accident, I want to have the bebby.'

'It must've been lonely in London.'

'I was used to being lonely. I was very introverted as a girl, full of complexes, always by myself. But my mother came to visit me in London.'

She had a son and called him Patrick. Then they both went to live in Rome and she forgot all her Arabic.

'The reason I'm an actress is because of him, to work to keep my son. He now lives in New York and has a bebby too, a little girl, so I am grandmother. He's English, has an English passport, though he's never been to London since he was born. But for a long time people didn't know his story. I tell them that Patrick was the little brother of my secretary or something.'

'Hard work bringing up a boy that way.'

'Yes, and I'm not careful with money or anything. I spend it.'

Home is – 'We have a house 20 minutes from Rome, in the countryside near Flaminia, very big with a park, a pool, a river. Lots of old furniture and lots of dogs.'

Lots of invitations to Roman parties?

'Oh, lots, but I never go.'

But lots of friends now.

'Not lots. I never had a close woman friend. For me the best friend is the man I live with.'

'Your present man is?'

'Pasquale Squitieri. A film director. He's *very* direct. He lives without compromise.'

'What do you like in a man?'

'Intelligence.'

'But you won't marry Mr Squitieri? He sounds intelligent.'

'He would like to marry.'

But not marrying is traditional with her.

'Yes. But maybe.'

(2 days later I had to phone her back. 'Miss Cardinale, I've just read that you married Franco Cristaldi.' He was Patrick's father and the man who first contracted and created Claudia Cardinale the Film Star. According to the records they married in Atlanta in 1967.

'Oh yes. Not really . . .' she says.

'Not really?'

'I did sort of marry him in America. But it doesn't count in Italy.'

This is getting complicated. But she is after all an Italo-French Tunisian with an English son-who-lives-in-America . . .

'What do you hate about looking beautiful?'

'Every woman can be beautiful. For me, in the beginning, it

was very helpful of course. But the disadvantage was they consider me the sex symbol. Also when I started, Alberto Moravia wrote a book about me as the next Goddess of Love.'

Miss Cardinale does nonetheless play all these madams and mistresses, and plays them well.

'What film of yours do you really hate?'

'*Popsy Pop.*'

'I haven't heard of it.'

'Good.'

'And what do you hate about being a film star?'

'That nothing is private, even if I fight.'

'Do you hate opera?'

'I don't like it.'

'A lot of Italians hate opera.'

'That's true. I love adventure. I like islands. Before my hobby was to travel. Now it's the bebby.'

'Your grand-daughter.'

'No. The same time I became a grandmother, I became a mother again, at 40. There's only 2 months between them. It's marvellous after 20 years, because the first bebby – I was so young, we almost grew up together. He never called me Mother. It was always Claudia. Now I have a little girl, also called Claudia. But when I was pregnant with her, I had such a terrible time with the paparazzi.'

Indeed Mr Squitieri, direct and uncompromising, shot one of them with a gun.

'Oh, it was all blown up. They climbed into the house. We thought they were robbers. We were having lunch in the garden by the pool. The son of the Italian President was with us. So Pasquale . . . but nobody was hurt or anything like that.'

'You've just finished *Princess Daisy*.'

'Yes. Ringo Starr was in it. I play the mistress of Princess Daisy's father.'

'Your next film?'

'Is with Pasquale. It's about Clarette Petacci.'

'Who's she?'

'Mussolini's mistress.'

'You've never played a religious woman, have you?'

Thinks hard . . . 'No.'

323

Liza Minnelli at the Savoy

There is Liza in the corner of the flower-filled room, hunched over the telephone in an ice-pink trouser suit, chattering into the mouthpiece and covering her free ear with her free hand. The current husband – tall, good-looking, super-coiffed Mark Gero – extends a welcoming arm before disappearing discreetly round the corner. He is described as 'producer-cum- sculptor' and the firmness of his handshake suggests one might add 'bouncer'.

An American PR man says 'Come and look at the view'. This is the Savoy's fourth floor, so the view is the wide stunning one across the Thames curving away in both directions. 'The service isn't that great but the view makes up for it,' says the PR man, pining for robots. Then he disappears round another corner.

Liza turns on what were once voted the best legs in the world, but they are now concealed in ice-pink pipes. 'Hi,' she says with the famous, everso-kooky face. It is charming, tomboyish, and at the moment both pleasure and pain are twitching about in it. The whole thing is just held together by a smile. The smile is her anchor but the other features, especially the eyes, frequently express contrary emotions of their own.

'It's a beautiful view,' I say.

'It *is* a beautiful view, isn't it,' she replies, locking onto the view like a lamprey, as though she wanted to hug the view to death. When in 1973 she won the Oscar for best actress (as Sally Bowles in *Cabaret*), it wasn't for nothing.

Liza loves London and knows it well. She went to school here for a few weeks – she went to school everywhere for a few weeks – 'but I already had a crush on this city from the Mary Poppins books'. And she chose London for her second honeymoon. That was her 1974 marriage to producer-cum-Lothario Jack Haley Jr. who was considerably older than she (Liza was born in 1946, Hollywood). Sculptor-cum-producer Mark is her third husband and 5 years younger. Miss Minnelli has been associated with various men apart from her husbands: Alice Cooper, Desi Arnez Jr., Peter Sellers, Charles Aznavour, somebody called Rex Kramer from Smackover, Arkansas, John Gorton who was Prime Minister of Australia –

'John Gorton! Can you believe that? It was all – excuse the word – bullshit. It would have been easy to sue. But I can never be bothered to sue. It takes too much time and effort and gets you upset,' and click goes the lighter, up go several thick plumes of Marlboro smoke, as Liza sits back in the armchair, crosses her legs, and momentarily takes up the position 'relaxed but urban'.

'Why did they always want to believe the worst about you?'

'Do you know – I don't know,' she says, lurching forward into a frown. (It seems not to occur to her that the worst is more fun.) 'Perhaps it was Sally Bowles rubbing off. Well, it's nice to be convincing, but really! Give me a break; I'm not that character. I'm quieter than her.'

Liza's failure to develop a thick skin, despite life's torments, is the key to her appeal. She's uncertain and dizzy – and very capable.

'Do you have to be tough to be a star?'

She has a quick twitch and a double puff. 'You have to be strong. There's a fine line between tough and strong. Coz tough sounds vaguely nasty, and I find it difficult to be nasty.'

As a young girl, one of her household duties, along with washing the pots or handing round the pistachios, was regularly salvaging her mother from pills and booze and razorblades in the bathroom. It was a sharp beginning and she early on developed techniques for keeping pain at bay. One is called 'wafting'.

'Ha, that word crept up on me somehow. Wafting, it's like the smoke from this cigarette. You just kinda . . . float away, dissolve . . . that's when things get *really* tense.'

'So what makes you angry?'

'Oh . . . inanimate objects. If I can't open a bottle I'll get just furious with the corkscrew. Have you seen the new tops to those aspirin bottles? They're so complicated that if you had a headache, by the time you get the thing open you've got a migraine!'

But Liza hates violence. Her favourite words are 'terrific', 'lovely', 'wonderful', preferably all at the same time. This doesn't mean that she isn't genuine, just that she likes to look on the bright side. Liza clings to the idea of brightness with the

325

same vehemence with which she almost strangled the view, because life can be pretty stormy.

'Have you ever tried to commit suicide?'

'Oh, God. No. Why?'

'People do from time to time.'

'No, it's so, so . . . yukky. Ugh, no, horrid.' She pushes it away with thin pale arms covered with fine black hairs, with small muscly hands with their uneven nails. The gesture is both touching and brave as a child's sometimes is. Then she goes wafting. Her mother finally went out on a Seconal overdose.

Liza would like life to be a big warm pool where everyone is swimming about being famous and well-off and terrifically lovely. She is determined to defy negativity in personal encounters. She knows everybody and everybody's a friend and she would rather be indiscriminate than cause offence. In fact she asks me to ring her if ever I'm in New York City and go round 'because it can be a tough, lonely town'. Which is terrific of her, wonderful, but slightly weird too.

Who is her favourite actress? Liza lunges forward onto the edge of her seat, pink silk knees wide apart. 'There's so many of them I admire now, it's just amazing. Barbra Streisand's terrific.' Then recalling that this is a British interview, she adds 'and Billie Whitelaw, I think she's wonderful. I mean, I like everybody, I really do.' And probably she really does.

Who is her favourite director? 'Oh God, there are so many good ones now, I don't know where to start. Have you seen *Tender Mercies*? No?! Bruce Beresford. What a movie!'

Who is the most exciting actor she's ever worked with?

'Robert de Niro in *New York New York*. He's just . . .'

Terrific?

'. . . consummate.' Then she adds with a characteristic gulp 'But I mean, Albert Finney is up there with him.'

Miss Minnelli loves the English countryside, especially up around Windsor where she used to stay with Michael and Shakira Caine when they lived up around there. She also loves the American countryside, especially up around Lake Tahoe where they have a country home. And she loves Italian food, adores Elton John – and Puccini, thinks Aretha Franklin is just, I mean, phew! and adores Johnny Mathis too. Marvin

Hamlisch is a genius, Paris is wonderful, as is Australia. She loves reading, loves Florence, likes red wine, and likes *small* parties. And big opening-night parties (hers was at the White Elephant on the River: champagne, crab, strawberries, buckets of celebrities). Black-and-white-and-red together she loves, but she likes pink too, and is starting to like softer colours generally. She hates smoking, but does it anyway.

Miss Minnelli is more at ease now which means that instead of being somewhat nervous she's become somewhat cautious. She is small, utterly untanned, considerably thinner than she appears on stage, and the speaking voice is noticeably elegant with its rich tone and slightly English intonation – except when Liza remembers how important laughter is to her and goes ha-ha-ha with a sound like tiny porcelain plates hitting the ceiling.

'What sort of things depress you?'

She flinches as if struck in the face, thinks hard. The seconds tick by like hammer blows. The personal negative looms. Then inspiration.

'The News!' she expostulates, with such relief that it seems a smile is going to disfigure her face but she recovers quickly. 'The News upsets me – everywhere I go – so depressing.'

'But there's hope?'

'Oh God, yes! I *love* children. I spend 2 weeks a year at Philadelphia's Institute for the Achievement of Human Potential which isn't mystical, isn't wafting, but hard work where they cure kids. For example, if you have an accident and they say you'll never walk again you will go to a place where they teach you to be crippled, but at the Institute they want to teach you to walk again. And I'm involved with another school for well kids, ordinary kids, not genius kids, but at 4 they can speak Japanese, English, Russian, play the violin, swim, because no class is longer than 15 minutes, they're brilliant at Greek grammar, things that blow your mind.'

'What's your favourite hotel in the world?'

'The Plaza in New York! But we have a flat in Manhattan now. It's the first home I've ever had and I'm very house-proud. It's like a big house up on the 21st floor. I've got the big furniture which makes a man feel comfortable, then the lighting that makes a woman look good, then everybody's cool. I think women look good in men's furniture, they kinda curl up . . .'

'You don't have lots of property? Some vagabonds collect houses.'

'No, I collect artwork. My husband's a sculptor besides being a producer. I've got a terrific collection of Andy Warhol's.'

'Is he a friend?'

'Andy? Sure.'

'What is your most treasured possession?'

'My sense of humour, ha-ha-ha. I *love* laughing. It's a great cure for the soul. Also it's very good for the diaphragm. It cures all sorts of diseases, laughing, isn't that funny?'

But this laughter can be a bit eerie, like the operation at intervals of a curse, as though 'Liza' had to spell 'pizzazz' at all costs. Perhaps it is part of the show-business armoury, just as that great grinding singing voice of hers is, that 'born in a trunk/ the show must go on/ roar of the greasepaint/ you gotta come back a star' voice. All her uncertainties and corniness solidify the moment she walks on stage which is the place where the ghosts – Mama, Daddy, the miscarriages, the divorces – finally get laid. Yes, the show – a handful of songs from way-back-when woven into a dramatic sequence, punched up by a tight brassy band, with some newer beat numbers thrown in, and Liza belting it out on a megawatt burn. It is a classic American act and in her class, the song-and-dance girl of the grand tradition, Liza Minnelli is the best there is. In fact she is almost the only one there is.

On the cold data she should have sunk without trace: no obvious beauty, alternately spoilt and rejected in childhood, the crushing ego of a spectacular mother. Once when Judy Garland was on a downer, a friend told her not to forget the rainbow. 'Rainbow, rainbow!' she replied. 'How can I ever forget the rainbow? I've had rainbows up my arse!'

With Liza it isn't rainbows, it's mothers. So this time Judy Garland hasn't been mentioned in the conversation at all. Nor for that matter has her father, Vincente Minnelli, a successful maker of film musicals but a dull man. Miss Garland was a brilliant 22 carat mess. She died a wreck, being fired even from the set of *The Valley of the Dolls* which is about the wreckiest thing anyone could manage. But failure has its own endurance and the way Judy Garland continues to live through her daughter's performance gives a mesmerising ambiguity to Liza Minnelli's stage personality in which many generations of show-business are somehow blended.

'Do you use psychiatrists?'

'No. I guess I've been lucky. I haven't found the need.'

Surprise – but it is easy to forget, among all the glitz and tragi-comic PR, that even the untidiest case histories are flooded with normality.

'Do you have any friends from childhood?'

'Oh yes. My girlfriend's coming over to visit and see the show. Her name is Pam Reinhardt. She's in real-estate.' And as if to underline the point, she continues 'I'm *starving*. Say, have you eaten?'

'No.'

Jeanne Moreau at Claridge's

Jeanne Moreau, born in Paris in 1928, became famous in Louis Malle's films of the late 50s as the female face and soul of the Nouvelle Vague: direct, emotional, versatile, intelligent, un-expected, strange-looking but appealing, vulnerable, aggres-sive, sexy. She remains all of these things. Moreau has also worked with Antonioni, Truffaut, Peter Brook, Tony Richardson, Buñuel, Joseph Losey, Orson Welles, Elia Kazan. She has recently starred as the brothel madam in Fassbinder's final film *Querelle*, based on Genet's novel.

'I think Britain was the last country to give it a certificate and it's been cut a little bit,' she says, with one leg tucked under her on the sofa. 'There was a problem with Italy too but it's been showing there very successfully. It's not what you see that's the problem. It's what's in the mind. What really outrages people is the way other people think.'

Fassbinder is the best of the garage film-makers. He is about intense emotions in a tacky world. Like Genet's, his work is both subversive and sentimental.

'I don't find this a sentimental film, I must say,' she protests. 'I think it's an important film because it's been made by Fassbinder who is a true artist, and it deals with sexuality, passion, and death.'

She doesn't have the kind of killing beauty which falls like a sheet of steel between the actress and the audience. But she is beautiful in that her face is inviting, human, and full of stories. She chainsmokes.

'Fassbinder was interviewed about it on television – he was clearly drugged to the eyeballs.' (Fassbinder died from an accidental overdose of cocaine and sleeping pills in 1982 at the age of 36.) 'Did he make the film on drugs?'

'On the set I've never seen him with drugs. He was very in control, very precise. The film was made in 42 days – extraordinary. I adored him, I loved him as a person, and was very surprised by his death.'

'Sentimental wasn't an insult by the way. Was he an unhappy man?'

'Oh, yes. The cause – his search. He was an artist, so he always wanted to discover, to develop, to try new things. Like people who are so sensitive, he was full of questioning and a violent person which his films show very clearly. All artists are violent – emotionally violent.'

'Was his homosexuality – '

'I would say his sexuality. Because he was bisexual. At the time of his death he lived with a woman who was his editor. He always had both men and women, but when he had a love affair he didn't go with anybody else, just that person.'

'The part you play, Lysiane, is a painful part for a woman: a woman still hungry for sexual appreciation but marginalised by (a) increasing age, and (b) the more intense homosexual relationships around her.'

'I didn't find it so painful.'

'Have you ever had an affair with a homosexual?'

'Well, I lived 5 years with Pierre Cardin.'

'Was this different from a straightforward heterosexual sort of . . .'

'Oh, fuck off! Homosexual, heterosexual, I never thought

about it. An affair is not this. An affair is always individual. He wasn't exclusively homosexual – because he lived with me.'

'And you made love in the so-called usual way?'

'Yes.'

'Have you ever had an affair with a woman?'

'No, I haven't.'

'What are the problems for you in getting older?'

'No problems.'

'Rewards, then.'

'Not to have to put up with things you cannot stand, with imbecility. You are your own. You don't have to submit. Getting older I feel stronger.'

'Looking back on the past – '

'I don't look back on the past.'

'What about the problem of self-pity?'

'Never, never. Self-pity is dis*gusting*.'

'But you must have experienced emotional pain.'

'Oh, yes. That's quite different. When one knows how to be happy, one also knows how to be unhappy. It only leads to self-pity for imbeciles. I'm not an imbecile. My response to emotional pain is . . . I try to find out why it is so painful and how I am responsible for that pain. In this way I discover a lot. Many people like to put their suffering onto other things, other people – if only this, if only that. But I always thought I should take responsibility for these accidents in my life, good or bad. I do have temper, I do get angry and upset, but less and less these days. Emotional pain for me comes from private difficulties with people. An unfavourable reaction to a piece of work doesn't cause this sort of pain. But work is essential, any work, essential for self-respect.'

'Are you hard on yourself?'

'Yes, because I tend to be lazy. That's why I work a lot. I love to be idle, daydreaming and reading.'

'I see you've got a book about Mahler on the sofa there.'

'Yes, I bought it just this afternoon. Dreaming without intention, about eternity, the unknown – that's beautiful. It's also addictive. My other weakness is I can't hold onto money.'

'Have you met Genet?'

'I knew him very well, then I stopped seeing him. He's

fascinating but not easy to be with. Nobody knows where he is now. Even his close friends don't see him any more.'

'I heard the Communist Party was looking after him in Paris and that he was dying.'

'He's been dying for a long time.'

'When you were younger, did you search for love?'

'No, I was expecting, not searching. I knew it would come. And it came all the time. Sometimes I wonder what it is to love – not to be loved, but to love. It is easy to speak about love. It's another thing to do it. I never thought there was just one true partner and you must spend your life to find him and then stick to him and if you don't it is a failure. No that's not it. I had many affairs, all different, all important. It's one's destiny, that's all. The accident of life. Sometimes you can have an affair that has nothing to do with love, that is an excitement. But always when you are close to someone, the physical bond is very important.'

'How do you recognise love?'

'That's easy. You want to see the person more and more, know more and more about them.'

'What about unrequited love?'

'What's that? No, it takes 2 to make love.'

'Have you ever had an affair with a younger man?'

'Oh yes, but I never thought about their ages, nor they about mine. When I was 44, 45, I had an affair with a young man of 19, a French boy. But we didn't carry our ages in front of our eyes. We were so involved with ourselves that we didn't think about age.'

'You are very European.'

'But I'm violently attracted to those huge pioneer continents like Australia and the States where people have fought to make a life. I was going to make a film in Hollywod with John Bennett but the producer's wife betrayed him and the producer shot the wife's lover, so it wasn't made. I love the West Coast – Griffiths used to say that California was very good for the body but not for the soul, so don't stay too long there.' Puff-puff.

'Have you been to Russia?'

'Once, for the film festival. The impression everywhere was – a desperate world. Even in festival time they cannot

332

hide it. From my hotel room I could see the back of the restaurant with these men and women who were serving the lunch, they got drunk round the back there and fought among themselves, it was terrible. By the way, my mother is English, from Oldham in Lancashire. She was a dancer in Paris but I lived in England as a little girl at the beginning of the war – in Hove, in Southwick, in Littlehampton. In my character there is something English – no self-pity, and to make right decision in violent, dangerous or important moments. Tragic events find me cool, organised. Also, this ability to discover other countries and be at ease anywhere, to have an adventure anywhere – that's the sailor side of the English. I want to go to China.'

'You are cool about a lot of things.'

'I'm not, I'm a warm person. But I can get upset by small details. In the Chinese horoscope I'm the dragon. Dragons can handle the big things but they get so much worried about small things.'

'What makes you nervous?'

'I hate to wait. I like people to be exact. I'm a perfectionist – this can be a problem. Also my incapacity, my limitations make me nervous. But if you are a performer or an artist you have to go outwards, push back your limitations. It's courage to write something, have it printed and people read it. You expose yourself to attack constantly. But the marvellous thing is that in doing this you take the lead in your life, you grow, you don't repeat yourself. I'm more curious about the unknown than the known. I know that beyond everything we see, there is something else. Now I am directing films too – I always want to do new things, to go further.'

'As a director – no, generally – how do you get someone to do something they don't want to do?'

'I wouldn't give them a chance to think they didn't want to do it.'

'And the future . . .'

'I prefer to keep quiet about it because one must deal with things one at a time. Very soon you discover as you pull out the thread of creativity, that all sorts of other things come out too and you have to say "Be quiet, not now, your turn will come later". If you give them all a bit of attention, then you become as we say in French "velléitaire". A new idea every week but nothing is ever finished.' Puff-puff.

'But accidents are important.'

'Oh, the accidents are essential.'

Yes, she certainly does chainsmoke. Liza Minnelli smoked a lot, so did Claudia Cardinale, but both are amateurs compared to Jeanne Moreau. Pure tar flows in her veins. She moves in a choking, sensual fog, her voice ripped and her skin ravaged by nicotine.

'Do you always stay at Claridges?'

'I stay a lot here and a lot at the Connaught.'

'What's your favourite hotel in Paris?'

'I never stay in hotels in Paris but I love the Ritz because of all the great writers associated with it.'

'Did you know Cocteau?'

'Oh yes, he was fascinating. He would tell a fantastic story. Then you'd rehearse a play and go to eat and some people would come over, then he would tell the same story again, and then at night over supper with some different people he'd tell the same story – and I thought oh God, this story, it's always the same story, then 6 months later he would publish a book and the story was in the book. So I learned that he was working on this story over and over again in public. He was important, he was provocative.'

'Are you ever lonely?'

'No.'

(all 1983)

IL PLACIDO DON
1 Day in Moscow

NATURALLY THE VISA was a slight problem. Being a spur-of-the-moment, non-tour-group trip, meant that a letter of invitation from a Russian was essential – which materialised only the day before departure. Aeroflot was fine, packed with Indians voyaging to the Subcontinent. Only a trickle of us got off at Moscow. Russian immigration procedures were hassle-free – what a pleasure compared to landing at Bombay or New York. First impressions driving into a dark December 6pm city: busy, no houses anywhere, blocks, some good art nouveau buildings, queues, washed-out colours in hard lights, clean, but everything at ground level painted with brown slush.

The Savoy Hotel is the best (but not the most beautiful) in Moscow, opened in 1912, currently run by Finnair, recently refurbished with peculiar oxblood panelling which doesn't quite fit. Remarkably graceless statues of naked women hang about in the foyer but the bar is mad-grand and the dining-room sensational belle époque rococo. The place is a dollar ghetto, massively overheated and sealed off from the outside world. Russians can't use it unless meeting a hotel guest – which quite a few of them seem to be doing.

Rupert Everett phones: 'Good God, you're here, I'm amazed! It was a forgery.'

'What was?'

'The letter of invitation.'

'Oh – will we be sent to prison?'

'No, no, but there was nobody here who could send one – so

I sent one, in Russian, full of spelling mistakes. I don't know if I'm working to-morrow. They've been on strike.'

'Who have?'

'The Italians – they'd not been paid. And the studio – they'd not been paid. It's chaos. We were going to the Steppes at the weekend. Now we're not. I expect the Steppes haven't been paid. I'll send my car for you to-morrow at quarter to 12.'

Howard (a photographer) and I go for a walk. It's cold, not windy, not a problem. In fact I feel electrified and thoughts come in an untidy rush. They're better dressed than I'd expected. No junkies, no beggars, one drunk. Superb faces. One type seems to be classic Russian: silvery gold hair, wide apart green-blue eyes, full lips, square or oval faces, and not stringy like the Scandinavians but sensual. Generally the people seem very sexy and alive. This is perhaps the effect of the racial mix, Asian with European, northern with southern.

We are entirely visible as westerners, despite a low-key wardrobe, and streetboys make repeated but surreptitious approaches for dollar deals. 'You want military watch, rabbit hat, military belt, postcards, caviar?' Charm, passion, shyness, good spirits, fear (the activity is illegal) characterise these encounters. For the moment Moscow lacks mugger tension. Less frequently girls approach, asking for a cigarette light, usually in pairs – for company (it's boring work). Groups of people constantly form in the streets for some indecipherable purpose then disperse again. Any kind of personal transaction gives them all an orgasmic thrill, not so much because of the money, though that is welcome, as because it was an activity so long forbidden.

Turning into Red Square is a major experience, James Bond with a Rimsky-Korsakov soundtrack, familiar and exotic simultaneously. Moscow is not a city of colours but the sense of colour and fantasy, a traditional feature of Russian culture until the 20th century, explodes here. The military presence – fur hats and greatcoats with gold buttons – is crucial, as with the guardsmen at Buckingham Palace. And the rotating, illuminated red stars on top of the Kremlin towers are a glamorous finishing touch. On the far side of the Square, down a road beside the mescalin riot of St Basil's Cathedral, a group of boys pause and fan out in front of us. Is this the moment of disillusion? My body tenses waiting for the knife and the demand. One of them steps forward and asks bashfully 'You want to buy military medals? Not expensive.' Oh, they all want to sell their medals!

That's quite enough for one walk. Back at the hotel, we scan the menu which is a terrific rip-off. A party of American film-makers are staying here and their confident, good-time voices occupy the bar, killing the atmosphere.

Rupert *is* working to-morrow, so his French assistant Bruno turns up for us, accompanied by Rupert's placid black labrador. 'There's no quarantine in Russia,' says Bruno who is small and lively with a crisp haircut which the studio does for him. The Mosfilm site is a dilapidated Stalinist monster on the outskirts of town, a complex of gloomy hangars and long corridors in which vast archaic heating systems shudder and hiss. Rupert is playing the lead in a 10-part Italo-Russian TV series of Sholokhov's *And Quiet Flows the Don*, the master-piece of socialist realism in Russian literature. He doesn't have a dressing-room but he does have a bed near the set.

'Do sit on my bed,' he suggests considerately. He's very tall and dressed as a Cossack. 'It's a tragedy – all the Cossacks get wiped out in it. Do you like my false moustache?' It doesn't look false. The studio is very dark; only essential lighting is allowed. And in the dinge he resembles a Beirut bandit. 'This is Tania.'

She is Russian liaison and has that beautiful pearly blond look and tells me that the director is Sergei Bondarchiuk. My immediate thought is 'Anthony Powell'.

'Bondarchiuk is very famous here,' explains Rupert in his voice of bruised plums. 'He won the People's Artist of the Republic when he was only 35. The Russian David Lean.'

'But I should say that he is not Russian but Soviet director,' adds Tania with a little frown. 'There's a difference, you understand? He is conservative and now many are against his work. How do you find Moscow?'

'I find the Russians fantastically attractive! I don't know why . . .'

She giggles and says 'Look, Rupert will work now. Come this way, you can see better.'

Through the gloom we make offensive noises clambering over random poles and boards. A man I presume to be Sergei Bondarchiuk says 'Action'. He's about 65 with thick white hair, brown jacket, and spectacles in heavy black frames. He doesn't waste gestures. A young maiden of the Steppes in her simulated log cabin intones 'I wasn't expecting you. It's a long time since you were here.' This must be the love interest. Rupert, a greatcoat thrown over one shoulder, mumbles something surly and inaudible in reply. He's emoting well. Then they all stop.

Lunchtime. The Russians go off to their cabbagey canteen. The Italians have their own chef and eating-place. We follow the Italians through the giant Mosfilm maze. There are aromas of gas and oil and urine and gravy – the whole of the Soviet Union is leaking. One understands Chernobyl at once. And eventually we find ourselves at a passable mock-up of a trattoria in Bologna.

'How do you cope with food in Moscow, Rupert?'

'I'm fine. I've Bruno to cook for me at the flat. And we take vitamins. Taste that Moscow mineral water.'

A curious taste which reminds me of the dentist's chair. Bruno, who has the true Gallic animation and nerve, is a well-known figure in the Central Market where most things can be found if you have dolllars. If all else fails there's always caviar – the best is pale grey the colour of Moscow skies.

Bruno says 'I had a problem with one of the neighbours in our building. I was feeding the birds with leftover porridge. The woman upstairs saw it and went crazy, saying how dare you, and she called the police – it was terrible.'

'Do you join the food queues?'

'No, because I have a dealer who gets me things. Queue 3 hours for a bit of sausage? You're joking. They drink vodka to stay alive in those queues and sometimes there are fights.'

In the Russian winter you drink to stay abreast of reality – like smoking dope in India. I've also developed very quickly the reflex of eating anything I bump into because you never know when you'll be eating again. You can't just pop into a restaurant. You have to book and they might be full or have run out of provisions. There are no over-the-counter snack-bars around the town that I've seen. McDonald's is the only takeaway – another immense queue. Some things simply don't exist here, not even for hard currency – milk for example.

So how does one rent a flat in Russia?

'There's diplomatic buildings where you can rent flats,' says Rupert, 'which aren't expensive but not cheap either. It's pretty spartan. There were bedbugs when I arrived. But the heating's thrown in. The only real problem is you can't telephone out of the country. You have to go through the operator who's always engaged. But you can receive calls.'

'So what do you do when you're not working?'

'Read. Go to the gym. There's no bar or café life here. I love being in nightclubs. Did you ever go to Troll in London? Fantastic club. And the Kit Kat in Paris is another fantastic one. The clubs here are not good, full of businessmen, and the Russians go for heavy metal.'

The latest Moscow club is Syever (meaning 'North') near McDonald's – admission $10 – the hangout for the city's precious few yuppies. Rupert was refused entry because he was in running shoes. He had problems at another club too. An Italian was coarsely manhandling the breasts of a Russian girl he'd bought and Rupert told him to stop treating her like that in public – there was a fight. Some Italians don't look their best in Moscow. The following day I see 2 well-to-do Italian couples in Red Square all done up in designer finery. The women were parading in full-length minks with noticeable self-satisfaction. There are those who might find this magnificent. Perhaps I should, in a different mood. But in the circumstances they appeared vulgar and cruel. This is one of the superpowers laid low. Bewilderment and humiliation are widespread.

The Italians' spaghetti however is extremely welcome. We wolf it down and Howard and Rupert take off to do pictures. I wander the poorly lit buildings until I find myself outside a room from which light is pouring into the corridor in a magnesium blaze. A notice on the door says 'Il Placido Don. Make-up.'

'Where's Rupert, have you seen Rupert?' I'm asked. 'He's disappeared everyone's looking for him!'

Bruno trundles round the corner and says with his palms turned upward 'They've lost Rupert.'

'What do you miss most in Moscow?'

'Small talk,' replies Bruno.

Tania trundles round the corner, smiling: 'Rupert has been localised!'

'What did you do during the August Coup, Bruno?'

'Rupert and I watched it on CNN in our Moscow flat.'

Mr Everett walks onto the set, straight-backed, scuffing the floor with his boots. 'We started filming the First World War episodes with the Russian Army as extras and one Monday we all arrived at work in the trenches but the Army was nowhere to be seen. They'd all gone off to do the Coup. The Italians of course went crazy. We went to have a look at the barricades in town – and there were all our extras, my companions, popping their heads out of tanks and shouting "Gregor!" which is the part I play, this folk hero.'

He goes to work again and one hears that plaintive voice from the log cabin. 'I wasn't expecting you. It's a long time since you were here.' Followed by the Everett mumble. Something in it isn't quite working for Sergei. He takes it again and again. High budget pressure has not yet hit the Bondarchiuks of the Soviet Union. They have a starting date for the film, but not an ending date. For Sergei it's an open-ended, a-commerical enterprise, as in the old state-funded days. Rupert returns to the bed, then takes me to a vast indoor set of a typical Russian village of the Steppes. He's called away but returns directly (false alarm), holding Stendhal's *The Charterhouse of Parma*. 'You know, I am a hooray. My background is hooray. I used to hate it – now I feel a great affection towards hoorays.'

'What brought that about then?'

'Getting away from them. Leaving England. The hooray junk phenomenon in retrospect is very touching for me and has had no public sympathy at all. No one felt sorry for the poor old junkie hoorays.'

'What's the clinic they all go to?'

'The Priory in Chelsea.'

'No, I'm thinking of the one near Weston-super-Mare, you know, with a Cavendish wing, a Macmillan wing, a Guinness wing, a Tennant wing. Broadway Lodge! I know a considerable number of people who met their spouses there.'

'In retrospect it was the sensitive hooray who became a junkie,' he continues, warming to the subject, 'because we were brought up by the very last generation of Empire rulers who injected us with all these Empire-ruling class attitudes of superiority – but there was no Empire any more, so we were all scuffing around. Some went to Lloyd's or the City or Sotheby's but many were lost. At the end of the 70s my generation – punk, drugs – didn't even try any more. They just sort of gave up – which I think was a rather dignified gesture. I can't stand the mentality of the British establishment of my parents' generation. I mean, just look at them, half-wits with hideous inbred faces – I couldn't get together with it.'

'Do you think the young Russians feel something similar about their parental generation?'

'Oh God, I hope so! But life is much harder here. We get so spoilt in life by comparison. I've a Russian friend who's got an asthmatic child and he can't get any Ventalin so every day he wonders if his child will have an attack and die. Often they go to a dentist who has to pull a tooth out without anaesthetic. I find it more shocking than India for example which has greater poverty.'

Near the hotel a band of top-quality out-of-work musicians imparts true gaiety to the scene. They often give concerts in private flats too. Because of the uselessness of the institutions and the overwhelming primacy of personal contact, Moscow feels like a village. Over at the Tomb of the Unknown Warrior, newly married couples arrive in cars with gold bells on the roof for the traditional photograph. Above them hangs the luxuriant grandeur of the Kremlin which is open for anyone to walk in, a collection of golden domed byzantine cathedrals and classical palaces eccentrically disposed within a triangle of red mediaeval battlements. Gay boys in the public loo blow kisses and one makes a suggestion: 'You want military greatcoat?'

GUM, the huge shopping arcade built in Moscow's distinctive Dracula neo-gothic, is busy but serene. The lack of goods, number of soldiers and muted colours give it an air of the 1940s. How can such an immense and rich country have so little? This is the constant question and all I can say is that it must have taken a lot of organising. And now the vortex of collapse is underway. It's thrilling when yesterday and tomorrow do not resemble each other, but people are worried and ask what will happen? what will happen? A surreal society is in free-fall. Nobody knows what will happen. The uprush of mixed vapours is terrifying and intoxicating.

Piotr, 2 years a law student, now selling souvenirs for dollars, keeps one eye open for the police. He says that you may get 4 or 5 years in prison if caught with more than $46 you can't account for. Meanwhile in the background the major crookery flourishes – as always. He says he makes a good living and can now afford an old Lada but when I suggest he will become a rich man he says 'I want to give it up, it's too tension. And I'm not really interested in money.' Well, his refusal to swallow whole the god of capitalism is very encouraging.

The Godfather is on TV. Switch. The doings of Princess Di. Switch. Trouble in the Middle East. Switch. Scriabin's *The Divine Poem* live. Stay with Scriabin and slugs of whisky. Sticky sleep. On the way to the airport the taxi driver plays the Cure. Oh Russia – part squalid old cynic, part passionate virgin! There is something astounding going on. One day is absurd! I shall return . . .

(1991)